Utterly Other Discourse

Literary Criticism from Dalkey Archive Press

Utterly Other Discourse

The Texts of Christine Brooke-Rose

Edited by Ellen J. Friedman
and Richard Martin

Dalkey Archive Press

Christine Brooke-Rose's "Remake" is published courtesy Carcanet Press Ltd (U.K.), from the forthcoming book of the same title.

The following essays first appeared in the *Review of Contemporary Fiction* (Fall 1989) and are reprinted by permission of the publisher: "A Conversation with Christine Brooke-Rose" by Ellen G. Friedman and Miriam Fuch, "'Just Words on a Page'" by Richard Martin, "*Thru* the Looking Glass" by Hanjo Berressem (in shorter form), and "Memory and Discourse" by Susan E. Hawkins.

Ellen G. Friedman's "'Utterly Other Discourse'" first appeared in *Modern Fiction Studies*, ©1988 by Purdue Research Foundation, West Lafayette, Indiana 47907. Reprinted with permission.

Damain Grant's "The Emperor's New Clothes" first appeared in *Annali-Anglistica* (1991). Reprinted with permission.

Annegret Maack's "Narrative Techniques in *Thru* and *Amalgamemnon*" first appeared (in German) in *Beckett und die literatur der Gegenwart*, ed. M. Brunkhorst, G. Rohmann, and K. Schoell (1987). Reprinted with permission.

Richard Martin's "'Stepping-Stones into the Dark'" first appeared in *Breaking the Sequence: Women's Experimental Fiction*, ed. Ellen G. Friedman and Miriam Fuchs. © 1989 by Princeton University Press. Reprinted with permission.

Brian McHale's "'I draw the line as a rule between one solar system and another'" first appeared (in different form) in his book *Constructing Postmodernism* (1992). Reprinted by permission of the publisher, Routledge.

Susan Rubin Suleiman's "Living Between" first appeared in the *Review of Contemporary Fiction* (Fall 1989), and was reprinted with additional material in her book *Risking Who One Is: Encounters with Contemporary Art and Literature*, published by Harvard University Press. © 1994 by the President and Fellows of Harvard College. Reprinted by permission of the publishers.

Library of Congress Cataloging-in-Publication Data
Utterly other discourse : the texts of Christine Brooke-Rose / edited by Ellen J. Friedman and
    Richard Martin. — 1st ed.
    Includes bibliographical references.
    1. Brooke-Rose, Christine, 1923- —Criticism and interpretation. 2. Women and litera-
ture—Great Britain—History—20th century.
I. Friedman, Ellen J., 1944-   . II. Martin, Richard, 1934-   .
PR6003.R412Z99   1995   823'.914—dc20   94-36950
ISBN 1-56478-079-1

Partially funded by grants from the National Endowment for the Arts and the Illinois Arts Council.

NATIONAL
ENDOWMENT
FOR 💙 THE
A R T S

Dalkey Archive Press
Campus Box 4241
Normal, IL 61790-4241

Printed on permanent/durable acid-free paper and bound in the United States of America.

Contents

Books by Christine Brooke-Rose: References and Abbreviations

LISTED BELOW ARE ALL of Christine Brooke-Rose's books in order of publication. All references in the present book will be to these editions and, when necessary, will use the abbreviations noted in parentheses. References to the four novels *Out, Such, Between,* and *Thru* will be cited as *Omnibus* when taken from Carcanet's omnibus edition of those four, otherwise by individual title when taken from the original editions.

Gold. Aldington, Kent: Hand and Flower, 1955.

The Languages of Love. London: Secker & Warburg, 1957. (LL)

A Grammar of Metaphor. London: Secker & Warburg, 1958. (GM)

The Sycamore Tree. London: Secker & Warburg, 1958. (ST)

The Dear Deceit. London: Secker & Warburg, 1960. (DD)

The Middlemen: A Satire. London: Secker & Warburg, 1961.

Out. London: Michael Joseph, 1964.

Such. London: Michael Joseph, 1966. (S)

Between. London: Michael Joseph, 1968. (B)

Go When You See the Green Man Walking. London: Michael Joseph, 1970.

A ZBC of Ezra Pound. London: Faber & Faber, 1971; Berekely: Univ. of California Press, 1971.

Thru. London: Hamish Hamilton, 1975. (T)

A Structural Analysis of Pound's Usura Canto. The Hague: Mouton, 1976.

A Rhetoric of the Unreal: Studies in Narrative and Structure, Especially of the Fantastic. Cambridge: Cambridge Univ. Press, 1981. (RU)

Amalgamemnon. Manchester: Carcanet, 1984; Normal, IL: Dalkey Archive, 1994. (A)

Xorander. Manchester: Carcanet, 1986; New York: Avon, 1988. (X)

The Christine Brooke-Rose Omnibus. Four Novels: Out, Such, Between, Thru. Manchester: Carcanet, 1986.

Verbivore. Manchester: Carcanet, 1990. (V)

Textermination. Manchester: Carcanet, 1991; New York: New Directions, 1992. (Tx)

Stories, Theories and Things. Cambridge: Cambridge University Press, 1991. (STT)

Remake. Manchester: Carcanet, forthcoming.

The Resisting Author: An Introduction

Ellen G. Friedman

THE READER LOOKING FOR biographical information on Christine Brooke-Rose will find only bits sprinkled in the essays of this volume devoted to her fiction. Brooke-Rose resists biographers' queries; for her, the text and only the text is germane. In this belief she is influenced by New Criticism, the reigning critical school while she was at university, as well as poststructuralism, which she has theorized in several works of literary criticism. Both approaches abandon the author: While the text is at the heart of formalist criticism and the writer a detached creator, in poststructuralism the text is a reader's construction and the author—if she has a place at all—is just another reader.

Brooke-Rose demurs even when asked to promote her books; as she explains in *Stories, Theories and Things:*

I have long thought that to promote or protest, to scramble and scheme, is a waste of my precious energy because, either my work is of value and will therefore be more widely appreciated one day even if I am dead, or it is not, in which case, *pourquoi me fatiguer?* I have had little enough time to write what I wanted as it is. My only concern has been to be at least available in print, a bottle in the sea. . . . (3)

The dazzling virtuosity of the linguistic play that is her signature as a writer keeps her critics glued to the intricacies of her texts. Yet her intricate verbal choreography, together with her reluctance regarding biography and promotion, has contained her reputation in the category of "difficult writer." The result is that certain resonances in her work are unheard or undervalued. Perhaps, then, some biographical and personal talk is in order.

As I write in March 1994, Brooke-Rose is house-sitting in Cambridge, England, for Frank Kermode. She is having an urban and winter respite from her Provençal villa in Les Maquignons, where she lives. A blurb by Kermode decorates the back covers of several of her texts: "If we are ever to experience in English the serious practice of narrative as the French have developed it over the last few years, we shall have to attend to Christine Brooke-Rose." Although Brooke-Rose has done her share in advancing the "serious practice of narrative," and thus may be good grist for the academic conference and doctoral dissertation mill, her books are narratively engaging, a quality of her fiction that too often gets marginalized. Unlike Thomas Pynchon, whose disappearance is his best publicity, Brooke-Rose's own posture of reticence has been less accidentally successful. Most readers, I think, would like to know, for instance, that her brilliant farce on the issue of the literary "canon," *Textermination*, in which she takes characters such as Emma Bovary and Captain Ahab out of their texts for a walk at a San Francisco convention, was provoked by the 1987 Modern Language Association Convention in San Francisco that she attended, where Richard Martin organized a session devoted to her work and where there were many sessions on canonicity. It adds emotional resonance to the fact that of the hundreds of characters and authors Brooke-Rose mentions in *Textermination*, the one most anxious about her survival is her own character, Mira, a writer.

Most of the biographical material included here is informed by reference works such as *Contemporary Authors*, *Contemporary Novelists*, *World Authors*, and even *Who's Who of American Women* (quite a find since she's a British citizen). In using these sources, I may be reiterating inaccuracies, but some factual errors concerning Brooke-Rose may also make sense, given her suspicion of things offered as "fact" and the profound undecidability that is her most enduring theme. This undecidability extends even to biography, since the essay that launches this volume is the first chapter of Brooke-Rose's experimental autobiography *Remake*, a text motivated by resistance to personal revelation, by an "almost" refusal of the genre. In chapter 4 of this autobiography, she meditates on time's compulsion to reassemble, to "remake" the objects of memory:

Memory is thought of in time, but time is always represented spatially, hands round a clock, decades aligned, and today all the terms for memory are spatial, screening, filing, effacing, storing, labelling, visualizing, doors opening on doors, scope-gates on scape-goats, representing the data-structures of the world as if all philosophy and history were not Herodotage, Clio's clangers, Erato's errata, rearticulation and disarticulation in the blindness of new logics.

The biographical entry on Brooke-Rose in *World Authors* serendipitously relies on her own account of her life, perhaps given before she solidified her anti-biography position. After informing us that she was born in 1926 (more reliable sources say it was 1923), the volume offers three columns on her life in her own words. Readers can learn much from it. In addition to biographical information, they may glimpse Brooke-Rose's personal voice as a young writer. They can also glean something of the growth of the poet when they compare it to her "autobiographical" essay included in this volume. She begins:

I was born in Geneva. My mother was herself half Swiss, half American, and married an Englishman, but separated from him early in my childhood, so that we went to live with my grandparents in Brussels, where I was brought up. I was bilingual, but French was my first language. After my father's death I was sent to an English school and remained in England throughout the war.

Before attending Somerville College, Oxford, Brooke-Rose joined the British Women's Auxiliary Air Force where she worked as an intelligence officer, translating intercepted enemy communications. After studying English philology and medieval literature at Oxford, where she married Jerzy Peterkiewicz, a Polish poet, she then read for her doctorate at London University. Her thesis consisted of a "grammatical analysis of metaphor in Old French and Middle English poetry, comparing methods of expression in both at a time when French had considerably influenced the development of English."

Of her literary ambitions, she writes:

I had always wanted to be a writer. But I was a slow developer. I think that bilingual children often are. During my teens, when girls who want to write are scribbling diaries and reading voraciously, I felt neither in one language nor in another. Certainly my later urge to study both thoroughly was due to this feeling of uncertainty, and although I never pursued pure Philology or Pure Linguistics professionally, I have never regretted this grounding and have remained deeply interested in language.

After she finished her thesis in 1954, she published *Gold* (1955), a book of poetry, and began *A Grammar of Metaphor*, a study of metaphor in fifteen poets from Chaucer to Dylan Thomas, published in 1958. When her husband became seriously ill, Brooke-Rose worked as a writer for hire doing book reviews and also began her first novel, *The Languages of Love* (1957), a satire about philologists. She followed with three more humorous novels—*The Sycamore Tree* (1958), *The Dear Deceit* (1960), and *The Middlemen* (1961)—before deciding to write in a self-consciously experimental way. She describes the transformation:

The crisis came in 1962, when I fell desperately ill for two years—oddly enough in France, where I first remained for six months. It was like a return to my essential self. Already before this I had, as a critic, become extremely interested in the experiments of certain French novelists, especially Nathalie Sarraute and Alain Robbe-Grillet, both of whose critical essays on the problems of the novel were a revelation to me, although their individual solutions were not, in any direct way, to be mine. Also influential was Samuel Beckett, as a novelist rather than as a playwright. . . . *Watt*, an early novel, . . . was a turning-point for me. The almost mathematical precision of language, the humorous play with all possible permutations of the simplest situation, as if each had its own philosophical existence, the mock-"scientific" but also in some essential way truly scientific attitude behind the poetry, all these delighted me, and seemed to me the only possible way of dealing with both inner and outer reality in this age of the uncertainty principle in physics, an age of undermined causality, an age in which subjective and objective have almost merged through the strange colloidal chemistry of psychic and physical energy.

At any rate, during my long illness, I found that I couldn't read novels, good or bad, about love-affairs, class-distinctions and one-upmanships, or portraits of society on any scale from parochial to professional: the sort of novel, in fact, that I had been writing. I devoured scientific books, which bred their own curious poetry:

"Each molecule can expect five thousand million collisions per second." "Weight consists of the attraction between two bodies." "In this kind of communication the echo decreases with the fourth power of the distance rather than with the square." Such phrases, of precise significance to the scientist, fired my imagination as poetic metaphors for what happens between people, and people are and always will be the stuff of the novel.

It was perhaps this scientific reading that led to her translating Alfred Sauvy's *Fertility and Survival: Population Problems from Malthus to Mao Tse Tung* (1961).

Her first experimental novel, *Out* (1964), written a few sentences at a time while she was recovering from kidney surgery, was quickly followed by *Such* (1966), *Between* (1968), and a collection of short stories, *Go When You See the Green Man Walking* (1970). Her admiration for the guru of the French nouveau roman, Alain Robbe-Grillet, resulted in her translating his novel *In the Labyrinth* (1967).

One of the institutions to grow out of the 1968 student revolution was Université de Paris VIII at Vincennes, an open-admissions university organized partially by Hélène Cixous and Jacques Derrida. Cixous invited Brooke-Rose to join the faculty in 1968, and except for occasional visiting professorships in the United States, Brooke-Rose worked in the English Department there until her retirement in 1988, writing criticism mainly during the academic year and novels in the summer.

Accepting its risks, she has steadfastly claimed the role of the woman experimental writer who refuses to play the *auteur*. Her essay "Illiterations," for instance, attempts to locate experimental women writers such as herself in the literary landscape and finds it an unfriendly place: "it seems to me that the combination of woman + artist + experimental means so much hard work and heartbreak and isolation. . . ." Yet true to her pattern, she claims its soil as her own: "every individual needs a mixture of withdrawal and belonging. And it seems to me that the woman artist needs more withdrawal and less belonging" (STT 262). Elsewhere in *Stories, Theories and Things* she spends a paragraph assessing the categories under which her fiction is considered:

I am one of the many authors who have a brief existence at . . . the interpretation level (the "meaning" or simple reading of the text as syntax, for instance by reviewers), but who have little or no existence at . . . the critical level (the "significance" or what others call interpretation, that links the text to other things/ realms of thought . . .). This can only begin to happen, for better or for worse, when an author enters a canon, however shifting, and I have a knack of somehow escaping most would-be canonic networks and labels. (4)

But she ends defiantly: "On the whole I regard this as a good sign."

Her fiction offers permutations of this theme. Outsider status is followed by resistance, sometimes covert, and then is absorbed in endings that offer at least partial victories. *Amalgamemnon's* opening sentence casts the protagonist, a professor of classics, as the outsider, indeed, as the rejected: "I shall soon be quite redundant at last despite of all, as redundant as you after queue and as totally predictable, information-content zero" (5). She combats this rejection through linguistic invention, by making up words and stories, trading university bureaucracy for the "madlanes" of her imagination. These inventions will not help her get a new job, but it is a way of inscribing herself in a world. Similarly, the protagonist of *Between* is a simultaneous translator who lives, as Brooke-Rose once said in an interview, "between languages, between ideas, between cities" and thus not inside anywhere (Hayman 5). But at the end, Brooke-Rose saves her from disappearing into the unstable and shifting material of languages that marks her professional life, by asserting her subjectivity and the materiality of the body. Asked in German and French by the customs agent whether she has anything to declare, she replies in English, "No, nothing at all, just personal effects." This claim of subjectivity— "personal effects"—together with the text's poetic and oracular last sentence, which reclaims the material body from language, "Between the enormous wings the body floats," counters the indeterminacy of the linguistic universe the text proposes, despite the obvious irony that we never leave it. The sense of the material body and the feeling of selfhood defies the wisdom that these are linguistic constructs, "just words."

Textermination opens in midsentence with a quotation from Jane Austen's *Emma* about getting into a carriage with Elton. However, Brooke-Rose puts Goethe into the carriage instead. The entire chapter, in fact, is composed of quotations from other novels about traveling in carriages. Emma, Goethe, and hundreds of characters and authors are, the narrator explains, "on their way to San Francisco, to the annual Convention of Prayer for Being. There they should recover, after an unimaginable journey, to savour what remains of international ritual for the revival of the fittest" (8). The candidates for rejection in this text are all of the literary characters Brooke-Rose manages to cram into an almost 200-page novel. The story that Brooke-Rose continues here is, of course, the one about the canon, She renders the crisis in literary studies from the point of view of the characters who are in danger of being disappeared in these literary upheavals. After all, if they are unread, they do not exist. Emma, for instance, thinks: "For roughly two centuries she has been totally sure of her personality, flaws and all. . . . But now everything has become confused, she lacks reality, as if the Reader her Creator had somehow absconded, like God, behind a Cloud of Unknowing" (14). Brooke-Rose complicates issues of the canon by having the convention invaded by television characters, who are also interested in survival. From one angle, Brooke-Rose has wittily turned the tables on her own perceived obscurity. Since canons are being dismantled, even Jane Austen is in danger. With great wit, Brooke-Rose thus makes possible obscurity a populated place, where, if that were her fate, she would be in good company.

In *Xorandor* (1986) computer-whiz fraternal twins attempt to tell the story of their discovery of Xorandor, a nuclear waste-eating rock that produces offspring with a similar ability. While the story of Xorandor repeats the Brooke-Rose topos of resisting outcast, this plot has feminist implications. The name "Xorandor," evoking not only computerese, but also unnamed alternatives and additions ("or" "and" "or"), that which is under erasure ("x"), as well as outside of conscious knowledge or control, represents the hidden, semiotic disposition that disrupts and subverts dominant or symbolic discourse—the discourse of authority and judgment (Kristeva 19). Although the patriarchal, political establishment thinks it is destroyed, Xorandor survives—like the semiotic—unseen. Brooke-Rose suggests it is gathering strength and producing offspring for that crucial moment in which it will return to defuse destructive phallocentric narratives—here, of nuclear holocaust.

The fiction of, say, Borges (e.g. "The Library of Babel" or "The Book of Sand"), Barth (e.g. "Lost in the Funhouse" and "Night-Sea Journey"), and other fabulists displays a nostalgic yearning after and grieving for the comforting authority of linear narrative, its teleology, and its Newtonian laws (see Friedman). In contrast, *Xorandor* declares itself on the side of ruptured and unreliable narrative, for in the spaces created by the ruptures and the anxiety provoked by the unreliable, the semiotic "x-or-and-ors" live. Their presence, this novel implies, provides a healing balance to the symbolic order which, if left alone and unchecked to direct the course of history, may steer the world to annihilation (Friedman and Fuchs 39).

Brooke-Rose writes—as woman, as experimentalist, and as woman experimentalist—from a position of otherness, eloquently claiming and resisting it. In *Remake*'s last chapter, she poignantly sums up her life:

On the long drive back to Provence the old lady muses again to Tess [a younger self] on how elements of pure chance, rather than merit, can govern a life: born and brought up in non-calamitous zones, never facing dole-queues or regular rush-hours or the drug temptation, being on the so-called winning-side in a safe and instructive war and surviving, meeting a wondrous partner in a library, getting a government-paid education, never having been a battered woman, a single parent, or a parent at all, sexually alive between VD and AIDs, landing a job at the top late in life, able to prepare a solitudinous and independent old age of invisibility, invisible as woman, as old, as English in France and French in England, as off-beat writer still barking up the wrong tree become a tree of life, enjoying the invisibility like an enclosed order preparing for the final invisibility, apart from close and stimulating friends.

The authors of the essays in this volume come from four different countries, a tribute not only to Christine Brooke-Rose's international background but also her reputation and readership. The volume opens with her own witty, pensive autobiographical piece "Remake," the first chapter of her forthcoming book of the same name. Here, at the same time that she interrogates the nature of memory, she offers her own recollections, which she characterizes as being as much constructed as contemporary television news, as "remakes," with as many indeterminacies as fiction. The critical essays that follow approach her texts from a variety of critical perspectives: feminist, structuralist, poststructuralist, and formalist. The interview, "A Conversation with Christine Brooke-Rose," with Miriam Fuchs and me, which took place at the same Modern Language Association Convention that inspired *Textermination*, may be a good place for the reader to be introduced to Brooke-Rose's narrative methods in her own words. Conducted in the year before she retired, the interview shows her in a reflective mood, looking back on her career. In it she confesses her late start as a feminist, gives her views on her own experimentalism, and tells of the challenges she set herself in each of her post-realistic novels.

Feminist literary critics are increasingly interested in the relationship between experimental form and feminism in Brooke-Rose's texts. Judy Little argues that Brooke-Rose's feminism has broad philosophical effects: "the ideology of (sexual) difference—and the usually related myths of textual origin and authority—. . . transforms or deconstructs most ideological structures, grand or small, in her work." Susan Rubin Suleiman's essay, "Living Between: The Loneliness of the 'Alonestanding Woman,' " argues that the protagonist of *Between* is both an incarnation of the "alonestanding" woman and a harbinger of a "different" future, one that veers off the historical course towards destruction set by "masculine upward myths." This insight is reiterated and particularized in Karen R. Lawrence's "'Floating on a Pinpoint': Travel and Place in Brooke-Rose's *Between*." Lawrence feels "the text's exploration of chance, randomness, accident directly relates to the special significance that Brooke-Rose's novel claims for the *gendering* of travel and translation. For drift, chance, passivity, symptomatic of the workings of history, might offer a new technology of narrative, an alternative to masculine teleological paradigms."

Employing the strategy of close reading, Richard Martin in "'Stepping-Stones into the Dark': Redundancy and Generation in *Amalgamemnon*" studies the first page of this text. After an elucidation of its complications, he moves on to the rest of the novel, concluding that the "dominant female strategy" is, in Brooke-Rose's pun, to "mimagree" dominant discourses because implicit in mimagreement, in redundancy, and in deconstruction is disagreement, generation, and regeneration. Lincoln Konkle's "'Histrionic' versus 'Hysterical': Deconstructing Gender as Genre in *Xorandor* and *Verbivore*" views these two works of science fiction as inverting Brooke-Rose's usual privileging of experimentation over concerns with gender. In these two works, Konkle asserts, she attempts "to deconstruct the binary opposition of masculine and feminine . . . in favor of a paradigm of androgyny, showing that qualities or roles or prose styles traditionally associated with masculine and feminine can be possessed, played, or written by anyone."

My own essay, "'Utterly Other Discourse': The Anticanon of Experimental Women Writers from Dorothy Richardson to Christine Brooke-Rose," argues that Brooke-Rose's texts are a recent addition to the work of women writers who have challenged the so-called Great Tradition by rejecting its standards and by "relocating their own work outside of them, a relocation that has over the course of the twentieth century accrued into what may now be viewed as an oppositional canon—an anticanon."

These feminist examinations of Brooke-Rose's texts vie with structuralist ones for dominance in this volume. Lacanian theory amplifies the structuralist tools that Hanjo Berressem applies in "*Thru* the Looking Glass: A Journey into the Universe of Discourse." Of all the essays in this volume, Berressem's goes the furthest in illuminating the significance of linguistic theory at the heart not only of *Thru*, but of all Brooke-Rose's texts. As Berressem's essay takes the measure of structuralist theory in *Thru*, "Reading *Amalgamemnon*" by Jean-Jacques Lecercle assesses the philosophical implications of Brooke-Rose's language games. (*Amalgamemnon* is written without realized or actualized tenses.) Lecercle is particularly interested in the relationship between Heidegger's notion of *Dasein* and the language universe in *Amalgamemnon*: "The world of the novel is not a possible world because it is the world-coming-to-worldness (*Welt weltet*), gathering the four elements, *das Geviert*: the mortals (as named in the genealogies), the gods (the numerous mythological references), the heavens (the stars), and the earth (that little pig farm)." Taking as his point of departure the image of the "Emperor's New Clothes" that appears in both *Thru* and *Textermination*, Damian Grant writes about the theme of authorial anxiety in *Thru* and Brooke-Rose's playful treatment of it.

A number of the essays provide introductions to the Brooke-Rose universe, such as Annegret Maack's "Narrative Techniques in *Thru* and *Amalgamemnon*," and Heather Reyes's "The British and Their Fixions, the French and Their Factions," appraising the influence of Brooke-Rose's British and French residences on her texts. The most comprehensive of these essays is Richard Martin's "'Just Words on a Page': The Novels of Christine Brooke-Rose," which traces thirty years of Brooke-Rose's fiction and introduces the reader to the texts' essential furniture. Brian McHale's astute essay, "'I draw the line as a rule between one solar system and another': The Postmodernism(s) of Christine Brooke-Rose," locates her postmodernisms in the "principle of hesitation." He distinguishes the poetics in the tetralogy of the sixties and seventies from that of the eighties and nineties by examining how various aesthetics of hesitation transverse, zigzag, or are recapitulated in her texts. McHale also identifies the places science fiction occupies in her poetic topography. For Susan E. Hawkins, Brooke-Rose constructs a "narrative of the near future," science fiction, to palliate the "dangers of the present and the past."

Thus the volume serves those who need an introduction to Christine Brooke-Rose's universe as well as those who, having already been introduced, want greater intimacy. The wide variety of vocabularies deployed to analyze her work—stretching from Heidegger to science fiction, from linguistics to feminism, from Lacan to fairy tales—demonstrate that her texts are hermeneutically, as well as literally, multilingual.

WORKS CITED

Friedman, Ellen G. "'Where Are the Missing Contents?' (Post) Modernism, Gender, and the Canon." *PMLA* 108 (1993): 240-52.

———, and Miriam Fuchs. "Contexts and Continuities: Women's Experimental Fiction." In Ellen G. Friedman and Miriam Fuchs, ed. *Breaking the Sequence: Essays on Women's Experimental Fiction.* Princeton: Princeton Univ. Press, 1989. 3-51.

Hayman, David, and Keith Cohen. "An Interview with Christine Brooke-Rose." *Contemporary Literature* 17 (1976): 1-23.

Kristeva, Julia. *Desire in Language: A Semiotic Approach to Literature and Art.* Trans. Leon S. Roudiez, Alice Jardine, and Thomas Gora. New York: Columbia Univ. Press, 1982.

Wakeman, John, ed. *World Authors: 1950-1970.* New York: H. W. Wilson, 1975. 223-25.

Remake

Christine Brooke-Rose

THE BLACK CAR limousines along the colonnade.

The Secretary of State descends the White House steps towards the car door held open onto a beige leathered emptiness, larger and larger as the viewer enters. The Secretary of State descends the airplane steps to be welcomed by the Russian Foreign Minister and delegation before being engulfed by the first of a waiting fleet. From the windows the viewer sees the sudden Kremlin surge. The overvoice continues to prognose problems to be discussed in the way of nuclear dismantling internal opposition for support at the U.N. in the present conflict elsewhere. In a national election this would be called buying votes but then, the two ex-rival blocks have been doing nothing else for forty years, in different configurations.

The viewer, an old lady of seventy, has professed literature, retired to Provence. The old lady knows this is routine remake, the cameraman having got into another limousine rented and drawn up for the purpose along the colonnade, into the beige leathered emptiness looming at the lens, into a no doubt smaller car driving towards Moscow and the Kremlin.

But then, everything in the old lady's life is remake now, as is the world viewed in cartoon strips. Mention of anything at all, person, place, problem, package deal, needs an image, a map a landscape a city a street a house a head, the Chancellor of the Exchequer at a desk in Number 11, turning the page of a large ledger by the open bright red dispatch case, brand new, so unlike the darkened old dispatch case displayed on Budget Day, black on old newsreels, dirty mahogany on TV. A new library picture has to be made whenever a new Chancellor is appointed. Images of ministers walking along the railings of Downing Street and into bobbied Number 10, the door opened by an invisible hand, party leaders in the hall of the Assemblée Nationale, ministers shaking hands in Brussels, Edinburgh, Geneva, Rio, standing at summit buffets about global warmongering awkwardly holding plate and glass or coming out to face a cluster of toffee-apples with a toffee statement carefully licked out to say little, ponderously hesitating towards the expected clayshit and getting into a drawn-up limousine to drive away, external shot. The overvoice on the French news mistranslates: A la fin de la journée . . . un accord. The old lady laughs alone, will check on the BBC an hour later, for clearly the English delegate has used the current fuzz-phrase "at the end of the day," and no agreement will be reached that evening.

The old lady thinks about the techniques of fiction, now regularly used in documentary. Getting inside the mind of a character, seeing things the character sees, thinking things the character thinks, seeing the character as well. But the author knows the inside of the character's mind because the character has come out of the author's mind.

Not out of the author's mind comes a knock at the door. Rachid, one of the cherry-pickers, with an offering of cherries in a plastic bag, also wants to come and weed this evening, when the sun has cooled. Voices chattering from the green trees, invisible human birds on ladders, the cherry orchards and the vines stretching far towards the wooded hills. How kind of Rachid, although the old lady has the friendly farmer's permission to steal.

Difficult to get into Rachid's mind through fragmentary French. Rachid looks eighteen but is twenty-eight and has five children in Morocco.

The little girl, aged two, is singing "Sur le Pont d'Avignon" to daddy in the dining room. The dining room is in Chiswick, at the back of a long deep flat, 15 Fairlawn Court, in a dark red building overlooking Acton Green. The dining room has chairs covered in dirty yellow plush. No, says mummy some forty years later at seventy-two, St. John's Wood, not Chiswick, Joanne at three was left with granny and grandad in Geneva, Chiswick was later, with both, several times. The old lady has no memory at all of St. John's Wood at two.

So le pont d'Avignon only half exists, stretching out broken into the flat slow yellow Rhône, so tumbling green in Geneva.

But learning the paternoster and the alpha beta gamma delta at daddy's knee in the dining room, Chiswick. And the paternoster in a dark red dressing gown on the small triangular balcony of the drawing room at the front of the house overlooking Acton Green. Paternoster waves good-bye to mummy bundling the two little girls into a big black cab on a last return to Brussels, in the long badminton of sending for and sending away. Is that a remake? Or a self-confrontation?

Self-confront many selves or one? A confrontation of two entities, as in the folktale, a hero (small but cunning and brave) and a villain (huge but stupid and cowardly), or a white knight and a black in a murderous clanging joust, or at most a giant green knight and at mostest a flaming golden dragon? But the entities are not of equal status and stature, the confronter is a speck in time compared to the army of confrontable selves.

Clearly grammar supports self-confrontation. John$_1$ confronts John$_1$. The rule of reflexivization requires a coreferentially repeated noun phrase in the deep structure to become pronominalized. And the definition of a personal pronoun?

A pronoun is an anti-noun, an anti-name, an anti-person.

A substitution.

A simulation.

An identification.

A possession and a dispossession.

Une fuite en avant.

Grammar doesn't say how many Johns or how many selves (and what color), or whether some past Johns are confronting one present John or one present John is confronting one or all or a selection of past Johns.

John is whole languages. John has as many selves as utterances, virtual or realized, as many selves as there are words in lexicons, each word an aetiology, a phoneyetic fragility, with semiantic sea changes, infinite contiguities and tall spokes of paradismatic possibilities. John is the excitement, the pursuit of knowledge, the donor with the magical auxiliary, an eagle, a flying horse, an invisibility ring.

Sometimes the old lady hates John, for at the surface John is both eager and easy to please, but differently positioned in each case, agent and patient, the pleasing John or the pleased John, the eagle John and the uneasy invisible John. John builds a house but cannot be built by a house, John can't be admired by sincerity, nor can John elapse.

Flying planes can be dangerous.

The old lady quantums back to pronominalization. Surely no metaphors are possible on pronouns except grammatical metaphors, using the pronoun as noun the way Donne did, or Cummings an adverb as adjective, the way American blacks do and vice versa in a pretty how town? *How can a town be, *hower than another town? Bruxelles est une ville loin, the little girl once said, or is reported later to have said, on a long train journey in a wooden-seated third-class carriage from Geneva or wherever to Brussels.

The old lady, having zapped to adverbs and fluffing out short grey hair, confronts the little girl with sidetracks, substitutions, and simulations about pronouns. Some people never use the other's name, but Monsieur, Madame, or darling or pussycat even in anger. Some parents replace the child's chosen name with a diminutive or an early mispronunciation. Some ill-mannered persons making jokey transformations of any unfamiliar name, and French news presenters colonize all foreign names into French phonetics, yet would not be pleased if the English rhymed Mitterrand with rand or Juppé with dupe or pronounced Dumas as dumb ass or Delors as delorse. People are frightened of names. Of otherness.

The world confronts the world in cartoon strips, sidetracks, substitutions, and simulations. The world is violent but the cameras are never there for the violence, only afterwards for the damage and interviews. Why come and film the misery here, says a Bosnian woman to the journalists, when the world won't help? Or else, exceptionally, the cameras are there but botch. Kennedy lying in the car, the pope being raced away, Monica Seles after being stabbed on the tennis court, surgical bombing on a surgical image from way up. Dying on the news is not allowed, only at most corpses. Yet there is a daily dousing of dastardly deaths in telefiction, viewers want those but would outcry at real dyings.

On Saturday evenings the old lady watches a program on the French cultural channel called *Histoire parallèle*, showing the newsreels of the same week fifty years ago, German, English, French, later American, Russian, Japanese. This is the world news in pictures, Pathé Gazette screening. With two historians hind-citing omissions and lies, the old lady hind-siting irrelevance, knocked into long-lost images. The Germans use film directors, slicing the distant battle scenes with brilliant shots of soldiers sailors airmen in tanks submarines cockpits, while the English make dubious jokes about Wops and Eyties, Huns and Jerries, and cheerily show the king and queen visiting bomb damage, the home guard training, the football matches and war fashions and factory girls. Life is normal. Well, the Germans show all that too, and generals meeting and Hitler Youths in happy holiday homes, more and more so as battles get lost and soldiers look more exhausted, less enthusiastic, just as the British later show more battles being won, as well as generals meeting plumply battle-dressed Churchill in North Africa and such. The French revel in sport, and speeches delivered in a mixture of priestly intoning and Comédie Française declamation, a style retained by Malraux well into the sixties. In all the newsreels the voice is cracked and hysterically hearty. In all presentations, the naturalization of war, to loud European military marches or Beethoven or Wagner, even in Japan. Things have got cleverer, not truer.

The young WAAF officer sits in a hut, later in a brick building, reading and evaluating German messages all day for priority lists to the intercepters and cryptographers. So many keys, daily to be broken, as fast as possible, sometimes within minutes of emission. Einsatzbereitschaftsbericht, Einsatz-meldung, Einsatzbefehl, from Keitel to Kesselring, from Kesselring to Rommel, from Von Rundstedt to subordinate divisions, from divisions to smaller units. The real war, seen from the enemy point of view at nineteen, twenty, twenty-one, twenty-two. Like watching different national newses today.

The old lady sits at seventy, feeling sixty, fifty, forty, in a burotic study overlooking the orchards and vineyards and wooded hills and lavender plateaux. There is a word processor and printer, an electronic typewriter and a Xerox machine. For the file of life.

Why is the old lady trying to intercept all those interseptic messages? Old-age self-indulgence? No. The old lady's publisher has asked for an autobiography. But the resistance is huge. The absorbing present creates interference, as well as the old lady's lifelong prejudice against biographical criticism, called the laundry lists by Pound. Only the text matters, if the text survives at all. But the insistent request has needled the interception. In earlier days the image would have been more of a brain tossing in a launderette machine, a sort of brain-washing, often by mentors. Or a manhoovering. But mentors come and go. There are no mentors now, except John, reaching Krafft ebbing through Freud by means of a magic Adler Fromm the Klein Jung. John is not easy to please, nor eagle neither, and seems to have elapsed after all.

On the roof is a vast dish, pivoting like an ear-eye to capture the news of the world, in English, German, French, Spanish, Italian, Polish, a monotonous variety of natiocentric views.

All the other programs are alike, intermediaocre, just as there are only four species of apples now, standardized taste, that is none. The Wheel of Fortune, Glücksrad, the candidates doing all the work, cheaper than paying professionals, even with the prizes. And long-amortized soap, old slices of life in fragmented scenes flung together, no dialogue more than two sentences, today's attention span being about thirty seconds. Just like life. Some feminists, the old lady remembers, insisted on both flux and fragmentation as female specificity in art. Perhaps such feminists were reared on soap. The old lady also wonders why American soap is always about the very rich, European soap always about doctors and lawyers and journalists, and English soap always about the working class. Perhaps only the workers watch, now there is no work, or only organized stupefying work requiring organized stupefied leisure.

But the dish is not for that. The dish is for watching the journalists provoking pseudo-events on the square of the high pother news and the political behavior of the participating public, unaware of being manipulated for profit and crowd-controlled in the best thirties tradition: le bo-bo, le nu-nu, le? BONUS! For the first time in the old lady's life there is all the time in the world to watch the world, a world never watched before, not as professor, not as literary journalist, not as student, not, of course, as WAAF officer, a world totally strange though so familiar to all the rest of the world watching the world in blaring baring uncaring despairing detail. The dish keeps the old lady in touch with languages once known or half-known, and with English as now spoke: Having said that, hopefully at the end of the day the bottom line will be a level playing field, on the line, but at the present time there's still a long way to go. Luckily there's also reading, for pleasure at last, not for an exam, a thesis, a review, a class, a seminar, or a conference paper. The old lady is not yet going blind.

One day there will come the shrinkage into a smaller space, in England perhaps, on the Kentish coast maybe, a terraced cottage along the seafront in Hythe for example, facing the same grey Channel as once did the schoolroom and the dormitory of the semi-posh school on the cliffs above Hythe, the address nevertheless Folkestone to sound posher. One day or sometime soon, here after all maybe, there will have to come the helplessness, an old people's home, being lifted from the bed into the armchair with a catheter to sit head bent in an outward stare, an inward gaze. But for the moment there is still the world to be watched at last, in its unsparing detail of simulation.

The dish causes trouble with the two immediate neighbors on either side, Simone to the east, a psychoanalyst, and Suzie to the west, a painter, the two serpents according to the rest of the hamlet, well-matched, the two Ss, gland in glove, S_1 and S_2, uncoreferential.

The old lady doesn't meet Simone until six months after settling there, five years ago, at five o'clock on Christmas Eve, on Simone's doorstep. The old lady, a little younger then and newly retired, asks about psychoanalysis, maybe gushing about Lacan. But Simone is suddenly abrupt, Simone's son is about to arrive. That means no passing the threshold. Perhaps Simone is an anti-Lacanian. Of course, the old lady says, do both come round for a drink over Christmas.

The son isn't in fact arriving till the next day, and there's no coming round.

Six months later the old lady tries again. Sorry, plenty of friends already, no need for more. Plonk. But in a saccharine psychoanalytic tone.

Suzie has a large black dog, kept in a close, or muzzled when let out, but the dog nevertheless digs up all the gardens. Simone's house has a pipe sticking out and flooding the village lower down whenever the hose is used. The village mutters but doesn't complain. Live and let live. Oh, is that Israeli music, Simone asks breezily into the open window. No, says the old lady, Hungarian. Ah, says Simone, anti-Semitic, eh?

A curious form of humor perhaps. The old lady has given up all but polite greetings, wondering occasionally whether Simone is as rude with patients. But when the dish is put up, Simone calls with psycharine reproaches. Not in the style of the region. And no consultation either. The old lady admits the unprovençal effect, but replies dryly, if the neighbors had been more companionable there would have been no need for spatial visitors. Ah bon, les voisins sont donc les méchants?

Simone and Suzie mount a cabal against the dish and this peculiar foreigner, not quite right in the head, but the rest of the hamlet defends the old lady, the two enchanting old twins, retired astrologists, and old, sick Madame Bernard, visited often by the old lady, partly in real concern, but partly no doubt self-righteously to show neighborliness as should be. What does that mean, say the twins, the whole region is up in arms? Has a house-to-house been done? And what about Simone's new garage opposite, with that pretentious false ruin of a wall sloping down sideways, blocking the view? Nobody was consulted on that. And what about the water, and what about the dog? Move with the times. And so on.

The local life opens no life. The flight from patriarchy is matriarched.

But then, things would presumably have been much the same if the old lady had retired in Kent. Used to big cites, where neighbors don't exist, only chosen friends. Big cities spoil people.

The old lady has spanned almost the century, the end in anticipation, the beginning in hearsay, La Grande Guerre, le Kaiser, le roi Albert saying NON, les tranchées and horror, Verdun, Ypres, la Somme, nettle soup, la Guerre and Belgium the center, though the grownups, the old lady now realizes, were not in Belgium at the time, grandpère, grand'mère and two sons in Geneva, the four daughters in America on girl jobs. And the same dramattitudes years later, after the second war, on a visit to the Geneva branch with Janek. What were things like during the Blitz? Well—Yes and every night the Allied planes could be heard rumbling over, on the way to bomb Italy! And there was no rice!

Schools teach their national version of history, but learning the history of Belgium in the thirties means learning the history of Europe, for Flanders belonged to many powers. Napoleon or Pépin le Bref, Charlemagne, the Duke of Burgundy, Maximilien d'Autriche, Charlequint, Philip II, le roi soleil, Guillaume d'Orange—le soleil an orange on some man's head like the apple on William Tell's. History is chiefly battles and the names of kings and alliance marriages lending legendary personality and glamour, the people being just armies moved on maps or rebels and riots put down. The little girl thinks how much easier to learn if kings and popes had the same numbers as the centuries reigned in, Louis the Ninth in the ninth, Gregory the Seventh in the seventh. True, some would have to share, Louis the Fifteenth and Sixteenth being the eighteenth a and b.

For Belgium, apart from being a region called Belgica by the Romans, has only existed for a hundred years since 1830, *le belge sortant du tombeau*, heard so much more vividly as *tambour*. Childhood is strewn with mishearings and mistranslations, le lendemain is le lent domain, un fait divers is a winter fact, the flick of a coin is le flic du coin, une arrière-pensée an afterthought, a bas-relief a base relief. And the family deranges the range with trilingual jokes, quelle est la matière, what is loose, have a good Fahrt, there is no what, taking something mit, grandpère a été délayé, like a sauce.

Geography consists of a straight coast sloping down westwards, Belgium humped behind it like a headless hamster, cut into strips to be learnt: la zône limoneuse, la zône calcaire, la zône ferrugineuse. The little girl transforms: la zône limonadeuse, la zône calamiteuse, la zône vertigineuse.

And today the old map of Europe learnt at school is resurging with calamitous zones from under the leaden palimpsest, not to mention the old map of Africa, ah, le Congo belge so proudly thrust into the children's imagination with jerky films at the Musée Colonial of black-breasted women pounding meal and savagely garbed black men stamping out war dances in happy honor of the white chiefs.

Once upon a time there is a little girl born in French, of an English father and a Swiss mother born of an American father and an Anglo-Swiss mother. The English father lives in London, the American-Swiss mother in Geneva, with the now Swiss grandpère and the Anglo-Swiss mother in Geneva, with the now Swiss grandpère and Anglo-Swiss grand'mère. That's the first split. Très wagon-lit, as Ian the joker, a brief wartime husband, says.

Back to London, back to Geneva, back to London, back to Brussels, back to back. Forgetting French, forgetting English, relearning French, relearning English, learning Flemish, learning German, forgetting Flemish, relearning English not really forgotten. Etc. That's the thirteenth split or so, scatterings and smatterings, French kindergarten in Geneva where the little girl at three stands on a stool by the Christmas tree reciting *Maman tire les rideaux*. English kindergarten in Brussels at four where the little girl and sister Joanne learn reading and multiplication tables in English singsong, and steal roses, hidden in elasticated knickers of pink cretonne, pregnant and prickly. At five a brown-uniformed day school in Chiswick, Brussels and the kindergarten again, at six a blue-uniformed school in Chiswick. And mysteriously, to cover the transition back to Brussels, a brief governess called Miss Enoch, with an atlas. Joanne remarks triumphantly, France is bigger than England. The little girl looks and sees a sort of solid square for France and, for England, a crochety old lady with stretched legs driving a motor-car, Ireland as the wheel. But Miss Enoch turns to the world page and says Look, everything pink on the map belongs to England. The little girl looks at the dot of England and the huge expanses of pink and asks, Why?

What was the answer? says John$_{13}$.

Can't remember. An answer to how, probably.

Pseudo-memory, more probably.

Sometimes the old lady hates John for the things John can't do, elapse.

Bifografy is always part fiction, John continues. First in the singulative birth, then in the iterative background, then in the singulative splits. Incoherent inchoative, incognitially punctuated. A situation, an event, another situation. Hero meets donor, is tested, receives a magical auxiliary, brains for instance or an eagle, is translocated to fight this or that dragon and returns incognito to perform another impossible task like emptying a river with a sieve, for recognition, then the whole cycle can start again and does, the recognition of desire being the desire of recognition (Lack-on). Pretty redundant, eh?

Pretty how?

Redundant.

Yes. A joke. Sorry. But girls in fairy tales are never heroes, girls must either be Cinderellas or marry the prince, girls are a statue, a tower-prisoner, a block of ice, deep sleep until a man comes along. Fogs lift, John, other fogs rise. People are fogs, fogs of experience, of talent, of knowledge. Each separating intelligence from talent, content from form, thought from feeling (etc.). Neither man nor mentors can endure otherness. Oxford or Cambridge? the girls at the blue school ask, about some unheard-of boatrace. Well, choose a rosette, pale blue or dark blue? Pale blue. But daddy is not pleased with the pale blue rosette. Daddy went to Oxford. This turns out, many years later, to have been one of many lies.

Why does talent belong to others?

In Brussels, asked the usual question about wanting to be what when grown up: an écrivain. Guffaws. Joanne, oui, Jean-Luc, oui, there's imagination. Talent belongs to others, brains to the little girl. That seems very fair, brains at school and the inner games at home, for a quiet mouse. Yet on that day the little girl becomes a writer, Joanne and Jean-Luc never do. Or perhaps John is the writer, John a whole language, or more, a worldword memory. Or perhaps later, the sixteen-year-old girl whispering down a rabbit hole on the Sussex Downs soon after the declaration of war: Hear O earth, a future writer, this is a solemn vow. The earth is very old and may have smiled benignly. Or guffawed malignly. But the little girl hears only silent approval and awe. That's the twenty-ninth split.

What does "that" refer to?

Anything, the hole, the earth, the vow. Other splits are wrenched school friendships now forgotten, passions of intense brevity. The mentors, coming and going.

Mentors are sometimes tormentors, says John, imposing to destroy, creating a pigmylion illusion of structure, preferring to ignore rather than absorb another.

Tor-mentors, that's good, the old lady says kindly. For mentors are sometimes mentowers, usually alas dead, or imagined, Athene to Odysseus, Homer to Virgil, Virgil and beady Beatrice to Dante, Dante to Pound and innumerable other strands, infinitely interwoven and sometimes shredded into—

Litter richer, says John flatly. The rat race. The mousetrap in the House of Fame or Fiction. John IS built by the House, flying reputations can be dangerous. Great, great, great, on cold grey stones of seachange, Stock Exchange, the Dow Jones Index of Authors closing at minus seven and a half tonight. Masterpieces, and occasionally mistresspieces, pieces of author, morceaux choisis in infinite morsels of the body politic of litter rats.

John, being stylistically guileless, is not eager to please, nor eagle neither.

All writing, all work, says the old lady, is necessarily a piece of master, a piecemeal attempt to master a file, a life. Alter ego et galore.

Yes, says John, ignoring the anagram, in the lie-prairies a million straws lie trampled by the tractors of intractability, how's that for paranomasia, snarls John$_{13}$, stung at being called stylistically guileless, to be rounded up in rectangular packages like books and bundled out by the inexorable combine-harvester, stacked in scattered yellow groups of miniature skyscrapers, isolated remnants of cities regimented along the fields, fodder for beasts, the grain thrashed out by the inexorable machine and stored away in braineries elsewhere, in universities perhaps. Before the traitors came the bundles were forked up by hand and tied together in steeple-shapes, rows and rows of golden chapels more haphazard over meadows. How's that for imagery?

John$_{13}$ is eager but not easy to please, now will John quite elapse.

There are so many others to confront, the credits rolling up the screen after the telefilm, the art director, casting adviser, location manager, script consultant, continuity girl, camera supervisor, focus-puller (*puller*?), director of photography, production assistant, composer, floor manager, prop buyer, graphics designer, costume designer, makeup consultant (but everything is made up), lighting engineer, executive producer, director, and innumerable others contributing to the life remade, alter ego et galore, the old lady can't help repeating, for a laugh, a smile, in vain, all the mentors and all the selves, the baby in Geneva, the little girl in Chiswick, in Brussels,

Folkestone, the young girl in Liverpool, in Thornaby-on-Trees, in Bletchley Park, in Occupied Germany, the student in Oxford, in London, the young wife and writer in Chelsea, the traveler in Spain, Austria, Italy, Eastern Europe, Turkey, the less young wife and writer in Hampstead, the middle-aged professor in Paris, in New York, Buffalo, Brandeis, Jerusalem, Geneva, Zurich, the old lady in Provence.

A Conversation with Christine Brooke-Rose

Ellen G. Friedman and Miriam Fuchs

San Francisco Hilton
29 December 1987

Q: IN YOUR ESSAY "Illiterations," which you wrote for *Breaking the Sequence: Women's Experimental Fiction*,[1] you mention the difficulties experimental writers face when they are male, but you say also that the differences are compounded when the experimental writer happens to be a female. Will you talk about those difficulties for the woman writer?

A: Yes, although it took a long time to become aware of them. Once in Paris, quite a long time ago, Hélène Cixous rang me up and asked me to write something about the difficulties I've had as a woman writer. Naively, I said, "Well, I haven't had any difficulties as a *woman* writer. I've had difficulties that *any* writer would have: can I write about that?" And she said, "Oh, no." She wanted something feminist. I was a bit antifeminist in those days in the early 1970s. I didn't consciously feel that I *had* had any difficulties. My later revision of that feeling came from genuine experience. As I look back over my career I realize that, in fact, I did have difficulties, but took them for granted as part of the nature of things. From the moment I went experimental, however, when I wrote *Out*, and my then-publishers couldn't understand it and turned it down, I did actually start having difficulties. And when I wrote that essay for you, I started looking back and thinking about it, trying to fathom it out, and I become aware that the woman experimental writer has more difficulties than the man experimental writer, in the sense that, however much men have accepted women's writing, there is still this basic assumption, which is unconscious, that women cannot create new forms. They can imitate others, they can imitate their little lives, tell their love stories and their difficulties and so on, and they do it extremely well. I'm not downgrading that kind of writing. But if by any chance they dare to experiment, then they are imitating a male movement, and usually one that's already dead. In my case, I always get the label *nouveau roman* in English because *nouveau roman* is, from the English point of view, safely dead and no one talks about it anymore. In other words, all one is capable of as a woman is to do what the men do, and not so well. There is an unconscious refusal, really, to look at what I'm doing in any kind of detail. Whereas men experimenters or innovators of any kind do get that sort of attention.

Q: What does the phrase "utterly other discourse" from *Amalgamemnon* mean for you? Do you feel that you are writing "utterly other discourses"?

A: In *Amalgamemnon*, it doesn't actually mean that. It doesn't refer to the writing, it refers to the woman reading and thinking quite other things until she has to switch back to talking to the man. In fact, though, I do feel that my writing is different. I haven't actually seen other writing quite like mine, but it is very difficult for me to say how "other" it is, or even whether it's any good. I can't really judge it, so I can't really answer that question. I do what I want to do.

Q: But you did make a conscious decision at one point in your career to write the indeterminate novel, rather than something realistic?

A: What a strange opposition. The realistic novel has its own indeterminacies. But anyway, it didn't happen that way at all. It was much more negative than that. I was simply dissatisfied with what I was doing. I had written four novels, my early novels, which are really quite traditional, satirical, comic novels. I did experiment with time in one of them, which was written backwards, for instance, so that in each chapter the hero gets younger and younger. But that was still classical irony. They were basically traditional modern novels, if I can use such a phrase, in that the main concern was, like most novels, epistemological, concerned with reality and illusion. But I felt it was too easy. It was great fun, but it wasn't what I wanted. Originally, when I was very young, I used to write poetry every day, but I soon discovered that I was not a poet; but that urge to write poetry . . .

Q: But you are a poet.

A: Perhaps, but I had to get around to it in a very different way. I then thought I had found myself as a novelist, but after those four early novels I realized it still wasn't what I wanted. So eventually—yes, I do now write very poetic novels, more deeply poetic at any rate than the poems I was writing every day. At the time of this dissatisfaction, I suppose it was Nathalie Sarraute's *The Age of Suspicion*, and her putting the modern novel in question, which was the first turning point for me, much more so than her novels, for although I like them very much, I can't say there's a direct influence of Nathalie Sarraute on what I write. Whereas Robbe-Grillet did have a direct influence, at least on *Out*. But I soon got out of it. So it wasn't a decision not to go on writing as I used to write. But the other thing that happened was much more important. I had a very serious illness, lost a kidney and had a very long convalescence. I fell into a semi-trancelike state for a long time. I was very much thinking of death as the meaning of life. And I began to write *Out*, which is a very "sick" novel. I think one can feel that. I imagine a time when the whites are discriminated against; the whole color bar is reversed. But the reason the whites are discriminated against is because they are sick, dying from this mysterious radiation disease to which colored people are more immune. My protagonist is a sick old man who cannot get a job and cannot remember his previous status. This exactly reproduced the state of illness that I was in, so in that sense of protection it was still a very mimetic novel. But I wasn't consciously trying to do anything different. I started writing a sentence and fell back on the pillow exhausted. I didn't really know where I was going, and it took me a long time to write it. I was groping. So I don't think it was a conscious decision. But then with *Such* I really took off on my own. I don't think there's any more influence of Robbe-Grillet on *Such*. I would say that *Such* is my first really "Me" novel, where I don't owe anything to anyone else.

Q: Can you characterize that "Me"-ness?

A: I think *Such* is much more imaginative, for one thing. It's still, of course, concerned with death since the man dies and is brought back to life. Again, I don't explain why. I get much more interested in fact, in the impact of language on the imagination. I suppose it's really with *Between* that I discovered what I could do with language. With *Such* it's still a fairly straightforward use of language, but very much in another world with this slow return to reality as the man comes back to life, but he then sees the stars as radiation. And having hit on that idea but not really knowing where I was going I then had to do a lot of work, learn something about astrophysics, for example, since I was using it as a metaphor for the world. It's in *Such* that I discovered that jargon, of whatever kind, has great poetry. For instance if you take a scientific law and use it literally, it becomes a metaphor. Of course, this is a schoolboy joke. If the teacher says, "Weight consists of the attraction between two bodies," everybody giggles. But if you take it further and use more complicated astrophysical laws about bouncing signals on the moon, for instance, to express the distance between people, then it becomes a very active metaphor. Yet it's treated as ontological in the world of the fiction, like a sunset or a tree. So this sort of thing, you see, isn't a conscious decision, it's a discovery.

Q: Is that how you would define the experimental novel?

A: Yes, in a way. People often use the term "experimental novel" to mean just something peculiar, or as a genre in itself (on the same level as "realistic" or "fantastic" or "romantic" or "science" fiction). But to experiment is really not knowing where you're going and discovering. Experimenting with language, experimenting with form and discovering things, and sometimes you might get it wrong and it just doesn't come off. When I discovered that there is great beauty in technical language (and this comes into its own in *Thru* where I actually use critical jargon as poetry), I also discovered that there's beauty and humor in confronting discourses, jostling them together, including, for instance, computer language. In *Such* it's astrophysics and in *Between* it's all the languages, the lunatic, empty speech-making of different congresses, political, sociological, literary and so on, and of course, actual languages, different languages, all jostled together, since my protagonist, who's a simultaneous interpreter, is always in different countries. Discourse became my subject matter. So discovery is one meaning of "experimental," and this would be, to answer your earlier question, my "utterly other discourse," where the actual language is different from the language you and I are using now, or that I find in other books. The second meaning is to see how far I can go with language, with vocabulary and syntax, and this is much more conscious. In *Between*, for example, a sentence can continue correctly, but by the end of it we are elsewhere in time and space. And I chose and imposed constraint, not using the verb "to be," just as in *Amalgamemnon* I decided to use only non-realizing tenses and moods like the future, the conditional, the imperative.

Q: Why did you write *Between* without the verb "to be"?

A: I wanted to get the constant sense of movement. She's always on the go, she never knows where she wakes up. It's amazing how once you don't use the verb "to be" (and it's extremely difficult not to), you're forced to find another verb, and it's usually an active verb. This gave a sense of constant movement. The other reason was the other sense of the verb "to be," the existential sense—she just doesn't know who she is, she is always translating from one language to another and never quite knows to which language she belongs, and in fact she belongs to three because she's German, French, and married to an Englishman, so the basic convention is English. The other languages are used to show that she doesn't know every language in the world. They block the text, rather like the ideograms in Pound. Things like "exit" in Polish, people don't necessarily recognize it. So I'm playing with disorientation, the disorientation of travel, we've all had it. And the double-reading jokes, too, are familiar. If you read a word in your own language, it can come out like a pun: "lecheria," in Spanish, for example, which means milk shop, but of course, she reads it as "lechery." And that kind of disorientation is very personal to me. I was brought up in a trilingual family, and we were always making these kinds of jokes. This loss of identity through language was very important. I don't know that the lack of the verb "to be" actually contributes to it, but that was the reason for it. It would be very indirect, but that was a conscious choice; I wasn't groping for anything. Experiment, then, means two things. One is that you're groping, you don't quite know where you're going, and you make discoveries about language. And the other is that you decide on a constraint, which produces a different style, the reader doesn't know why but he feels it, the physical signifier is made more physical, the signified less important. A year after the publication of *Between* (1968), Perec brought out *La disparition*, written (much more drastically) entirely without the letter *e*. In French, this mean far fewer feminine pronouns, and then only with the definite article *la* (*une* being outlawed), or abstractions in *-tion* (etc.), whereas all the masculine nouns have to be introduced by the indefinite article *un* (*le* being outlawed). This consequence alone, and there are others, such as rare words, foreign words, makes the language extraordinarily immediate, concrete, cliché-free. Obviously we had similar concerns.

Q: But not using the verb "to be" in *Between* had a thematic purpose.

Does using only the future tense in *Amalgamemnon* also have a thematic purpose?

A: If you like. But my original purpose was purely technical. Genette shows how language is so structured that you have to situate yourself in time, but not in space. You have to use tenses so that the narrator is either speaking after the event he is telling (that is the large majority), or before, with the future, the event hasn't occurred yet. The future is theoretically impossible over a whole narrative; it occurs only in a mini-narrative such as a prophecy or a marching order. Even SF is written in the past and postdated, so is the Apocalypse. This is because the reader needs to know that the story he is reading has happened or is happening. So that was a challenge, a purely technical one. But the more I explored narrative in the future tense, the more I realized that we're living all the time in a kind of pseudo-mini future. A lot of the news is given in the future. I don't mean an actual event that hasn't happened yet, but there's a tremendous amount of speculation like "Tomorrow the prime minister will meet the president of . . . and they will probably discuss. . . ." By the time they've met and discussed it, it's gone, and they're speculating about something else, when will the summit be, and so on. We're always living in this kind of future so that when a thing happens, it's always a big letdown, not to mention *the* future of the death of the planet, which is hovering over all of us. This is something new that I wanted to explore, the sort of predictability of discourse, particularly political discourse, but also of much ordinary human discourse in private situations. Even more so since sociologists and psychologists have analyzed it, and we all understand each other's hidden motives. This is something which has taken surprise and wonder out of living. So, the original technical motive acquires a thematic "motivation" (in the Genette sense). Not the other way around.

Q: Each novel, since your first, seems to have more humor and vitality. There is a joyful tone that comes through each novel. Part of the tone is due to the language and its playfulness. Do you work intentionally to communicate that joy?

A: Yes, I am aware of it. Obviously, like everyone, I've known deep unhappiness, but I think I'm a very balanced person. Perhaps *balance* is the wrong word. It sounds as though I never lose my temper, but that's not true, I'm very impatient. Serene is perhaps what I mean. And humor is one of the ways to achieve that serenity and the bubbling result of it. Almost out of disillusion, if you like, that you don't expect anything else. It gives me, at any rate, a tremendous . . . how shall I put it . . . self-reliance. Some people are so terrified of being alone they'd rather be with a bore. I love interesting people but I'd far rather be on my own than with a bore. To answer your question, the only moments in life when I'm 100 percent happy, almost deliriously happy, are when I'm writing, so that there is this feeling of creation of what you do with words, this joy when you hit on something. Well, I know what Freud would say about all this, but that doesn't worry me. I'm just very happy when I'm writing. I think this probably comes through in the joy of each text. *Out* was probably a sad text, and some people think that I'm actually a melancholy writer beneath the "dazzling wit" and all that. This is the sort of thing that tends to be said by the reviewers.

Q: There is a sense of solitude in *Amalgamemnon* and *Xorandor*.

A: Yes, well you can't hide what you are. I *am* alone, but I think I've become a far better writer through being alone. It's amazing the exploration one can do when one is never interrupted. My kind of writing takes immense concentration and single-mindedness. I think this is also one of the difficulties most women writers experience if they have children and families and they're always interrupted, then they get scattered. In that sense, my being alone has been a blessing. It probably means that I put a tremendous intensity into it because it's all I've got, so that probably explains this feeling of joy. It means, of course, that I lead a very selfish life, too. I never have to think about feeding a man, and if I want to work until five in the morning, I work until five in the morning. I mean, I live *only* for myself. There are always students who need help, and friends, but basically I don't have this constant pull that most women have. But after all, artists are selfish people. If you really want to give yourself 100 percent to your art, then it's better to be alone. Most male writers have found this out. They've used their women very badly, or just as slaves to bring them cups of tea or do their retyping.

Q: Could you talk a bit about the idea of redundancy in *Amalgamemnon*?

A: Socially, being redundant means that you're out of a job. This is in England, I don't know if it has the same meaning in America. But in information theory, redundancy means that something is marked over and over again. For instance, some languages are more redundant than others. French is more redundant than English. If you take a French sentence like "Les petites filles sont jolies," you've got the plural marked in five times. In "the little girls are pretty," it is marked only twice. The feminine is marked three times in the French sentence and only once (lexically) in the English. Redundancy here means that an element is said many times in case of noise or disturbance. In that particular opening of *Amalgamemnon* the first meaning of "And soon I shall be quite redundant at last despite of all" is the social meaning, but when I come to "like you after queue," I play with the two meanings. Because of course the letter *u* coming after *q* is redundant, since it always comes after *q*. Its information content is zero. It is merely a marking of the *q*.

Q: How would you say the idea of redundancy is carried through thematically in *Amalgamemnon*?

A: I don't know. It's an interesting question, because originally it didn't start like that at all. I forget how it did start, it was just this use of the future, this Cassandra theme, and this predictability, and by predictability, of course, I mean redundancy. The social meaning didn't come until later. What concerned me was this predictability of the news. Politically, if somebody is interviewed about something, let's say the leader of the Communist

Party, you know just how he's going to answer, same with other parties. Everyone's playing his role. That's what I wanted to explore, this predictability. The Cassandra theme in the novel refers not only to Cassandra in the Greek myth, where she is prophesying the end of Troy, and nobody believes her. That's one side of prophesying. But prophesying can also come from this predictability that is just so obvious that you wonder why nobody sees it. For forty years the economists have been telling us, "Oh no, there couldn't possibly be another stock market crash like 1929." Well, maybe technically the crash of 1987 wasn't like 1929, but I'd been waiting for it, and I know nothing about finance. So this is what I was trying to explore, why it is we are led by people who can't even predict what it's their job to predict. I was trying to explore on all sorts of levels—political, psychological, metaphysical, and so on. And then precisely to make things easier, because originally it was quite a difficult text, and since I'm accused of being difficult, I made a conscious effort to motivate this, as the theoreticians would say, to place this Cassandra creature in some sort of context, and I hit on this idea of making her a redundant professor, and it fit in very well since she's reading Herodotus. In other words, I gave a realistic motivation to all her inventions. She's got nothing else to do now since she's redundant. It was like a sop, to help people understand, and naturally all the reviewers picked on that and said the novel was about a redundant woman professor!

Q: Your work, for many readers, is extremely demanding. Although novels like *Amalgamemnon* provide realistic details as a frame for the abstract elements, it's often difficult to separate them. In fact, the text seems quite porous as the abstract and realistic commingle. One must read in a new way, so to speak.

A: I don't apologize for that at all. One of my aims in writing the way I do is to teach people to read. They have forgotten how to read. I want what Barthes calls the writerly text as opposed to the readerly text—the readerly text is the consumer product, which can be flicked through. I'm not against that—to read on the train or in the bath—but where is the pleasure of reading if, in fact, you're just going to skip things such as description? The very word *redundancy* comes back here because, as you know, structuralists did a lot of work on this—what is description, what is the effect of the real, how is the effect of the real provoked, and so on. There is a vast amount of redundancy in the realistic novel that the reader skips. That was the point, swelling the detail to fantasy pitch, the fetish object. But today people get that from other media and read just for the plot, for the event, and they don't really want to know what the writer is doing. I think this is a tremendous loss. So what Barthes calls the writerly text is the text which the reader is writing with the writer—I want to share my writing with the reader. Of course, that means the reader has to wake up and see what I'm doing. All the writers of the postmodern movement are doing this; I'm not the only one. Many people say that my novels are difficult; indeed, a lot of people complain about it, but when my fans say that, it's a compliment. They go back and see that I've done this, or that. They say my books are slow reading, and consider this a pleasure. If I achieve that, then I'm very pleased.

Q: *Xorandor* is somewhat easier but still requires a great deal of attention to every word.

A: Yes, but that book is a much more "realistic" novel. SF always is realistically anchored. I was very pleased with Ellen's paper on it, which treats it still as a self-reflexive experimental novel, because a lot of people thought that Brooke-Rose was having a rest and writing "just" science fiction.[2]

Q: Your two most recent works, *Amalgamemnon* and *Xorandor*, seem, in many ways, more readable than some of the earlier works—also innovative, but more accessible. Are you doing this intentionally?

A: Probably, yes. It's a little exasperating to be told all the time that one is difficult and unreadable, but also don't forget that my path had to go through *Thru*, which is a very special sort of unreadable book. I had to write it because—there I was teaching narratology and being a writer. The contradiction, the tension, was such that I had to write *Thru*, which is a novel about the theory of a novel. It's the most self-reflexive novel that it's possible to write. It's a text about intertextuality, a fiction about fictionality. But it is very difficult, and I knew that I would be rapped on the knuckles. Still, I needed to write it, I needed to send up the structuralist jargon, also to use it as poetry, to use the very jargon of narratology as metaphor, in a way, to deconstruct it. It's a very Derridean book. In fact, all the things it spelled downwards in the beginning, announcing certain themes acrostically, are straight out of Derrida. I was influenced by Derrida at the time, but I didn't want to do just a deconstruction of realism. . . . Yes, that really is a very difficult novel. It was written almost tongue-in-cheek for a few narratologist friends. I never thought it would be accepted. It was something I had to do. My publisher loved it; at least my editor loved it, the publisher was perhaps not quite so pleased, and of course, it didn't sell. And after that I did realize that I had probably, career-wise as they say, done myself a lot of harm because I was really dismissed as completely potty, doing surrealistic tricks and typography, and so on. It's written for people who understand narratology and the crisis of representation. If you like, it's a little bit as though I wrote a book entirely on engineering that only engineers could understand.

Q: However, many readers, particularly American readers, know narratology in fairly superficial ways, and they probably could follow much of *Thru*—more than you might think.

A: That's good, because I had so accepted the fact that people found it unreadable that, I suppose, with *Amalgamemnon* I really did make a big effort. There were many versions of that. It took nearly nine years to get it right, although I did produce a critical book as well. It took me so long to get it right, partly because of this question of tone, because the future tense can sound very portentous, and I didn't want that, but also because I wanted it to be readable, and the first versions were not. They were kind of thick and dense. So yes, there has been a conscious effort. I don't know. Perhaps it's also come naturally. I'm more at ease, and I'm happier in my writing, as you pointed out yourself. Perhaps I communicate better and have simply learned my trade. It's taken me a long time! But it's true that in *Xorandor* I went back to telling a story, though I still had to do it in this way, with the kids quarreling about how to tell it themselves. Yes, I quite agree. The two novels I have in my head that are to follow will probably be easier to read. But I still think that people should take pleasure in reading, that it is up to the writer to write in such a way as to direct the attention of the reader to the richness of the possibilities of language. Because otherwise we're just going to lose language, this sloppy, almost un-English English that everyone is talking. People are just not aware of the solidity of their language. It's sliding away. Of course, something always comes to replace it, but I still think that unless we do something the whole reading and writing capacity is going to just disappear. Do what? Well, all one solitary writer can do is to fight against this consumer-product attitude, to make people enjoy working with you.

Q: Then can we assume that we do not need to worry that you're moving towards realism?

A: Were you worrying? Well, I might be, you know. Why not? I think I say somewhere in *A Rhetoric of the Unreal* that realism may come back, but in a new form, refreshed by all this. We already have magic realism and hyper-realism, after all. Fantastic realism. The real made unreal and vice versa. Sometimes there is a period of tremendous experiment, and then somehow the old thing comes back again, renewed by all the experimenting that's been going on. That may be the only useful purpose of such experiment, I just don't know. But that doesn't concern me too much. I also think that the way "experiment" is set against "realism," the way I and others are said to be working against the "realistic" novel, is a great oversimplification. Even the most experimental, most postmodern writer is still basically realistic. They may not be "imitating" reality, in the sense of reproducing a familiar situation, but ultimately they're representing something. There's always a representative function simply because language is representative. There have been very naïve attitudes towards representation, and we've all become much more self-conscious about it, but I don't think we can actually get out of representation.

NOTES

[1]Ellen G. Friedman and Muriam Fuchs, eds. (Princeton: Princeton Univ. Press, 1989), 55-71. Rpt. in Brooke-Rose's STT, 250-64.

[2]Ellen G. Friedman, "Feminine Narrative, Science Fiction, and the Science of Fiction: Christine Brooke-Rose's *Xorandor,*" Modern Language Association Convention, Special Session on the Works of Christine Brooke-Rose, December 1987.

"Just Words on a Page":
The Novels of Christine Brooke-Rose

Richard Martin

> Whenever I slide into a realistic scene, say a love scene or some-
> thing like that, something happens later to destroy it, to show that
> these are just words on a page.[1]

CHRISTINE BROOKE-ROSE'S first novel, *The Languages of Love*, opens with
a discussion of "palatal dipthongisation in fourteenth century Kentish" during a doctoral oral examination; her most recently published tenth novel,
Xorandor, concludes with an agreement by the narrators to delete the
computer files containing their entire text. These moments are representative of two major concerns of Brooke-Rose's writing: a fascination with
language, and an insistence upon the unreality of fictional discourse. The
concern with language in action which she formulated at the outset of her
writing career —"I'm interested in language as a process, not a thing or an
essence" (LL 66)—became the consistent keynote of her subsequent books,
together with the assertion that the mastery of language is of necessity an
ambiguous achievement: "language is your strength and your strength is
your weakness" (T 136). At the same time, the mastery of language leads
to a carnivalesque exploitation of the interplay between the semantic and
phonological dimensions of words. Brooke-Rose's novels abound in both
sophisticated and appalling puns; from the ex-soldier, now a hearse driver,
who sums up his career as "from the Service Corps to serving corpses" (ST
130) to the multileveled pun of "a dictator who will be venerhated as a
sacred milchcowtow" (A 95).

In Brooke-Rose's novels, fiction is continually put forward as that which
is essentially unreliable and yet also essentially human. It is the product of
the imagination in its eternal toying with what it likes to think of as the truth
of the past: "Strange how the reality of the past comes to our mind most
immediately as fiction. Some even say that all our knowledge of the past is
fiction" (DD 29). It is the writer's ability to create new worlds with words
that is essential to the fictional process and, at the same time, itself the
source of the fragility of the narrative discourse: "You start with nothing,
treat it as something and in no time at all you have infinity or thereabouts.
Storytellers do the same I believe" (S 71). The necessity to go on telling
stories is central to Brooke-Rose's writing; her novels suggest that the

38

compulsion to narrate is a universal human quality, whether it is the Italian policeman in *Thru*, who makes long notes about a minor traffic offense and, when jokingly questioned whether he is writing a novel, replies, "Ma, devo raccontare qualcosa" ("Well, I have to tell them something"), or the character near the end of the same book who states that "Narration is life and I am Scheherezade" (52, 133).

Such outspoken concerns with the nature of fiction and of narrative inevitably lead to textual comments upon the text itself. These tend to take the form either of warning asides to the reader or authorial remarks upon the ongoing narrative. In the early books such moments are rare, but still significant: "An adventure, especially an adventure of the mind, can begin anywhere, as long as the mind exists to experience it, imagine it, invent it, or whatever the mind does with an adventure" (DD 7). The reader—the mind experiencing the invented adventure—is accepted as a necessary partner in the realization of Brooke-Rose's narration, continually addressed and guided; warned, for example, that "we must place it in context, mustn't we . . ." (S 140), or, more frequently, exhorted to skepticism about finite meanings: " 'one has to understand immediately because the thing understood slips away altogether with the need to understand' " (B 41).

Although Brooke-Rose's novels seem to avoid the explicitly autobiographical, some knowledge of the salient features of her life is perhaps necessary, if only to give a possible explanation for her interest in languages, and to suggest sources for some details of her plots.[2] Christine Brooke-Rose was born in Geneva, Switzerland, in 1923, the daughter of an English father, Alfred Northbrook Rose, and a Swiss mother of American descent. After an education at schools in Switzerland, Belgium, and England, Brooke-Rose joined the women's branch of the Royal Air Force in 1941. After the Second World War, she studied English at Oxford, going on to do graduate work at London University, where she received her doctorate, with a dissertation on Middle English, in 1954. With the completion of her academic education, Brooke-Rose took up cultural journalism, writing regular review articles and essays for major British weekly publications such as the *Observer*, the *Sunday Times*, the *New Statesmen*, and the *Times Literary Supplement*. In 1968 she accepted the offer of a professorship at the University of Paris VIII, where for the next twenty years she taught courses in English and American literature, literary theory, linguistics, and translation. During this period she built up a considerable international reputation as a literary scholar and critic. Brooke-Rose retired from her post at the University of Paris in 1988 and now lives and writes in Provence.

Both *The Languages of Love* (1957) and *The Sycamore Tree* (1958) are concerned, in the first instance, with conventional human relationships. Julia Grampion, in the former book, bears a superficial resemblance to her creator—a recent Ph.D. in English Philology, who earlier served with the Air Force in Germany. As the book opens she is at the end of her academic training, and more or less engaged to Paul Brodrick, lecturer in Afro-Asian Philology. The relationship breaks down over the barrier to Paul, a practicing Catholic, of Julia's divorce from a wartime husband. She finds physical solace in an affair with Bernard Reeves, the author of a book on courtly love. In this novel, the conventionalities of the main plot pale in comparison with the more colorful subplot, which involves Georgina Raymond, a poet and a friend of Julia's, and her devoted lover Hussein Abdillahi, a native of the fictitious African country of Sanuri, whose love is expressed by the traditional gift of a camel, and in numerous poetic outbursts.

The first novel introduces features that become characteristic of Brooke-Rose's fiction. There is, for example, the obtrusiveness of her learning, which itself dictates the nature of her linguistic wordplay; contemplating the offer of a university job teaching English philology, Julia sees herself going through "the minutiae of scansion, dialect forms, emendation, haplography, *hapax legomena* and *anacolutha* in Beowulf. That wasn't what she wanted at all. She began to invent a whimsical love affair between Anna Coluthon, who was too inconsequential, and Hapax Legomenon, who was too unique" (LL 34).[3] At the same time, language is not merely a vehicle for intellectual games, but a suspect quantity in the relationship between the sexes. While Paul complains to Julia, "we don't even seem to talk the same language" (43), Julia attacks Bernard at the height of a lovers' quarrel for the very ease with which he is able to deploy language as a form of protection: " 'You have easy labels to dismiss every shade of feeling, haven't you? But the feelings are just as real, however they are expressed. . . . You think that by giving an emotion a name that makes it sound silly, the emotion will go' " (174). The outcome of Julia's relationship with Bernard remains deliberately ambiguous; for Brooke-Rose it is not the happy ending that matters, but the ability to assimilate the significance of the difference between the emotion and its expression: "Julia," the novel ends, "had learnt the languages of love" (239).

Nina Jackson's search for happiness with a man in *The Sycamore Tree* is as unsatisfactory as the novel itself. Married to an American novelist who teaches philosophy at Oxford, she falls in love with someone she dislikes, Howard Cutting, an ambitious literary critic. In this second novel, Brooke-Rose's hand is less sure, and she forces her narrative into unlikely plot devices culminating in the shooting of Nina by a Hungarian refugee poet. After a brief recovery, and having made her confession to her husband, Nina dies in a melodramatic conclusion.

In the early chapters of the novel, Nina Jackson is presented as a vehicle for Brooke-Rose's comments on the role of the physically attractive educated woman in a male-dominated society: "She was one of those women who make sweet, devoted wives to sweet devoted husbands, but to whom most men find it impossible to talk without making some crude reference to her physical attractions" (24). Nina has already revolted against the roles of the ex-academic turned mother and the "intelligent-modern-mother personality" by "grooming herself into a frivolous dumb sweet thing" (42). Thus she becomes the perfect fiction within a fiction that later characterizes so many of the personae of Brooke-Rose's narratives. She takes on a further positive characteristic in that she is invested with the ability to gameplay with words, as when she, like her creator, is tempted by the possibility of taking conventional formulae literally: " 'How many are you, madam, one?' a waiter had asker her in a restaurant that morning, and she wanted to say, 'There are at least a hundred of me today' " (218). However, the attempt to turn the novel and the figure of Nina into some clearly positive statement fails, so that her sudden end comes as a merciful release.

In her third and longest novel, *The Dear Deceit* (1960), Brooke-Rose turns her back on the contemporary scene in order to explore the possibilities of retrospective narration. The novel begins and ends with Philip Hayley, who attempts to reconstruct the life and personality of his father; Alfred Northbrook Hayley is, in many respects, a conventional figure of his times, a charming wastrel, an exploiter of others, in particular of women, and a professional fraud. Seen in the context of Brooke-Rose's later work, the plot of the novel is less interesting than the structure employed; Alfred's life is traced backwards from his death to his early childhood in the 1880s, so that a composite picture is built up in reverse. The justification for this procedure is contained in the conviction that stories are subservient to their narration, since fictionality implies an intellectual adventure, whose fascination is rooted in its own imaginative invention. In addition to its structural premises, *The Dear Deceit* is also of interest for the way in which Brooke-Rose's penchant for language games leads her into stylistic experimentation. In the fourth chapter of the novel, in which Arthur Hayley is dying, she creates a remarkable deathbed interior monologue which is the first example of the disembodied narrative voice of her later work:

Somebody was dying, evidently. But he didn't look good, no. Old Flabby. His belly must be a mountain, or had it sunk? How did one rescind an order? If he moved his little finger perhaps. So heavy. How did one revoke a life? There shall be weeping and gnashing of teeth. But it was so heavy. His little finger, that was it. . . . (62)

If *The Dear Deceit* gives evidence of dissatisfaction with linear structures and conventional narrative patterns, the book which followed, *The Middlemen* (1961), makes it equally clear that Brooke-Rose was still uncertain about the direction she intended her fiction to take. Basically a satire on the growing importance of the intermediary in the culture of the early sixties, the novel reveals its author's impatience with plot, and a growing interest in vocal collage. Brooke-Rose offers the reader a satirical collective portrait of representative "middlemen"—an advertising man, a public relations expert, a psychoanalyst, TV personalities, a literary agent, lawyers, realtors, and critics. Only the most tenuous of threads links the various characters before nemesis overtakes a number of them on a Greek island, where their author kills them off in a volcanic eruption. Everything and anything becomes material for Brooke-Rose's narration: advertising slogans, publicity campaign material, and psychoanalytic jargon. In *The Middle-men*, the language of narration begins to demonstrate the plurivocality that is so characteristic of her later work. An overall intelligence exploits the nuances of even the most banal of utterances. Near the end of the novel, for example, Brook-Rose quotes from a travel brochure describing the fatal Greek island:

The island of Hephaestos is the most fantastical in the world that will furnish you with most incredible dining conversation for many years back home. In two hours of one another you can indulge in spearing numerous big fish beneath its saphire waters . . . then visiting the most horrific landscapes like the moon, a petrified foretaste of our immediate future perhaps. . . . (192)

By simply offering this to the reader as an authentic transcript, Brooke-Rose seems to invite a conspiratorial enjoyment of its absurdities. Whereas here she clearly delights in the ambiguity of phrases such as "in two hours of one another" or the implicit wordplay of "a petrified foretaste," in later novels she incorporates such *objets trouvés* into the fabric of her own narration, thus indulging in that fusion of various discourses that particularly interests her. In *The Dear Deceit* and *The Middlemen*, Brooke-Rose was beginning to discover the basic elements of the novels that were to follow: the abandonment of narrational linearity based on the exigencies of a unified plot; the incorporation into the text of extraliterary discourses; a multiple narrative voice; and finally, the planned subversion of illusions of authenticity.

Having proved that she could write straightforward, conventionally structured, naturalistic fiction, Brooke-Rose completely broke with this tradition during the sixties and early seventies. The next four books play a variety of disruptive games with the form and language of the novel. In *Out* (1964), there are no characters in the conventional sense; rather, as to some extent in *The Middlemen*, there are unmediated voices who, either directly or indirectly, impart information, or who are overheard in conversation with one another. Nor is there any great resemblance to a conventional plot, since language is more important than content. It is characteristic of Brooke-Rose's experimental fiction that the novel is set in an undefined future; these "out-of-time" narratives grant her the same sort of freedom from convention that the science fiction writer enjoys, and also free her from any necessity to adhere to principles of verisimilitude. What action there is takes place at an undefined time in the future, after the so-called "displacement," when the white races lost their former supremacy; now called the "Colourless," they live in settlements as workers and servants. The elderly "protagonist" of the novel spends most of his time endeavoring to gain employment as a gardener. He proves to be a failure, a misfit, and is sent to undergo "psychoscopy" to make him content and amenable. The novel ends with him back at work as an odd job gardener once again.

There is a pervasive air of depressed solemnity about the eavesdropped utterances in *Out*, and thus also a lack of the playfulness that one has come to associate with Brooke-Rose's work. In keeping with this hopelessness and gloom, views of human existence are expressed that are reminiscent of Samuel Beckett, as, for example, the final words of the novel: "We are merely marking time and time is nothing, nothing. A moment of agony, of burning flesh, an aspect of the human element disintegrating to ash, and you are dead. But that's another story" (196).[4] What, however, *Out* does introduce into Brooke-Rose's writing is that sort of self-reflexivity which became the hallmark of much American innovative fiction some ten years later. This tends to take the form of anticipating the reader's difficulties with the text by giving the speakers such comments as "it is difficult to tell who's talking in this type of dialogue" or "since you're inventing this dialogue you ought to give something to the other chap to say" (61, 17).

Brooke-Rose herself has commented on the difficulty that readers have found in her work, and attempts to defuse some of the criticism leveled at her on these grounds by suggesting that in her desire to "shift fictional conventions" she may even have deliberately attempted to make readers uneasy.[5] However, I think it says much about this mooted difficulty that the account she gives of *Such* (1966) in her article goes beyond that which even a careful first-time-round reader can hope to grasp. Although it is interesting to discover that distances between astral bodies are used as a generalized metaphor for the distances between people, or that the chief experiment of the book was the fusion of outer space and psychic space, neither piece of information is vital for an understanding of the novel. Such is the nature of Brooke-Rose's difficulty: it has in part to do with the inevitable gap between intention and reception, and not with the actual material difficulty of the proffered text.

The central character of *Such* dies and returns to life after having been transported to some "other" state, where he experiences various quasi-SF adventures as "Someone" together with a female partner, "Something," and their children (all named for a different blues number—Gut Bucket, Potato Head, Tin Roof, etc.). Back in his "real" life, Larry is a member of a team of scientists led by a professor of radio astronomy. In this existence he experiences his wife's infidelity, the suspicions of his teenage children and the unwelcome attention of an intrusive TV journalist, who tapes his confessional monologues for use in a television film on the morals of scientists. Far from having no plot, *Such* is almost overloaded with potential plots which tend to be only partially developed.

In many respects *Such* contains most of the characteristic elements of the four books that follow it. First there is the introduction of a basic strategy upon which the narrative rests, in this case a persistent use of the planned reiteration of phrases, sentences, and even whole passages. This device, which sends the reader back into the text, has the double effect of both underling the artifice of fiction and of giving the reader an increased sense of complicity with the author. It relies on the reader recognizing not only the repetition of a key statement such as "I have a name and no story," but also the variation when it reappears some hundred pages later as "I have a story but no name" (32, 173)—statements that neatly summarize Larry's two existences. It is also worth noting the way Brooke-Rose converts the self-imposed problematics of her narrative into a positive statement about fiction in general. Having introduced the complexity of the man who, while dead lives a full and eventful other life, she deliberately utilizes this "unreal" aspect of the narrative to state her firm belief in the infinite delights of the universe of the imagination. *Such* ends: "Out of the story of a death and amazing recovery and into the unfinished unfinishable story of Dippermouth, Gut Bucket Blues, my sweet Potato Head, Tin Roof, Really, Something and me" (194).

The creation of a foundation premise on which to build the narrative structure is further developed in *Between* (1968), whose title is its own guiding metaphor. From the first page announcement, "Between doing and not doing the body floats," the text plays multiple variations on the possibilities of definition by opposition—the state of being between. Initially *Between* exploits the potentialities of being between languages as exemplified by the central characters who, as professional translators, mediate between the languages in which they are competent. The protagonist (if that word has any meaning in such a context) is a young woman translator, born (between cultures) in France of a German father. There is, however, no plot worth speaking of—"no one does anything at all" (80)—rather the novel confronts the reader with a series of repetitious monologues (somewhat reminiscent of *The Middlemen*) that are uttered between plane journeys, international congresses, and tourist excursions, in cosmopolitan hotel rooms, and airports.

Between exists in the interstices of languages ranging from French and German to Polish, Turkish and modern Greek; it fascinates because of the total mastery Brooke-Rose displays over a text that, because of its own multiplicity, threatens to be erased by the complexity of its discourse. Beyond the linguistic fireworks lies the contrast between *langue* and *parole* in language as formulated in the theories of Ferdinand de Saussure. For example, the failed lights of an advertisement in New York set off a series of associations interwoven with items from conference translation:

Above Times Square five letters have gone dark in STU   ANT with the eye in an imprecision of nationality reading STUPEFIANT—The International Passport to Smoking Pleasure. Let us return for a moment to the central Saussurean dichotomy of Langue et Parole. La langue in a dumb show consists of le langage moins la Parole, une institution sociale, un système de valeurs which escapes from all premeditation since the individual cannot create it or modify it. La parole on the other hand consists of an individual act of selection and actualisation. (167)

The reader is at once reminded that Saussure has actually been quoted earlier during the translation of a conference paper:

Et comme l'a si bien dit Saussure, la langue peut se contenter de l'opposition de quelque chose avec rien. The marked term on the one hand, say, the feminine, grand*e*, the unmarked on the other, say, the masculine, grand. Mais notez bien que le non-marqué peut dériver du marqué par retranchement, by subtraction, par une absence qui signifie. Je répète, une absence qui signifie eine Abwesenheit die simultaneously etwas bedeutet. (32)

In both cases one inevitably becomes aware of a new ingredient in Brooke-Rose's writing: the integration into linguistic concerns of an insistence on the feminine, on the nature of the opposition between the genders. If in the first passage this is simply seen as latent in the grammatical necessities of French "*la* langue" which is in fact "*le* langage" minus "*la* parole," in the second quotation the additional weight of the clarifying effect of the interpreter's English leads to the realization that rules of grammar are being imbued with metaphorical overtones, and the translation into German adds emphasis to the subtext: the nature of the relationship of the masculine ("*le* non-marqué") to the feminine is contained in the implication of the latter's absence ("Abwesenheit"). Furthermore it is this absence that is meaningful ("die . . . etwas bedeutet"). Brooke-Rose increasingly employs such an interweaving of levels of discourse in her later books, thus injecting them with a dense semantic richness.

If *Between* is Brooke-Rose's most enjoyably accessible novelistic experiment, then *Thru* (1975) is her most personal and thus, perhaps, most "difficult." It is a novel about the writing of the novel, an exposure of fiction's fictionality, and, in the end, a deconstruction of itself in a riotous, typographical carnival that unites its author's two vocations, the novelist and the literary critic. It gave rise to some admiring narratological attention in scholarly journals,[6] but in the first instance it was a self-satisfying undertaking:

In my last book, *Thru*, I tried to join the two.
The two what?
Critic and creative writer came together in one textual act. . . . I am content, I did what I wanted, even though I won't do it again.[7]

Thru is partially generated by a university class in literature and creative writing; the characters in the stories the students write take over their own invention, thus becoming the embodiment of their own unreality and the cause of their own deconstruction. At the center of the narrative are exchanges between Armel Santores, both a character and, perhaps, the teacher of the class, and Larissa Toren, his creation, creator and partner— "if Larissa invents Armel inventing Larissa, Armel also invents Larissa inventing Armel" (108). Their names, apart from the letters *I* and *ME*, are anagrams of each other, emphasizing the self-reflexivity of their narrational inventiveness. In other passages (characteristic of the novel's insistent intertextuality) Jacques and his Master, borrowed from Diderot's *Jacques le fataliste*, exchange remarks on the process of the ongoing narration. In fact *Thru* contains any number of such quotations and comments by the fictional characters on linguistic and narratological topics: on textuality and interpretation—"within each text there is another text, within each myth another myth. The reader has to be prepared for the undecidable" (30); on transformational grammar and reality—"Generative grammar's the thing, it's the grammar of the universe and it's wildly poetic" (84-85); and in addition the novel contains almost outrageous moments of punning self-reflexivity:

Omni scient qui mal y pensent.
Ooooh.
My! That's a terrible pun.
Not when you think about it. I can do more.
So I noticed in your work. (28)

Brooke-Rose is at pains to point out the consequence of the essentially linguistic nature of fiction: that fictional characters, being nothing more than words, are hopelessly anti-mimetic and thus expendable. When Stavro Laretino, an Albanian linguist in love with Larissa, recounts his dreams to her, we read: "You are the sentence I write I am the paragraph, generating each other cutting off each other's word" (145). This reflection upon mutual, even auto-, generation and destruction is then expanded in the observation: "this is the text we are creating it verbally we are the text we do not exist either we are a pack of lies dreamt up by the unreliable narrator in love with the zeroist author in love with himself but absent in the nature of things, an etherised unauthorised other" (155).

Thru begins and ends with a multiple vision of reality expressed in the metaphor of images in the driving mirror of a car: reflections in reverse of the world behind already passed, and the observer's own present reversed image, both seen within the frame of the world ahead. These images are seen *through* the mirror, thus *Thru*, the text, reflects (upon) itself, but can only present a multiple, even false image. The text is thus a distorting mirror not only of events beyond itself, but of the process of its own generation. The novel ends:

. . . reflecting nothing but

T

E

X

(I)

U Я H T H R U

In other words, the exit from the text can only be through the text, the text is its own reversal, its own dismissal. With this conclusion it seemed that Brooke-Rose had got as far as it was possible to go with the relentless demolition of the novel.

For nine years after *Thru* she published no fiction, then in 1984 came *Amalgamemnon*. Once again a narratological problem forms the basic premise of the novel and its challenge: only future, conditional, subjunctive, and imperative verb forms are used. As a result everything is talked about but nothing *can* happen; actions, persons, even ideas, belong to the realm of the possible but indeterminate. For such a narrative the archetypical phrase of fiction "as if" becomes a thematic motif:

Soon the economic system will crumble, and political economists will fly in from all over the world and poke into its smoky entrails and utter soothing prognostications and we'll all go on as if.
    As if for instance I were someone else, Cassandra perhaps, walking dishevelled the battlements of Troy, uttering prophecies from time to time unheaded and unheeded, before being allotted as slave to victorious Agamemnon. (7)

Even this short passage reveals the basic procedures of *Amalgamemnon*: the text appears to generate itself—the mention of "smoky entrails" leads automatically to the name "Cassandra"—at the same time this Cassandra only exists in a possible variant of the future ("if . . . I were someone else"). Furthermore, reference is made to Cassandra's unheeded prophecies, so that she embodies redundancy both in terms of employment and of information. Throughout *Amalgamemnon* the potentially redundant text continuously generates further discourse, which no sooner generated, moots its own redundancy.[8]
    The narrating voice of the novel, Mira Enketei (the name is a variation on the name of the star Mira Ceti, stars and constellations being a favorite source for allusive metaphors in the text) is a university teacher of the humanities threatened with dismissal on grounds of redundancy. We are introduced to her students, to her friends, and to the men who offer self-interested assistance. As in earlier books, however, potential plot elements are not the main interest. Quite apart from anything else, Brooke-Rose exploits her gift for outrageous punning even further in *Amalgamemnon*, the puns being more intrusive because they form a part of the by now familiar pattern of significant repetition. One field of linguistic play makes use of the prefix "mim-" to emphasize only a surface version of the action concerned (mimed action), as in, "I shall mimagree, now should I not? Mimecstasy and mimagreement will always go together like sexcommunication" (14). Another of Brooke-Rose's favorite linguistic subterfuges is the wordplay based on the merging of two words into a compound that playfully comments on the word it phonetically resembles, as in "intergnashional farewell orgies" or "the slow gas-chambers of sibylisation" (102).

Although *Amalgamemnon* can be read with much surface enjoyment of
the language games and the virtuosity of the narrative confined by its tense
forms, the rich world of allusions will be lost on the reader who is not prepared to work for enlightenment. Apart from the numerous references to
astronomy, the basic source of the narrative is Herodotus, whose *Histories*
is used to juxtapose the classical past of literature, philosophy and history
with the daily events of the imaginary present as propagated by the radio
program the narrative voice is listening to, and with typical incidents of late
twentieth-century civilization. Not only does Brooke-Rose refer to figures
from Herodotus, but whole passages, suitably transposed into the future
tense, are quoted verbatim from an English translation as an ironic comment
on both the degeneration of language and the parochial localization
of events in the modern world. The rape of Europa by Zeus becomes the
first round of the European rugby football championship, and is accompanied by the plaintive cry "shall we ever make Europe," which is both a
modern-day colloquialism for Zeus's act, and an expression of despair at the
European Community's inability to act *as* a community. In *Amalgamemnon*
Brooke-Rose goes beyond the deconstruction of the novel she had practiced
in *Thru* to show that the novel survives, as all written discourse survives, on
the conscious understanding of its very nature as an adventure into the
unreal.

In spite of, or because of this, *Xorandor* (1986) marks a return to the
narrative with a clearly defined plot. The twins Jip and Zab (*John Ivor Paul*
Manning and his sister I*sab*el), computer whiz kids, discover Xorandor, a
stone that communicates in computer language. He, or it, feeds on radioactive material and has found an ideal home close to the nuclear waste dump
administered by the twins' father. With the discovery that Xorandor has the
power to reproduce, bizarre and exciting incidents are set in motion. The
most important of these is the escape of one of the stone's offspring, who,
due to a programming defect, turns terrorist, occupying a nuclear power
station and threatening to turn himself into a nuclear bomb. At the eleventh
hour the twins come to the rescue and disaster is averted.

Apart from the excitement of the story, the interest of *Xorandor* still lies
in the narrative strategy Brooke-Rose employs. Once again a foundation
premise governs her procedures: let the narrating voices be those of children; further, let them tell their story direct into a pocket computer with only
the aid of its memory and tape recording of past conversations. The introduction of the computer and tapes deals with the age-old problem of the
perfect recall of the narrator who is limited by age or education. An immediate result of these conditions is that *Xorandor* becomes a novel that plays
out reflections on the problems of narration while narration proceeds.

The novel also contains much of Brooke-Rose's familiar verbal playfulness, which leads to bravura set pieces of her dominant wit. As a computer,
Xorandor is not only capable of communicating with human beings, he
can also tune into radio broadcasts, including radio drama; everything that

has passed into his system is stored in its memory available to all who are connected to him. The terrorist stone occupying the nuclear power station thus recovers the name Lady Macbeth, and deals with the outside world in sets of appropriate quotations from Shakespeare's play:

You do but teach bloody instructions, which being taught, return to plague the inventor. That is what he said. Double double toil and trouble, fire burn and caldron bubble. I have isolated enough Uranium 235 and Plutonium 239 in this caldron to make an atom bomb, which I can detonate at any moment. When the hurlyburly's done. . . . (109)

The twins prevent disaster by persuading the authorities to send Xorandor and the offspring back to Mars (their presumed home) with plenty of radioactive material as food. This solution is based, however, on an error: in his communications with humans Xorandor has found it convenient simply to say what his questioners expect to hear. Therefore, when the stones were presumed to be Martian in origin, Xorandor supplied the desired confirmation. In fact that is not his home, and on Mars he and his offspring will probably perish. When it emerges that the offspring, who have been donated to other countries including the United States and the Soviet Union, have such a voracious appetite for radioactive materials that they can even discover and devour such useful deposits of "food" as the nuclear warheads of the military arsenal, international concern grows. Finally Xorandor makes a self-destructive sacrifice by agreeing to be returned to his Martian "home." He has, however, revealed to the twins that he and his offspring are by no means unique and the world's supply of nuclear deterrents remains threatened. After Xorandor's departure Jip and Zab agree to suppress this information by deleting the entire record they have so painstakingly created:

Meanwhile, do you agree, we dump the whole thing? No saving?
Accept. First thing tomorrow, Operation Scratch.
Promise, Jip?
Promise. (211)

Thus, once again, Brooke-Rose's discourse dismantles itself, or maybe is transformed. As Zab says to her brother, "what started as a language game had to go on as a lie, or a myth" (190). This returns the narrative to the narrators—for them the story exists even without the record, but it exists as a part of their lives, not as an artifact. The merging of fictional life and fictional narration is taken up when Jip complains that nothing is happening and Zab replies: "Something is happening to us, Jip, we're growing up. Even storytellers can change, during the story" (159). Here what appears to be a discussion of the relation of fiction to the "real world" is in fact a confirmation of the XOR AND OR of the title. This is an amalgam of computer terms for the non-exclusive alternative, AND OR, and the exclusive XOR. Thus at the center of the novel is the essential statement of Brooke-Rose's fiction to date: either fiction is mimetic, or it is a game played with words and purely fictitious, or it is both, or neither. The tellers existing only in language are as mutable as their tales. In the same way the fictional destruction of the twins' narrative at the end of the novel is a purely "as if" act. As readers of Brooke-Rose's fiction, we have now progressed from the assumption that events narrated in the written discourse can never actually take place (*Amalgamemnon*), to the discovery that not even the text we have read exists. Further, Brooke-Rose the writer has maneuvered herself into the role of pretending to write a text which we have no choice but to pretend to read.

Having traced the thirty years of Christine Brooke-Rose's novelistic career, having unfairly reduced her ten novels to snippet quotations, bald summaries, and insufficient appraisals, one begins to feel that she, too, has become as unreal, as fictitious as her character-narrators. Who will be the author of her next novel, *Verbivore* (completed in 1988)?[9] Commenting some ten years ago on the confrontation between her two personae, the novelist and the critic, Brooke-Rose, finding herself once again, as in childhood, in a French-speaking society, wrote of her other selves and of "that little girl who replied to the question Que veux-tu devenir quand tu seras grande? Un écrivain. Et la famille se pouffe de rire. Toi, un écrivain! (Oui, moi.) I must unite her with the girl who whispered down a rabbit-hole on the Sussex Downs"[10]—and, no doubt, with many more.

NOTES

[1]"An Interview with Christine Brooke-Rose," conducted by David Hayman and Keith Cohen, *Contemporary Literature* 17 (1976): 4.

[2]The biographical details that follow are largely based on information kindly made available by Christine Brooke-Rose herself.

[3]Anacoluthon is syntactical inconsistency or incoherence within a sentence, and *hapax legomenon* is Greek for something said only once. It is worth noting that the humanizing pun on *anacoluthon* is repeated more than twenty-five years later in *Amalgamemnon* (43).

[4]Compare Pozzo's comment in Beckett's *Waiting for Godot*: "One day we were born, one day we shall die, the same day, the same second, is that not enough for you? They give birth astride of a grave, the light gleams an instant, then it's night once more" (London: Faber, 1956), 89.

[5]"Illicitations," *Review of Contemporary Fiction* 9.3 (Fall 1989): 102.

[6]See Brooke-Rose's own comment, "perhaps my real fans are all narratologists," in "Illicitations." See too Emma Kafalenos, "Textasy: Christine Brooke-Rose's *Thru*," *International Fiction Review* 7 (1980): 43-46, and Shlomith Rimmon-Kenan, "Ambiguity and Narrative Levels: Christine Brooke-Rose's *Thru*," *Poetics Today* 3 (1982): 21-32.

[7]Christine Brooke-Rose, "Self-Confrontation and the Writer," *New Literary History* 9 (1977), 136.

[8]For further elaborations on this theme, see my " 'Stepping-Stones in the Dark':

Redundancy and Generation in Christine Brooke-Rose's *Amalgamemnon*" later in this book.

⁹This essay was written in 1988-89 and originally published in the *Review of Contemporary Fiction* in the fall of 1989. It had been my and the publisher's hope that I would be able to update it for this collection, but, sadly, production schedules make this impossible. Rather than attempt some superficial, brief comments on *Verbivore* and *Textermination*, I would refer the reader to the essays in this volume which deal, in part, with them—most notably those by Judy Little, Damian Grant, and Brian McHale.

¹⁰"Self-Confrontation and the Writer," 136. The French can be translated: "What do you want to be when you grow up? A writer. And the family burst out laughing. You, a writer! (Yes, me)."

The British and Their "Fixions," the French and Their Factions

Heather Reyes

Hors de l'espace asphyxiant du roman anglais contemporain lavé
dans ce pseudoréalisme national qui permet de fuir la réalité,
surgissent de rares rebelles, telle Christine Brooke-Rose.

—Hélène Cixous[1]

EVEN A BRIEF SURVEY of postwar British fiction is sufficient to make one
regret profoundly that Great Britain, after producing some of the most
exciting and innovative modernist writers, such as Woolf and Joyce, should
deny such an inspiring inheritance and return to the mode of so-called social
realism. There were, of course, one or two lone voices, such as that of B. S.
Johnson (1933-73), who tried to develop new forms and possibilities for
the novel but who ultimately despaired at the condition of British fiction.
"So many novelists," said Johnson, "write as though the revolution that was
Ulysses had never happened."[2] Elsewhere he quotes Nathalie Sarraute's
description of literature as a relay race in which the baton of innovation
is passed from one generation to the next, and adds, "The vast majority of
British novelists has dropped the baton, stood still, turned back, or not even
realized there is a race."[3]

Johnson was one of the few British writers of the period—along with
Brooke-Rose—to be aware of and to care about what was going on in
France with regard to new forms of writing and criticism. Others who were
aware rejected the "experiments" of the *nouveaux romanciers* with a mixture of petulance, xenophobia, and sheer unwillingness to countenance the
"different." British intellectual parochialism was no doubt why it took
structuralism a decade to cross the Channel. Even those at the forefront
of literary developments and with a natural interest in what the French were
doing remained unaware of just how rapidly theories of the novel had
advanced—even Brooke-Rose herself. Before going to work in Paris in
1968, she had submitted plans to write a book on the theory of the modern
novel and had received an advance from a publisher to do so. However,
when she became aware of what had already been achieved in this field
in France, she had to change her plans:

Since going to Paris, I realise that the contract I've signed and the synopsis I've done
are useless. It's all been done in Paris already and I'm ten years behind. I thought my

ideas were way-out and original but when I found what had been done in France, I realised I was completely naive. So now I'm just catching up. I don't want to write a book that's just a vulgarisation of what's already been done, so if I find I've nothing new to say, I won't bother writing it; I'll just repay the money.[4]

In February 1972, Brooke-Rose took part in a discussion on Radio 3's "Arts Commentary" program (along with Gabriel Josipovici and Julian Mitchell) that addressed these very issues of why new fiction and criticism took so long to cross the Channel, why so little was translated, and whether there was any common ground between the contemporary literary movements in France and Britain. Those attempting to find or establish common ground had a great deal of entrenched prejudice to overcome.

British resistance to new developments is widely recorded and commented upon. David Lodge, for example, has admitted that "There is a good deal of evidence to suggest that the English literary mind is peculiarly committed to realism and resistant to non-realistic modes to an extent that might be described as prejudice."[5] American critics, too, were aware of British literary conservatism, as Rubin Rabinovitch points out:

The critical mood in England has produced a climate in which traditional novels can flourish and anything out of the ordinary is given the denigratory label "experiment" and neglected. . . . The successful novelist in England becomes, too quickly, a part of the literary establishment. . . . All too often he uses his position as critic to endorse the type of fiction he himself is writing and he attacks those whose approach is different.[6]

In *Against Interpretation*, Susan Sontag applied the criticism to American novels as well as British. Suggesting that, compared with other art forms, the novel is painfully backward, she believed it had "sunk to the level of an art form deeply, if not irrevocably, compromised by philistinism" and asked for a mode of fiction to be developed that would be truly unfamiliar and challenging.[7]

But let us concentrate for the moment on the British scene. Rabinovitch's judgment concerning the "literary establishment" can be verified by looking at statements made by such "establishment" figures as C. P. Snow and Kingsley Amis. Snow appears to have regarded all experimentation to have died with Joyce and Woolf: "Looking back, we can see what an odd affair the 'experimental' novel was." He believed that it sacrificed reflection, moral awareness, and "investigatory intelligence," and that it was for this reason that it died "from starvation, because its intake of human stuff was so low." Kingsley Amis considers "experimental" to consist of "obtruded oddity, whether in construction—multiple viewpoints and such—or in style." With a jibe at those who write differently from himself, he characterizes experimental writers as those who "shift from one scene to the next in mid-sentence," and "cut down on verbs or definite articles."[8]

Brooke-Rose's earliest novels were in the "realistic" style acceptable to the establishment and earned her a solid reputation. Muriel Spark, reviewing

The Dear Deceit (1959), called her "a new George Eliot" while another review of the same novel links her with Iris Murdoch and Elizabeth Jane
Howard as part of the "formidable trio" of postwar women novelists. To be
fair to British critics, even the much more adventurous *Out* (1964) and *Such*
(1966) received some very positive reviews. Indeed, *Out* was awarded the
Society of Authors Travel Prize and *Such* the James Tait Black Memorial
Prize. It was only with the multilingual *Between* (1968) that responses became a little more equivocal, while the publication of the *very* much more
experimental and demanding *Thru* (1975) met with hostility on this side of
the Channel and admiration on the other. Unfortunately the labels of "difficult," "theoretical," "experimental," and, perhaps worst, "French" that
attached themselves to her after its publication proved difficult to throw off.
Brian Morton reminds us that, despite her "French connection," her work
should not be regarded as an English version of Robbe-Grillet:

> Like most fiction that falls outside the mainstream, her work has been labelled "dif-
> ficult" and passed over at top speed by the majority of critics and readers. Since, in
> England, "difficult tends to be a synonym for French," many reviewers were tempted
> to the assumption that they were reading a home-grown version of the French
> nouveau roman, a view reinforced by Brooke-Rose's interest in names like Alain
> Robbe-Grillet, though none the less inaccurate for that.[9]

Brooke-Rose herself asserts her difference from Robbe-Grillet, "I wonder if
the people who still lump me in with Robbe-Grillet have actually read him!
He wouldn't like what I'm doing at all."[10] However, the labels of "difficult"
and "French" proved difficult to remove and ensured that, subsequently, it
would not be easy for her to find either a publisher or a wide readership in
Britain. This was not helped by the fact that there was a gap of nine years
between the publication of *Thru* and her next novel, *Amalgamemnon* (1984).
    Comparing a typical French review of *Thru* with one in the British press
demonstrates how much more thoroughly the French are in tune with
Brooke-Rose's method. Most significantly, perhaps, there is an appreciation
of her humor—an aspect of the novel totally ignored or simply "missed" by
the sour British review media. The French critic Sylvère Monod does not
ignore the difficulty of the text: "Ce livre, ce texte, n'offre aucune des
facilités de lecture qu'un esprit traditionnel, nourri de Fielding, Dickens,
Conrad, Lawrence et Angus Wilson (ou même de Sterne et du Joyce pré-
Finneganesque) attend d'un récit. Il me semble qu'un première lecture de
Thru ne peut donner que des satisfactions fragmentaires, même si elles sont
aigues. L'auteur exige donc au moins deux lectures; dans l'ensemble, elle
les mérite." Monod proceeds with a lucid and intelligent analysis of the
book. While admitting that "Chez l'amateur de romans, *Thru* risque de se
heurter à des résistances considérables," the conclusion is one thoroughly
appreciative of Brooke-Rose's characteristic blend of intelligence, humor,
and "culture": "Il reste que *Thru* est un livre d'une grande richesse. Un
déploiement d'intelligence, d'humour et de culture comme celui que nous

offre ici Christine Brooke-Rose est un régal. Son livre peut être diversement défini: pour lui emprunter quelques-unes de ses propres expressions, il est permis d'y voir plutôt que des 'syntagmatrics,' une 'textasy' et surtout 'a grammar of narrative.' C'est du beau et bon travail."[11]

The British reception of the novel is typified by Michael Mason's review in the *TLS* in which he not only criticizes the book itself but seems to take exception to "Frenchness" in general—and totally misses the irony with which the text is imbued:

To start with, the book is persistently about narrative, and the more embracing topics on linguistics and literary theory, all approached with characteristically French emphases. It is crammed with allusions to "texts," "semiotics," Chomsky, *Tristram Shandy, I Promessi Sposi*, and phrases like "narrative matrix" and "linearity of the text"; Frank Kermode himself secures a mention. Part of its material is none other than French academic talk about those matters, and the figure of Christine Brooke-Rose in her actual French academic function—as a teacher at Vincennes—is constantly before us. This identity is established yet more firmly by the Frenchly chic photograph of the writer on the cover, her *foulard* arranged to display "Saint Laurent" in the V of her dress. The trouble here is partly the voraciousness of "semiotics" itself. Its tendency to generalize the idea of "text" is so strong that self-reference can hardly be avoided; texts are bound to be about texts, and in this book even sexual acts have, obscurely, a text-like character.

I also doubt if it is appropriate to speak of this work as a "narrative," except by courtesy.[12]

Brooke-Rose's photo (by Maurice Lemesle) from the dust jacket of *Thru.*

As this was one of the very few reviews of the novel in the British press, Mason's somewhat snide xenophobia probably had a more negative effect on the novel's reception than if there had been a wide range of reviews— particularly if there had been some that caught the book's tone and had read intelligently enough not to make misleading and irrelevant remarks such as Mason's one about the "text-like character" of the "sexual acts" in the book. It is a comment that, first of all, suggests that there is a great deal more overt "sex" in the novel than there actually is and, secondly, fails to take into account that the whole book is about the making of "text." And, in fact, the more direct sexual references (there is not much in the way of "acts") tend to be in the "text" produced by the creative writing students as they provide a further level of exploration of the making of narratives. But perhaps more important than the specific details of Mason's criticism is the sense of a mind closed to innovation—and encouraging others to be equally resistant on all fronts.

No doubt if Brooke-Rose had remained in England and had continued to produce the scholarly, witty novels of her earliest period, she would have secured a sound reputation and been widely read, enjoyed and fêted nationally. She was, however, too honest for that. She could see that the nature of the novel had to change if it were to survive and make a useful contribution to the exploration of what it is to be human in the twentieth century. She could see that the traditional novel was no longer appropriate as its role had been "taken over by sociology and all sorts of other disciplines" and that to go on writing the nineteenth-century novel was "simply pouring into old forms a reality that has completely changed" and that we have to "evolve new forms to suit this new reality."[13]

Brooke-Rose was not the only British writer to think thus. As already mentioned, B. S. Johnson was making determined efforts to renew the British novel and to take account of developments in France. The reasons both he and Brooke-Rose give for *not* being content with the so-called realistic novel, based on nineteenth-century conventions, are very much the same as those given by the French writers who first developed the *nouveau roman*. Johnson sums up his belief in the necessity for new forms to embody the new reality of the present in the following way: "The novelist cannot legitimately or successfully embody present-day reality in exhausted forms. . . . Present-day reality is changing rapidly; it always has done, but for each generation it appears to be speeding up. Novelists must evolve (by inventing, borrowing, stealing or cobbling from other media) forms which will more or less satisfactorily contain an ever-changing reality, their own reality and not Dickens' reality or Hardy's reality or even James Joyce's reality."[14]

This view was closely endorsed by Brooke-Rose, speaking on BBC Radio in November 1965:

I think that it's very important to remember when discussing what has or has not gone wrong with the modern novel to remember that the novel is a way of looking at reality and that any author of any period will look at the reality immediately around him through certain kinds of spectacles and that it's no use writing, say, in the twentieth century through the spectacles of the nineteenth century, any more than it's any use writing in the '60s through the spectacles of the '30s, because reality shifts all the time and it's up to the novelist to reflect the reality as he sees it and not the reality as other people have depicted it. . . . But it does change all the time, the more one looks at it. It's rather like the uncertainty principle in science . . . the more you look at an object, say in microscopic terms, the more the object is affected by the instrument observing it. . . . Every new novelist who looks hard at reality and captures it for his time is doing something difficult and is capturing something that is then unfamiliar and perhaps disturbing and which has meaning.[15]

Brooke-Rose's awareness of "what is real" is firmly located in the sense of science that is present both in the texts themselves and in her own theorizing about them. During another BBC radio broadcast—discussing the first of her more "experimental" novels, *Out*—the interviewer compares Brooke-Rose's interest in science with that of Nathalie Sarraute, whose "tropisms" take a term from science and apply it to the representation of human interaction in literature. He suggests that Brooke-Rose's fascination lies not with the concept of tropism but with entropy and symbiosis. Her reply shows, once again, to what extent she sees her work as dealing with "reality," although it is far from what is usually termed realistic fiction:

Yes, certainly, I am very interested, in general, in the French novelists' attempt to try and get with the modern world of science. I think we all have to, whether we like it or not, and it is a very difficult world for us to understand, but we have to understand it and we are all chemical beings. . . .

The modern scientific concept [is] that any object is affected by the instrument observing it. You can't actually see an electron jumping from one orbit to another, if indeed it jumps, and . . . the photon that you've got to use is going to affect its behaviour. And I think this is very important in the observation of reality; the moment you start observing it, it shifts. And I think this is a problem modern novelists have to face, that you can't just make a photograph of the reality immediately around you because it has already shifted by the very process of photographing it, and looking at it.[16]

Even in one of her early "social realism" novels, *The Sycamore Tree*, Brooke-Rose's interest in the nature of reality appears in the text when, in chapter 3, we find Gael Jackson, the philosopher, correcting his students' essays on that very subject. In fact the title and central concern of the novel is bound up with George Berkeley's theories of reality (that the world of matter only exists when observed). The characters even quote to each other Ronald Knox's famous limerick on the subject. In the later novels, however, talk *about* the nature of reality is replaced by an attempt to embody modern reality in the very process of the text. The foregrounding of language itself in these texts is inevitable in a period when Wittgenstein's ideas on the relationship between language and reality (that reality shapes language, in the early work; that language shapes reality, in the later) had to be taken account of by anyone attempting to work with language in a "serious" way. Despite Brooke-Rose's awareness of language, however, and her admiration for what the *nouveaux romanciers* were trying to do, she avoids the extremes of the autotelic texts that characterized a certain period of the French developments, and has managed to remain outside the various French "factions."

Perhaps one of Brooke-Rose's strongest claims to being a truly postmodern writer is the fact of her own "decenteredness"—the sense of her being always just outside, an exile both from her own country ("her perspective on British society and cultures is that of an informed outsider")[17] and from her adopted one, as well as from the theoretical groups with which she has much in common but to which she doesn't quite belong. Having always been "deeply suspicious of all movements and labels which create blind obsessions" (STT 225-26), she bears a continually shifting and very individual relationship to the cultural contexts in which she works. She herself sees this in a positive light :

I have a knack of somehow escaping most would-be canonic networks and labels: I have been called "*nouveau roman* in English" and *nouveau nouveau*, I have been called Postmodern, I have been called Experimental, I have been included in the SF Encyclopaedia, I automatically come under Women Writers (British, Contemporary), I sometimes interest the Feminists, but I am fairly regularly omitted from the "canonic" surveys (chapters, articles, books) that come under those or indeed other labels. On the whole I regard this as a good sign. (STT 4)

From the point of view of solidarity and a degree of exposure to a ready audience, being associated with an identifiable "group" can be useful. From the point of view of creativity and artistic freedom, however, the reverse may prove true—and certainly does, I believe, in the case of Brooke-Rose.

One of the obvious "centers" for Brooke-Rose would seem to be the *Tel Quel* group. She shares with those linked to the journal and all it stands for a particular attitude to language which has grown out of the modernism most significantly represented by Joyce and Beckett, an emphasis on wordplay, multilingualism, and a generally subversive attitude towards the making of text. But unlike the majority of the *Tel Quel* group—and more like Joyce and Beckett (though she didn't actually read Joyce until 1969)—she does not use it as part of an explicitly political program.

The factionalism within the *Tel Quel* group is well known: the extreme left-wing politics of its early days (in the sixties its editor, Philippe Sollers, was a Maoist who saw writing as "the continuation of politics by other means")[18] that united its contributors did not survive the aftermath of the failure or "les événements" of '68, and some of its original adherents (including Julia Kristeva) theorized themselves into other political directions. Significantly, Brooke-Rose has more in common with Maurice Roche than with the "political" Sollers. Roche, accepted by the *Tel Quel* group (though for a long time part of the *Change* splinter group), has remained determinedly independent, and, like Brooke-Rose, he may be described as "a writer's writer, creating novels for tomorrow out of a profound awareness of yesterday's art."[19] When she discovered his work and met him in Paris, it was, she admits, an "éblouissement." She admires the elements of his work that are not found as significantly in Robbe-Grillet and Sarraute—the "linguistic humour" and an "attitude toward language as a material which is in itself not only pliable and touchable" but also "funny."[20] In a "tradition" going back at least to Eugene Jolas's *transition* of the 1920s and the manifesto-like nature of that journal, the disruption of linguistic and literary codes is for Sollers primarily a political act and tends to partake of the "savage seriousness"[21] that often accompanies such acts. Roche, on the other hand, appears to have no such direct party-political project and thus is more comparable with Brooke-Rose. Like her, his project is more to extend the bounds of the novel, to find out what it can be made to do and what can be done with it, to glory in the very nature of language itself, its materiality and its possibilities. It would be argued by some that this is inevitably a "political project," yet it lacks the specified orientation of writers such as Sollers.

Although it is in *Thru* that Brooke-Rose appears to have most in common with Roche's typographical innovations, she shares with him, in her most representative work, the general characteristics of exuberant verbal playfulness (including multilingual puns and portmanteau words), what David Hayman calls an "almost classical lightness and control," and the fact that his books are about "pages, about words, about the rich culture in which he swims."

The *nouveau romacier* with whom Brooke-Rose is most frequently associated (though somewhat against her will) is Robbe-Grillet, and indeed her interest in his work and its influence on her is shown in the fact that her translation of *In the Labyrinth* won her the Arts Council Translation Prize in 1969. As previously mentioned, however, she suspects that those who "lump her in with" Robbe-Grillet may not have read his work (certainly not with due attention), and the first of her important novels, *Out*, can be read with Robbe-Grillet's *Jealousy* as an intertext; she deliberately inverts certain aspects of his novel while appearing to make use of some of the methods of the *nouveau roman*. The apparent emotional flatness and objective, scientific-report style of Robbe-Grillet's language (his actual objectivity has been questioned by some critics) is seen in the "chosiste" manner (though with a touch of humor) of the opening of *Out*, which describes two flies copulating on the knee of the "character" who forms the central focus or consciousness of the text, and throughout the novel in passages of detailed description. However, she satirizes the minutely accurate and apparently "scientific" description of the "chosiste" method by repeated references to microscopes and other instruments used to give detailed views of physical phenomena: "a microscope might perhaps reveal . . ." (*Omnibus* 11), "a teinoscope might perhaps reveal . . ." (18), "a bronchoscope might perhaps reveal . . ." (20), "a periscope might perhaps reveal . . ." (21), and so on. Brooke-Rose adopts a limited point of view, like Robbe-Grillet, and also uses his attenuated perspective, but by the contrasts that are set up by such deliberate association she attempts to "deny his now well-known theme that humanism is dead and metaphor outmoded because it implies human values."[22] The setting of *Out* suggests a future South Africa in which apartheid has been reversed and the poor, unhealthy plantation workers are the whites—one of whom is the novel's controlling consciousness (one hesitates to use the term "protagonist"). This is a direct reversal of *Jealousy* in which the plantation owner fills this role. In *Out*, the main view is from the workers' shacks up towards the big house, whereas in *Jealousy* it is from the owner's house out towards the regularly spaced banana trees, but with no evidence of the existence of workers and a total ignoring of any political issues. The famous centipede of *Jealousy* is recalled by the copulating flies in *Out*, while in *Jealousy* the husband's frequent views of A at her dressing table are ironically echoed in descriptions of the "toilette" of Mrs. Mgulu (mistress of the big house). Making a connection between the two texts is a strategy by which Brooke-Rose can install her project of combining the moral, humanistic concerns of the traditional novel with the new reality and the new ways of representing it as practiced in innovative forms such as the *nouveau roman*. It is this combination which gives her work something in common with the Claude Simon of *The Georgics*—although her work is so different from his in many other ways. The light playfulness of surface combined with deeper philosophical concerns that one finds in novels such as *Xorandor* and *Textermination* is reminiscent of Raymond Queneau—and she is certainly appreciative of the humor that marks him off from many modern French writers. ("One thing I have against the French school is," she has said, "on the whole—I don't want to mention any names—but on the whole there is very little humour . . . I can't get by without humour.")[23] But once again the connection is only partial; there is no real "identification with," and she manages, once more, to escape involvement in any "faction."

Brooke-Rose's response to the various French feminist factions has been characteristically complex. As the various strands of French feminism are broadly representative of those in other countries too, it would seem reasonable at this point to look at Brooke-Rose's relationship to feminism as a whole, although inevitably with some emphasis on French theories.

   In her overt statements she tends to distance herself from feminism, while admitting that, as a woman—and particularly as a woman experimental writer—she has received less than her fair share of critical space, being "fairly regularly omitted from the 'canonic' surveys," while she believes that "There's a curious prejudice that still exists—not against women writers . . .—but against women experimental writers. There's a deep-seated notion, which you can trace all the way back to Plato, against the idea that women can actually create new forms. Their writing is either supposed to imitate men or simply to imitate their own lives."[24] This last comment draws attention to her theoretical distance from that faction of feminism that sees the first task of literature by women to accomplish the "gender revolution" more by providing what Rita Felski calls "a critique of values" and "positive fictions of female identity,"[25] than through the feminist aesthetic strategy of disrupting logical male discourse in the manner propounded, most notably, in Kristeva's theory of the "semiotic." Brooke-Rose's main quarrel with many women writers—and with so-called realistic novels in general—is that they simply "put things down as they happen" and "just give you everything." *Her* aim is to involve the reader in "making" the text. Whereas a great deal of writing by women is what (using Barthes's categories) can be termed *lisible* (readerly), Brooke-Rose's work definitely aims to be *scriptible* (writerly). Although she admits that she may sometimes expect too much from the reader, she firmly believes that one "shouldn't underestimate the intelligence of the reader."[26]

Although she does not share Felski's views about the sociological project of women's writing, she is not an obvious exponent of *écriture feminine* in the same way as are Kristeva and Cixous, for example—or Mary Daly in America. On the other hand, she does practice certain forms of "logical discourse disruption" and language-play, strategies that form a significant part of *écriture feminine,* and in fact she has expressed a very positive response to the work of Cixous, in particular, as Cixous has of hers (see STT 229-30). In Brooke-Rose, however, these strategies are accompanied by an ever-present sense of humor, a high level of sophistication, and the agreeable stance of never taking herself too seriously. The comparison of a passage from Brooke-Rose (recent, nonfiction) with one by Mary Daly (written for a similar, though obviously not identical purpose) clearly illustrates the difference in tone and effect, despite the use of similar linguistic tactics. (It seems more reasonable to choose passages in the same language as certain nuances may be lost on a non-native speaker of French):

Once upon a time, in 1968, there appeared a novel called *Between*, by Christine Brooke-Rose, hereafter in this metastory or story-matter referred to as the author, author of *Out, Such*, and earlier novels. *Between* deals with (?), explores (?), represents (?), plays around with (?), makes variations on (?), expresses (?), communicates (?), is about (?), generates (?), has great fun with the theme / complex experience / story / of bilingualism. The I / central consciousness / non-narrating narrative voice / is a simultaneous interpreter who travels constantly from congress to conference and whose mind is a whirl of topics and jargons and foreign languages / whose mind is a whirl of worldviews, interpretations, stories, models, paradigms, theories, languages. (STT 6)

The deliberate avoidance of the absolute through the use of alternatives and emphatic nondefinitions achieves a fluidity, subtlety, and openness that some might theorize as "feminine," and that is echoed in the following passage from Mary Daly. However, it is easy to detect that Brooke-Rose is writing partly tongue-in-cheek—at least with a sense of fun in the method, which seems missing in the over-earnest (and therefore less satisfyingly complex) tone of this passage from the very end of Mary Daly's *Gyn/Ecology*:

Our beautiful, spiral-like designs are the designs/purposes of our bodies/minds. We communicate these through our force-fields, our auras, our O-Zones. . . .
    Spinning is celebration/cerebration. Spinsters spin all ways, always. Gyn/Ecology is Un-Creation; Gyn/Ecology is Creation.[27]

Brooke-Rose's awareness of the hidden possibilities and connections within words, her ability to draw out subsurface implications and to make enlightening use of puns (also a characteristic of "feminine" writing of the Mary Daly kind) is evident in the titles used in some of her critical writings (as well as elsewhere): we have "Id Is, Is Id?" "Ill Locutions," "Ill Logics of Irony," "Illiterations," and "A Womb of One's Own?" in *Stories, Theories and Things* and "The Squirm of the True" as the title of an essay on "non-methodology" centering on Henry James's *The Turn of the Screw* (rpt. in RU). And yet one cannot help feeling that such usage is more a result of Brooke-Rose's modernist inheritance than a conscious participation in feminist theories of language. The question that automatically follows is to what extent those theories themselves are a result of modernism. Brooke-Rose's close association with modernism is suggested by her important critical work on Pound's *Cantos*, *A ZBC of Ezra Pound* (1971). The critical method (or non-method) she adopts in this work could be interpreted as a deliberate disruption and demystifying of what some feminists would label the male-dominated logical discourse of literary criticism. I doubt very much, however, if Brooke-Rose herself would theorize it in such a manner. Her method of plunging "in medias res," adopting a casual but enthusiastic tone without relinquishing erudition, is a splendidly effective one for making the extremely complex *Cantos* accessible. Her tone and manner completely dispenses with the self-importance of the critic, the "look how clever I am to understand all this" tone that some critics seem to slip into. On reading the *ZBC*, one does not think of it as being a "disruption of traditional male logico-critical discourse," but simply how refreshing, how thoroughly enjoyable and inspiring. And that, I think, is the main difference between Brooke-Rose and some "innovative" feminist writers. She employs certain strategies because they seem the best way of doing things and not to labor gender differences. For her, personal vision and even craftsmanship take precedence over "politics."
    Brooke-Rose's contributions to the furtherance of gender equality is to be living proof of that equality in both intelligence, achievement, and sheer creative originality.

[1]Hélène Cixous, "Le Language du dépaysement," review of *Between*, *Le Monde*, 28 December 1968, vii.

[2]B. S. Johnson, Introduction, *Aren't You Rather Young to Be Writing Your Memoirs?* (London: Hutchinson, 1973).

[3]Quoted in Edmund J. Smyth's *Postmodernism and Contemporary Fiction* (London: Batsford, 1991), 19.

[4]John Hall, "A Novel Theory," interview with Brooke-Rose, *Guardian*, 16 November 1970, 9.

[5]David Lodge, *The Novelist at the Crossroads and Other Essays on Fiction and Criticism* (London: Routledge and Kegan Paul, 1971), 7.

[6]Rubin Rabinovitch, *The Reaction against Experiment in the English Novel 1950-1960* (New York: Columbia University Press, 1968).

[7]Susan Sontag, *Against Interpretation and Other Essays* (New York: Farrar, Straus & Giroux, 1966); from a *Partisan Review* essay that first appeared in 1963.

[8]Both are quoted in Lodge, 18-19.

[9]Brian Morton, "A Glimpse into the Future Tense," *Times Higher Education Supplement*, 5 October 1984, 10.

[10]Letter from Brooke-Rose, 28 December 1984, in *Letters to an Editor*, ed. Mark Fisher (Manchester: Carcanet, 1989), 220-21.

[11]Sylvère Monod, *Études anglaises* 29.2 (1976): 237.

[12]Michael Mason, "Textual Tensions," *Times Literary Supplement*, 11 July 1975, 753.

[13]Hall, 9.

[14]Introduction, *Aren't You Rather Young . . . ?*

[15]BBC Radio *New Comment*, recorded 25 October 1965, broadcast 3 November 1965 (transcript from BBC Sound Archives).

[16]BBC Radio *New Comment,* recorded 23 November 1964, broadcast 2 December 1965 (transcript from BBC Sound Archives).

[17]Letter from R. L. Marsack (Editorial Manager, Carcanet Press) to Susannah Clapp (*London Review of Books*), 7 August 1984.

[18]Philippe Sollers, "Écriture et révolution," in *Tel Quel: Théorie d'ensemble* (Paris: Seuil, 1968), 78.

[19]David Hayman, *In the Wake of the "Wake,"* ed. Hayman and Elliott Anderson (Madison: Univ. of Wisconsin Press), 27.

[20]David Hayman and Keith Cohen, "An Interview with Christine Brooke-Rose," *Contemporary Literature* 17 (1976): 15.

[21]Hayman, *In the Wake of the "Wake,"* 27. The quotations in the next paragraph are from p. 28.

[22]Morton P. Levitt, in *The Dictionary of Literary Biography, vol. 14: British Novelists since 1960* (Detroit, Gale Research, 1983), 126.

[23]Hayman and Cohen interview, 8.

[24]Jonathan Coe, "Writing the Rules of the Language Game," *Guardian*, 2 March 1992, 33.

[25]Rita Felski, *Beyond Feminist Aesthetics* (London: Hutchinson, 1989), 182.

[26]Coe, 33.

[27]Mary Daly, *Gyn/Ecology: The Metaethics of Radical Feminism* (Boston: Beacon, 1978), 423-24.

S(t)imulating Origins: Self-Subversion in the Early Brooke-Rose Texts

Judy Little

EXPERIMENTAL FICTION does not inevitably involve the overturning or textual deconstruction of long-standing ideologies or grand narratives. Although contemporary fiction on both sides of the Atlantic resists interpretation, yet even stylistically radical texts may still be "regressive" in their "treatment of sex," as Christine Brooke-Rose observed in *A Rhetoric of the Unreal*; more recently she also notes the "regressively phallocratic" preoccupation of much science fiction (RU 387, STT 176).[1] In her own experimental fiction, however, the ideology of (sexual) difference, and the usually related myths of textual origin and authority, become part of the playful mix of discursive simulation that transforms or deconstructs most ideological structures, grand or small, in her work. Brooke-Rose has expressed her agreement with the postmodern "incredulity" about grand narratives, all those large culture-structuring discourses or assumptions such as the unity of knowledge or the liberation of human beings; she cites Jean-François Lyotard's description of this "postmodern condition" in which a technological world allows only hypotheses or "little narratives."[2] Rejecting the totalizing narratives, Brooke-Rose—and most of the textual voices who speak in her novels—instead simulates and transforms a rich variety of discursive hypotheses, that is, of self-subversive texts ready for continuing creative metamorphosis.

In the fiction of Brooke-Rose there is little nostalgia for the ever more attenuated grand narratives that until recently defined the dominant culture of the West. Except for the ill and disoriented narrator of her first experimental novel, *Out* (1964), the voices in most of her fiction are content with the "self" as text, the self as an experimental narrative, the self as a continually simulatable new word. Perry Hupsos in *Verbivore* (1990), for instance, is only a few lines of advancing text on the screen of another character's word processor. He is literally a little narrative (a "sublime" work of art), and he wishes that Mira (who has been creating him on her computer) would continue with his story so that he could talk to her (188). Yet Perry, and the other subjectivities, generally take textual life as it comes; they do not seek an ultimate dialogue with an ultimate creator about ultimate meaning. As a recurrent phrase in *Between* affirms, "All ideas have equality before God."[3] The big ideologies such as "liberation" or gender "difference" are no more important than the phrases of conference jargon that the simultaneous translator of *Between* transforms skillfully and automatically from one language to another. In this ideological democracy, there is no despair over the demise of the totalizing text, the death of God, or the problematics of authority and origin.

In this respect Brooke-Rose differs from Samuel Beckett (whom she acknowledges as one of several influences).[4] Her characters and voices do not take themselves seriously enough to despair. They are not waiting for Godot. (Why wait? They can invent or simulate him and talk to him, and he—or she—can talk back.) Indeed the Brooke-Rose text explores the comic potential of the "simulations" in contemporary experience, especially the ever-available simulating machine, the computer. As she writes, "*Verbivore* (and less directly all my novels) are about all our suppositions being simulations of one kind or another."[5] The character Mira in *Amalgamemnon* indicates just how comprehensive "suppositions" and "simulations" are; she sees a world that will supply "simulating machines for opinions, arguments, loves, hates, imaginings" (52). This list includes much of what goes into constructing a "self" or "subjectivity." The suppositions that socialize a person, the attitudes that "call" one into a class or a gender, a set of codes that inscribe a life—all are feignable, constructable. *Amalgamemnon* is in a sense Mira's own elaborate simulation of a multiplex and paradoxical future, one that she creatively feigns in an extended monologue as she anticipates losing her job as a university professor.

The "opinions, arguments, loves, hates, imaginings" that shape a self or voice are simulatable, flexible, in the Brooke-Rose text. As a result, the main characters (or the prominent voices) tend to be flexible, creative, and courageous. They evade discouragement by re-writing, re-simulating themselves; they self-subvert. In an early critical study, Brooke-Rose described the varied critical theories that she was using in her analysis of Pound's "Usura" Canto. She pointed to the flexibility of her approach; such a method, she emphasized, avoided a "universal grammar" and instead could "be infinitely self-subversive like the text [Pound's poetry] itself."[6] Similarly the voices and selves in Brooke-Rose's fiction are self-subversive texts; that is, they are self-subversive *selves*. This capacity to self-subvert or deconstruct is also their capacity to simulate/stimulate further origin—to create additional experimental texts.

Although some of these textual voices, such as Mira's, appreciate (perhaps love) certain humanistic ideologies of the West, the voices are also prepared to face an experimental future, even one in which the grand narratives of "difference," origin, and (textual) authority are themselves hypothetical and simulatable. In an early novel, *The Dear Deceit* ("experimental" only in that it is written backwards, each chapter giving an earlier portion of the narrative), Brooke-Rose used the structuring device of the quest for (paternal) origin. This is the oedipal "family romance" pattern without which, Roland Barthes asserts, there would be no narrative at all.[7]

The pattern is certainly a "grand narrative"; it is the major psychoanalytic ideology as well as a literary and novelistic pattern. As a pattern in fiction it is usually a son's search for his father, and the role or voices of women are minimal and secondary.

Unlike *The Dear Deceit*, the more recent fiction of Brooke-Rose offers something like this "quest" pattern (a "simulation" of it) only in the highly modified and witty astrophysical/pseudo-Jungian quest of Larry in *Such*. Perhaps there is also a parody of the ancient grand narrative in the (re)quests for "origin" the sub-voices make in *Amalgamemnon*, for instance, as they seek the attention of their author. She is not their father, but their mother, Mira. In *Verbivore* also, the search of the child for the "parent" (the search of the secondary voice for its author/character) is not a major structuring device, and the quest becomes more a matter of a computer search.

In the work of others as well as in her own fiction, Brooke-Rose appreciates the ironic or disruptive inscription of these once-great narratives of difference and origin. She praises Donald Barthelme's *The Dead Father*, for instance, because the very ironic quest for the father in this novel is not, Brooke-Rose argues, the center or source of meaning in the text.[8]

In her critical prose Brooke-Rose has perceptively examined the ideologies of authorship and difference. She accepts Lacan's description of gender as basically a rhetoric or language, and she also finds valuable his concept of the unconscious as "Other." Emphasizing Lacan's notion that to speak at all is to limit, omit, or "castrate," Brooke-Rose points to her novel *Thru* as a textual enactment of his idea.[9] In *Thru* two major voices (one male and one female) seem to be authoring or deauthorizing each other, finally going "through" the mirror of the text, or deconstructing each other's texts. Brooke-Rose has also emphasized in her essay "Id Is, Is Id?" that psychoanalytic theory is distinctly text and not truth (STT 28-44). As Verena Andermatt-Conley notes, Brooke-Rose does not subscribe to the "current terminologies of difference."[10] Authority is not a matter of which gender but which text. Indeed, authority and origin for many of the computer "selves" in *Verbivore* are largely dependent on getting oneself written; for the already-written characters (Jane Austen's, Flaubert's, those of Brooke-Rose, and others canonized or not) in *Textermination* (1991) the quest is for readership—to get oneself read, the reader taking the position not precisely of "author," but of "authority" over the life and death of textual subjectivity.

In addition to this playful shuttling about with regard to authorization, the extremely voice-centered mode (a "diegetic" mode)[11] that Brooke-Rose uses also contributes to the self-subversive qualities of the text. These speaking "characters" do not provide, and are not given (by a narrator outside themselves), the wealth of descriptive detail or background typical of a more "realistic" or mimetic characterization. As Brooke-Rose has described similar characters in the experimental fiction of others, they can be merely "subthreshold sensibilities" as in the work of Nathalie Sarraute, or only a neutral "emitter" as in the fiction of Maurice Roche and Phillipe Sollers

(RU 325, 326). The characters or minimal subjectivities in Brooke-Rose's fiction have likewise been slimmed down to voices and sometimes to the texts that a computer is emitting. Origin, under these textual circumstances, becomes a hypothesis, a little narrative, a simulation or stimulation of authorship.

Further, the various strategies of wordplay in these experimental novels also stimulate the de-authorizing or liberating of discourses, grand or little, and so contribute to the experimental, open, flexible quality of the implied voices or "selves." Echoing Walter Pater, but referring to the creative new languages of feminist theory, deconstruction, and computer technology, Brooke-Rose has said that novels now "aspire to the condition of poetry" (RU 12; STT 178). She finds the "techniques" of poetry in many experimental novels, and she commends the poetry of the "word-play, repetition, inversion, paradox" in *Plus* by Joseph McElroy; such techniques are frequent in her own work as in the "poetry" of jargon (scientific, linguistic), a feature she describes, referring especially to *Between*, *Such*, and *Thru*.[12] The wordplay is dialogic as are the near-repetitions (near-simulations) of phrases; these phrases often recur, as Brooke-Rose says, "in a new context" that changes their meaning.[13] As a result, conflicting implications and even ideologies are juxtaposed; they deconstructively go "through" each other, enriching and stimulating more voices.

Her remarks about "suppositions being simulations" apply directly to *Verbivore*, Brooke-Rose indicated; yet she also affirmed that the rest of her novels as well concern the simulated quality of all suppositions. Since the scope of this essay will not allow me to do justice to the poetic strategies of simulation in all her novels, I offer the above sketch of these strategies (and my illustrations drawn from recent novels) as one way of introducing her work as a whole; the remainder of my discussion will focus on *Out* and *Between*, with a few remarks on *Such*. After all, these first three experimental texts share certain qualities. In them the "condition of poetry" is somewhat more lyric (even poignant?) than in the later novels, perhaps because these earlier novels (experimental and disjunctive in style as they are) can still be read as monologues. *Amalgamemnon* also is a monologue, but it, like all the later novels, gains in wit and stylistic hilarity what it lacks with regard to the nearly songlike "condition" of the three earliest novels. (And by "lack" I intend a positive; the buoyant cleverness of the computer text-selves quarreling and simulating is completely worth the sacrifice.) Yet it is a sacrifice; the three earliest experimental texts seem to hover "between" a mimesis that still sings a self and a textual self-subversion that s(t)imulates nearly infinite varieties of origin and discourse.

In the confused thoughts of the elderly, displaced man in *Out*, as he reflects achronologically on his postnuclear illness and world, there is indeed a certain "hopelessness and gloom," as Richard Martin asserts;[14] yet there is also considerable self-subversive humor in the man's inventive simulations, his perpetually revised requests and observations. He is continually trying to find a job as a gardener or groundskeeper; then he is trying to keep the job, though his illness thwarts his performance. He frequently composes letters, trying to redress racial injustice (white people are ill and oppressed while the darker skin has protected the upper classes). The text continues to revisit these repetitious activities, but the man's thoughts about them are inventive variations on the painful textual routines that are progressively "infecting" his sentences.

He is often asked (or was asked in the past by an agent or employer) what his "occupation" is, and the narrating voice is either recounting these occasions or facing new ones, or poetically inventing variations on the incidents. The worldwide catastrophe seems to have destroyed, or reduced to textual fragments, certain long-standing traditions; the catastrophe has destroyed the great narratives of the precrisis society. As a result the meditating voice searches ineffectively for "origins," for the person he may once have been and the person he now is. He tells a questioner that he was a "builder"; in fact he quips that he "built the tower of Pisa and it leant."[15]

His responses to this question of identity become wilder (and more comic and more painful) as he seems to realize that he will never find the "story" or text that is or was his. He even simulates responses to his responses; he says he was a "fortune-teller," and he hears (invents?) the response: "Yes well, there's no future in that, not nowadays" (62). His society seems to be a giant examiner, continually questioning and diagnosing his psychological, physical, and political legitimacy. He is continually being inscribed by others as this society attempts to construct or simulate its subjects. He responds that he was an electrician (24) or a welder (62); he is an odd job man, but his previous "occupation" was that of "psychopath," and the hospital receptionist (or the narrator's imagining of this person) carefully writes and voices the syllables as though "psychopath" were a profession (127). Later, the doctor who runs the "psychoscopy" machine (which zaps the patient with a condensed dose of psychoanalysis) admits, as he reads the "psychopath" on the form, "We have a sense of humor, yes?" (132). The elderly man does have a sense of humor, but he never can be sure whether anyone else really hears it (he may be only imagining scenarios of job-hunting and job-finding), or ever acknowledges that he is speaking (if he *is* speaking and not just reminiscing).

He has almost no sense of himself as a narrator, as a functioning self, an "author" or source of a text. The narrative style of the *nouveau roman* contributes powerfully to this effect, and Brooke-Rose acknowledges the influence of Robbe-Grillet.[16] In the novels of Robbe-Grillet the reader "hears" only what impinges on the consciousness of the speaking or thinking voice in the novel; the narrator seems not to be directing or shaping what moves into the field of perception and thought. Brooke-Rose intensifies this effect with what could almost be called the "theme" of many of the repeated phrases: this man continually inquires about—or overhears remarks about—identity, "story," his occupation, and what the various elaborate, diagnostic instruments might "reveal." Yet in this very controlled society, he is never diagnosed, never sufficiently acknowledged; or rather, his urgent repetitions about his subjectivity imply that he is never certain that he has been heard, never certain who he is.

It is as though the one voice in this novel increasingly regresses, in this controlled political climate, to a nearly presymbolic state. Indeed the man's ethnic group is now a "muted" culture, and he does not seem to grasp the "symbolic" system that rules him, rules his speech, and rules his capacity to narrate, to "tell" a story and simulate a self. If consciousness arises with the acquisition of language, as Lacan theorizes,[17] the speaker of *Out* is undergoing a dis-acquisition of language and a deconstruction of consciousness.

In one of many dialogic distortions of biblical phrases, an agent or employer seems to be advising a better diet, but he says, "Oh I didn't mean just bread. There's consciousness too, man cannot live by bread alone. He needs his daily ration of the whole world, blessed are the conscious for they shall inherit the earth" (181). The old and confused hearer wonders if this is "an article of faith" (181), a phrase he uses several times. Earlier in the novel, for instance, someone advised him "to identify with the flux" (63); the voice of the puzzled narrator wonders if this is "an article of faith," and he notes that "it is difficult to tell who's talking in this type of dialogue" (63). Indeed it is. The speaker's subjectivity is dialogically acquiring (or being indoctrinated with) the postcrisis articles of faith, the legitimating narratives of the new society.

The repeated phrases are often intertextual fragments, the revisionist phrases, of a former (and biblical) grand narrative of political inversion ("the meek . . . shall inherit the earth"—Matt. 5:5). The speaker's confusion about who is talking reflects his sense that more than one ideology is "talking" as well as more than one, perhaps hallucinatory, voice inside his head. The collapsing consciousness of the narrator cannot tell when he is being "fed" his society's "ration of the whole world" (his society's major ideology) and when he is just trying to get a job or hear a "story" that is at least reminiscent of the "self" he thinks he once was. He senses that "the conscious" will inherit and rule; they control the symbols of the discourses that construct or simulate all texts and institutions. In a severely restricted society, this man, who belongs already to a muted subculture, is becoming muted even to himself. He is becoming a self-subverting text and as a result is less and less conscious of *becoming* less and less conscious.

The novel can be read as a kind of dialogic elegy on the loss of the self (and of authority and origin). The man's subjectivity is one that is undergoing such a radical socially imposed and experimental rewrite that his consciousness is dying in the process (as his body is dying also). I suggest "elegy" because Brooke-Rose is here very successfully moving her prose towards "poetry" (to which, in her view, experimental novels aspire), and the repetitions, with their variations, have the quality of a refrain. The entire novel is a refrain—with no "stanza," no mimetic story, no "narrative" between the refrains. The story, the explanation or narrative, has been lost in the worldwide catastrophe and the radiation-illness epidemic. All that remains for the speaker is a disjunctive, fragmented but lyric response to the disaster. Although the reader has no mimetic "character" with which to "identify," I disagree with Shirley Toulson who says that the "reader's emotions" cannot become engaged in the fiction of Brooke-Rose.[18] An elegy, and lyric poetry, may also lack characters and plot, but they can still move (in all senses) by different means. *Out* aspires to the condition of poetry, and it arrives.

In her next two novels, *Such* and *Between*, Brooke-Rose continues her experimenting with the "poetic" strategies of repetition, paradox, wordplay, and again these become the narrative medium of a disoriented subjectivity. The main speaking voice in *Such*, however, gradually becomes less disoriented as he returns from the spiritual education of a near-death experience. In a way Larry's progress in finding and connecting discourses (especially the scientific and the personal) moves in the opposite direction from the thwarted attempt by the speaker of *Out* to simulate or narrate a "story" and a self. Brooke-Rose has said that the "experiment" in *Such* consists of the "fusion of outer space with psychic space"; it concerns the language of astrophysics as a metaphor of human relationships.[19] A gradual fusion of the outer and scientific (material world of objects, electrons, stars) and the inner (Larry's resurrected and more perceptive "self") results in a near-allegory of the spiritual journey. One of the inner voices, during Larry's experience of "death," asks if he remembers anything significant about the onset of his midlife, Dantean crisis—"some final decision for or against made in the light of the person you had become midway through life in the dark wood?"[20] Larry's midlife renewal, like Dante's, moves through cosmic imagery towards a gradual strengthening and revitalizing of subjectivity.

Larry is a kind of Lazarus, and many slightly varied repetitions also link him with the rebirth imagery of Jonah emerging from the whale (205, 271, 290, 313, 371, 344). Unlike the speaker of *Out*, Larry perhaps arrives at a greater integration of self and greater fusion of discourse. Evidently quite insensitive to his family in his pre-death "life" as a psychiatrist, he achieves a kind of integration of the formerly separated "texts"—the personal and the scientific. Larry seems to acknowledge during his recovery that the scientific and physical coalesce with the personal in an integrated "such" that shapes a "presence." A voice at one point describes and advises: "That ache, and blood vessels, muscle spindles, bones flesh and such that form some sort of presence to hold on to, such as your patients. Shouldn't you perhaps start seeing a few patients again?" (305) As words begin to assume and simulate new relationships during his midlife journey, Larry also grows into a relationship with his family and his clients.

Although the novel is distinctly experimental, it is subtly didactic (better relationships are needed). Larry's world comes together as his language does. Such a unifying movement is not the case of the disintegrating speaker of *Out* or for the perpetually traveling translator of *Between*. Like herself, her language must also continually travel. She is a simultaneous translator from French to German, and she has enough Italian, Spanish, and other European languages to talk about, and with, her lovers and colleagues, to locate left or right, to turn the cold tap or the hot (though she makes some mistakes), and to scream a rough translation of the kind of insect inevitably crawling in the hotel bathroom.

In addition she knows the specialized language, the jargon, of many areas of scholarship, especially linguistics, anthropology, history (and she knows these in French, German, and English). She travels from discourse to discourse. Or rather, the languages themselves travel, for they are personified somewhat in this novel; the translator makes love, and the languages also "fraternise."[21] They mingle; they slide, in the same sentence, from French to German or English, and from linguistic technicalities to the jargon of sociology or the clichés of a guidebook as the narrator, between conferences, fills in time as a tourist.

In this novel that never employs a form of the verb "to be," the narrator is always between; with the traveler's Saint Christopher medal between her breasts, she moves between conferences, between countries, between languages, lovers, and ideas. Acknowledging, as we noted earlier, that all ideas have equality before God, she merely translates those of other people. As she says to her friend Siegfried: "No one requires us to have any [ideas] of our own. We live between ideas, nicht wahr, Siegfried?" (413) She lives in effect between discourses, between any given society's languages and myths that might define or simulate into a steady subjectivity this continually experimenting consciousness and so give her a local habitation and a name. As Brooke-Rose has suggested, speaking of her own "trilingual family" which delighted in multilanguage puns and jokes, there is a "loss of identity through language" in such an experience and in her novel, *Between*.[22] Like the distressed speaker of *Out*, the translator in *Between* also acknowledges the fragmentation of grand narratives and of her "self"; yet for her, the uprooted, fragmentary scraps of various discourses are the medium of her professional life. The ever simulating subjectivity of this novel lives the "loss" of one identity, and the gaining of another, as nonchalantly as Virginia Woolf's *Orlando*.

If the translator is not quite "between" grand narratives (emancipation? the unity of knowledge?) she certainly travels the periphery of these. As a modern divorced woman with a career, she perhaps could be considered the product of the West's technology and its ideology of "liberation." Yet she is not by any means thoroughly inscribed into such an ideology. One of the repeated phrases reminds us (and reminds her) that the "Lord Mayor" wants her to "commit" herself "to one single idea" (413, 457, and elsewhere). Yet the translator's itinerant subjectivity is not wholly the product of a postmodern disintegration of "meaning," the collapse of the large legitimizing and explanatory narratives. She is *between* her betweenness and her still-nagging commitment to a "single idea."

Paradoxically she did make one very serious commitment—to her husband, to the "idea" and life of a marriage. Although divorced and thus free in a secular sense to marry a persistent lover, she either does not want to marry again at all, or she is delaying while the Church processes her annulment request. She seems to take seriously her nonbelief or perhaps her belief—her remnant loyalty to her former faith. Many of the repeated phrases, the "poetic" refrains that move through several languages in the same sentence, concern this almost endlessly processed and reprocessed annulment case. She reflects with comic frustration at one point that after seven years' processing in England and then in Germany, the subsequent reorganizing of witnesses and interviews in France has taken three more years, and "all this for four years of marriage, after seventeen years one can't remember exactly" (459). Obviously she takes this one single "idea" very seriously, seriously enough to wait for an official, "legitimate" emancipation from it.

This translator's ever experimenting consciousness for most of the novel (and most of her life) is in transit between her free-floating postmodern condition and her residual commitment to a life that was not so "between." The only "plot" in this novel (where "plot" or action or psychological direction derives from the repeated surflike collisions of language) seems to be a gradual chipping away of the notion of committing to "one single idea," to one loyalty, and—by implication—to one authority or authorizing source of one's life and self. And some of this tendency is her own persistent chipping; she insists on officially peeling away, on documenting—with the annulment declaration—her "between" status, her liberation from loyalties. Much of the dialogic mingling of discourse (conferences, tourist idiom, theological language, etc.) plays with the juxtaposition of phrases that imply loyalty or "belief," and those that suggest freedom from loyalties (and so from the oppressive, possessive quality that can accompany dedication to a single idea).

For instance, Coleridge's phrase the "willing suspension of disbelief" sometimes merges with the mechanical requests of Customs agents; these very long sentences also move into the imagery of planes, large wings, and a sense of the suspension of the body and of consciousness in space. With such meshed voices, the narrator reflects, "Have you anything to declare such as love desire ambition or a glimpse that in this air-conditioning and other circumstantial emptiness freedom has its sudden attractions as the body floats in willing suspension of responsibility to anyone . . ." (422).

This complex of discourse regenerates, resimulates itself often, the subtle variations indicating another stage of the traveler's ongoing translation of herself to herself, and perhaps a kind of de-authorizing or liberating of herself. The varied phrase passes through her mind with, "Have you anything to declare such as love desire ambition nothing at all just personal effects," and this time there is a "willing suspension of loyalty to anyone" as the plane moves from conference to conference: narcotics, timber, immigration (461-62). For the traveling consciousness of *Between*, declarations of responsibility, love, or loyalty have proved costly. The airport phrase assembles and simulates the implications, "Please declare if you have any love loyalty lust intellect belief of any kind or even simple enthusiasm for which you must pay duty to the Customs and Excise" (444). This sentence, traveling through at least two "ideas" or discourses (as though the Customs-phraseology were managing the ethic of commitment) parallels or "writes" the traveling ideologies of the narrator. In dialogue and in her silent, multifold reflections, she moves toward a greater freedom from the ideologies that have cost her something while they also authorized her life.

The most costly authorization, or cultural simulation, of her life seems to have been her marriage and the long arm of the Church's annulment process. Her subsequent refusals of marriage may be costing her something also. Sometimes the rising and subsiding repetitions imply her judgment on others, especially men; then again the surfacing or disappearing refrain-language indicts the translator herself. Talking with Siegfried, she says that he has tried "to undermine what little faith remained," but to this accusation she adds, "Everyone. And life. And Rome more than anyone" (514). When the annulment finally is granted, the words of a very long sentence at last reach this event, but only after traveling through references to "buttons" (both clothes and elevators), the translator's "lilt of the heart" (in the elevator and then as she begins translating into the mouthpiece), and a conference on sociology which merges into the official letter: ". . . this our masculine-dominated civilisation which has turned vital lies into fragile truths such as Madam, I have just received the notification of the Nullity decision in your favour at the Last Judgment and enclose it with great joy and felicitation at the happy outcome just in time for the menopause" (569-70). The cruel humor in this wonderful chain of discourse suggests that the woman perhaps wanted a new marriage and even children. Yet she clung to her hope of an official release, the *legitimate delegitimating* of her commitments. Was the oppressively high price of loyalty (and belief, love, responsibility, etc.) set by the Church and a "masculine-dominated" society, or by herself? The woman's subjectivity travels between the two convictions.

As another refrain-repetition often suggests, she may have injured her own heart; the end of a long, layered sentence often asks: "where when and to whose heart did one do that?" (464, similarly 500). The third-person disjunction between acknowledgement and pain (the gap "between" knowing and feeling) is more prominent when her questioning reflection varies as: "where when and to whose heart did one make anything matter?" (465) For this traveler, the highest price of loyalty (especially an ill-advised one? an oppressively restrictive one?) is an eventual *loyal disloyalty* to any "one single idea." To put it another way, this speaker is loyal to her disloyalty; she is disloyal on principle, and is not just a postmodern consciousness adrift in "meaninglessness."

She has fought hard for the costly meaninglessness, or betweenness, of her life. She declines a unitary quest for (her)self. She resists "origin" as though she has had enough of one civilization's discourses about it. She migrates between narratives (grand ones, little ones, jargon), simulating her life as a de-authorized text. She thus travels light—much lighter than Forster's Cyril Fielding in *A Passage to India*, who also was between loyalties and ideologies. Among her loving languages, the experimental subjectivity of the translator lives her "willing suspension" of belief, disbelief, love; she is quite "willing," indeed persistently willing, to suspend these things. The paradoxical multifaceted refrains tease her about what she has lost as they perpetually translate and imaginatively simulate and stimulate her playful if disorienting freedom.

In a way these first three experimental novels of Brooke-Rose are transition novels ("between," as I suggested earlier). They can be said to presage, indeed to predict or "authorize," all the later novels, and they do so progressively. That is, the disoriented voice of *Out*, though full of puzzled and irritated wordplay, is unwillingly forced by the worldwide catastrophe into a less secure subjectivity. On the other hand, Larry in *Such* positively responds to the disorientation of death, or a near-death vision; for him, self-subversion is an opportunity to resimulate a (new) self. Finally, the traveling voice of *Between* vigorously affirms her freedom to live in a rich complex, a creative welter, of narrativity and of (equal) ideas and discourses. Perhaps for this traveling heart, the annulment is a kind of passport into a fuller text. By de-authorizing, it authorizes textual travel and exploration. These voices in the early experimental novels give a progressively more positive acknowledgement of narrative dislocations, self-subversive texts, and the play of simulation.

NOTES

[1]Others have noted that "experimental" writing is often not experimental or radical with regard to gender. Molly Hite, for example, writes: "it would seem that in the contemporary period, fictional experimentation has everything to do with feminism and nothing to do with women—emphatically nothing to do with women as points of origin, as authors" (*The Other Side of the Story: Structures and Strategies of Contemporary Feminist Narrative* [Ithaca: Cornell Univ. Press, 1989], 17).

[2]Brooke-Rose quotes and paraphrases *The Postmodern Condition* in STT 18. See also Jean-François Lyotard, *The Postmodern Condition*, trans. Geoff Bennington and Brian Massumi (Minneapolis: Univ. of Minnesota Press, 1984), pp. xxiv, 34, 60.

[3]Christine Brooke-Rose, *Between*, in *The Christine Brooke-Rose Omnibus*, 424, 426; similarly, 462. Further citations are given in the text.

[4]Brooke-Rose says her "big influences" are Pound and Beckett; see "An Interview with Christine Brooke-Rose" by David Hayman and Keith Cohen, *Contemporary Literature* 17 (Winter 1976): 10.

[5]Christine Brooke-Rose, "Illicitations," *Review of Contemporary Fiction* 9.3 (Fall 1989): 108.

[6]Christine Brooke-Rose, *A Structural Analysis of Pound's Usura Canto* (The Hague: Mouton, 1976), 9.

[7]Roland Barthes argues that the quest for the father is central to narrative "pleasure," but he implies that the radically disruptive textual "jouissance" would violate this pattern; see his *The Pleasure of the Text*, trans. Richard Miller (New York: Hill and Wang, 1975), 10-14, 47, 53.

[8]Other critics have perceived the psychoanalytic quest myth as the "key" to *The Dead Father*, but Brooke-Rose takes issue with such a reading; see RU 377-78.

[9]Hayman and Cohen, 11-12. In *A Rhetoric of the Unreal*, Brooke-Rose offers an in-depth Lacanian analysis of *The Turn of the Screw*; see 47, 158-87.

[10]Andermatt-Conley's remarks occur in her overview of statements by writers on writing; see *New Literary History* 9 (Autumn 1977): 186.

[11]Linda Hutcheon describes the so-called experimentalist's favoring of story-telling (that is, use of a diagetic mode) as an emphasis on "process mimesis" rather than on the "product," the goal of conventional "realism." See her *Narcissistic Narrative: The Metafictional Paradox* (Waterloo, Ontario: Wilfrid Laurier Univ. Press, 1980), 1-6.

[12]RU 287; she speaks of the poetic strategies in *Such, Between*, and *Thru* in "A Conversation with Christine Brooke-Rose," above, 31-32.

[13]Hayman and Cohen, 3.

[14]Richard Martin, " 'Just Words on a Page': The Novels of Christine Brooke-Rose," above, 43.

[15]*Out* in *The Christine Brooke-Rose Omnibus*, 19, 20. Further citations are given in the text.

[16]"Illicitations," 102.

[17]Jacques Lacan, *Écrits: A Selection*, trans. Alan Sheridan (New York: Norton, 1977); see especially "The Subversion of the Subject and the Dialectic of Desire in the Freudian Unconscious," 292-325.

[18]Shirley Toulson, "Christine Brooke-Rose," in *Contemporary Novelists*, ed. D. L. Kirkpatrick (London and Chicago: St. James Press, 1986), 141.

[19]"Illicitations," 102, and Hayman and Cohen, 3-4.

[20]*Such* in *The Christine Brooke-Rose Omnibus*, 303. Futher citations are given in the text.

[21]The word or concept is one of the refrains: *Omnibus* 449, 517, 544-45, 548, 549 and elsewhere.

[22]Friedman and Fuchs, above, 32.

"Floating on a Pinpoint": Travel and Place in Brooke-Rose's Between

Karen R. Lawrence

> What would be the narrative of a journey in which it was said
> that one stays somewhere without having departed—in which
> it was never said that, having departed, one arrives or fails to
> arrive? Such a narrative would be a scandal, the extenuation, by
> hemorrhage, of readerliness.
>
> —Roland Barthes, *S/Z* (105)

CHRISTINE BROOKE-ROSE'S novel *Between* (1968) is a prime example of the
scandalous, "writerly" text hypothesized by Barthes in *S/Z* (1970); indeed, it
anticipates his hypothetical conjecture about a new kind of narrative based
on the trope of the journey. This multilinguistic narrative, which, as its title
suggests, thematizes travel and translation, presents both narrative *of* and
narrative *as* a journey severed from origin and telos. In other words, it
thematizes, in its travel plot, its own experiments with the traditional trope
of the journey that underwrites the trajectory of many classic narratives. In
the discontinuities and gaps of her narratives, Brooke-Rose does not reject
the crucial role of narrative and narrative journey, but proposes, with
Barthes, a new logic for it.

Barthes identifies what he calls the "readerly" text—that is, classic realist
narrative—as based on the model of a well-plotted journey, a traditional
sequence of events that he describes as "saturated": "To depart/to travel/
to arrive/to stay: the journey is saturated" (105). Like a well-guided tour,
this kind of narrative leads the reader from place to place, establishing an
illusion of continuity in the fullness of its presentation: "To end, to fill, to
join, to unify—one might say this is the basic requirement of the *readerly*,
as though it were prey to some obsessive fear: that of omitting a connection. Fear of forgetting engenders the appearance of a logic of actions; terms
and the links between them are posited (invented) in such a way that they
unite, duplicate each other, create an illusion of continuity . . . as if the
readerly abhors a vacuum" (105). In contrast, Barthes calls the "writerly"
text a "scandal," a "hemorrhage," language that suggests the violation or
wounding from within of the classic text, destroying its "logic of actions."
This text disseminates meaning rather than fixing it in place. This journey
without origin or telos thus serves as Barthes's paradigm for a psychological

76

freedom from the compulsion and anxiety betrayed in the figure of the "saturated" journey as sequentially plotted. The journey now funds an optimistic theorizing of a narrative mobility which, unlike conventional narrative, does not circumscribe or fix the movement of desire and free play. According to Barthes, there are pleasures, for writer and reader, in the discontinuities and silences of this "writerly" text.[1]

Published in 1968, two years before the French publication of *S/Z*, Brooke-Rose's novel anticipates Barthes's new kind of narrative journey, with its break from the logic of beginning, middle, and end. This is not surprising, given Brooke-Rose's own dual vocation as theorist and novelist. An international phenomenon herself, born in Geneva, the daughter of an English father and a half-Swiss, half-American mother, Brooke-Rose has lived in France since 1968 and is one of the few contemporary English writers thoroughly "at home" with continental theory, which her essays and fiction perspicaciously address. In Brooke-Rose's description of her own experimental style in *Between*, the journey figures a freedom from conventional syntax, an errancy or wandering that resembles Barthes's general idea of the writerly: "The syntax of *Between* is free-ranging in that a sentence can start in one place or time, continue correctly, but by the end of the sentence one is elsewhere" (STT 7). Syntax engages in transgressive travel in an unpredictable trajectory, a metonymic slide from here to there that produces a sense of random movement rather than purposeful direction.[2] In an interview in the *Edinburgh Review*, Brooke-Rose represents the experimentalism of her style in terms of an exploration that is not a quest but a kind of magical and pleasurable crossing of boundaries; as a writer she finds herself "on the frontier of something and I must twist language in some way to pass the frontier, and that's the pleasure" (Turner 31). The pleasure of the text resides in (or, more properly, lambently circulates in) a style that could pass the electronic screening at the airport, a sly smuggling across conventional borders.

In lieu of a "saturated" narrative journey, the entirely present-tense narration in *Between* offers reiterated passages of dialogue and description in several European languages (with English the hegemonic medium). The narrative settles on the European travels of an unnamed female translator, of French and German parentage, who "travel[s] in simultaneous interpretation" (*Omnibus* 408, 494), translating mostly from French to German. Narrative continuity is replaced by replays and repetitions, iterated scenes for the most part not clearly marked as having *taken place*, either temporally or spatially. We hear a dialogue about annulment; a marriage is inferred. One hotel room, one plane ride, one lover, blends into another. Informational or semantic gaps occur to disrupt the logic of narrative continuity.

The most persistent scene is the inside of a plane en route to one of many European and, occasionally, Asian cities. The novel begins:

Between the enormous wings the body of the plane stretches its one hundred and twenty seats or so in threes on either side towards the distant brain way up, behind the dark blue curtain and again beyond no doubt a little door. In some countries the women would segregate still to the left of the aisle, the men less numerous to the right. But all in all and civilisation considered the chromosomes sit quietly mixed among the hundred and twenty seats or so that stretch like ribs as if inside a giant centipede. Or else, inside the whale, who knows, three hours, three days of maybe hell. Between doing and not doing the body floats. (395)

The travelers go places but seem to exist in a limbo of movement and disorientation, traveling, but caught, like Eliot's hollow men, like Jonah in the whale, in an interstitial "between" of time and space ("Between the dawn and the non-existent night the body stretches out its hundred and twenty ribs or so towards the distant brain way up beyond the yellow curtain" [404]). "Welcome aboard this vessel of conception floating upon a pinpoint and kindly sit quietly ensconced in your armchairs, the women to the left of the aisle the men less numerous to the right" (442). The plane is a vehicle of transportation, a vehicle of metaphor (the "vessel of conception") that translates us from one place to another: "Beyond the wooden shutters and way down below the layered floors of stunned consciousness waking dreams nightmares lost senses of locality the cars hoot faintly poop-pip-poop the trams tinkle way down below in the grand canyon and an engine revs up in what, French German Portuguese" (396-97). In her latest collection of essays, *Stories, Theories and Things*, Brooke-Rose describes her conception of the novel in a Jamesian "metastory": "The I/central consciousness/non-narrating narrative voice/ is a simultaneous interpreter who travels constantly from congress to conference and whose mind is a whirl of topics and jargons and foreign languages/whose mind is a whirl of worldviews, interpretations, stories, models, paradigms, theories, languages . . ." (6).

There are references in the novel to the "freedom of the air," and the "inebriating attractions as the body floats in willing suspension of loyalty to anyone" (461), that is, to the liberating possibilities of such constant airplane travel, but the "intended effect" of the mobile, hectic style and plot, she goes on to say in the same essay, is "mimetic realism—in brief, perpetual motion in my central consciousness, and loss of identity due to her activity" (7). Brooke-Rose, who often cautions her readers against searching for authorial "intention," even the one the author hands you on a plate, serves up a metastory that, in its appeal to mimetic realism, partially tames the "scandal" of the writing. The errant style mimics the theme of anomie and rootlessness (see Herbert 73), a modern condition, which in the "now" of the writing (1968) is replaced by the banality of late capitalism, the global hegemony of mass culture that turns one European place into another. Like the official voice of the pilot and cabin crew, originating in some "distant brain" and amplified over the loudspeaker system, the detached, dispassionate narrative voice announces flatly that "air and other such conditioning . . . prevent any true exchange of thoughts" (399), as the body floats in "this great pressurised solitude" (406).

Translation becomes the central metaphor for the general loss of place in this global village. Despite the disorienting effect of the different languages on the reader and sometimes the main character, the rapid language changes in the text suggest an almost frightening fluency of scene, dialogue, character, relationship. The bilingual interpreter becomes the symptom of this frightening fluency; like the phrases passing through the microphones of simultaneous translation, she herself is a translatable sign. We are meant to hear the double meaning in the phrase "Bright girl, she translates beautifully don't you think? Says the boss" (414) The French/German translator crosses national borders, geographical and linguistic, with such facility and frequency that "home" and the destinations of travel cease to be oppositional—there is always something alien about home and something familiar in the foreign locations.[3] In her "metastory," Brooke-Rose insists that this is a particularly gendered travel—the female body transported across national boundaries is also the sign of a passive identity that circulates so freely across boundaries that it loses its own distinctiveness. In *Stories, Theories and Things*, Brooke-Rose describes her own false start with the novel, twenty pages in which the interpreter was conceived as "androgynous."[4] These pages, she tells us, were abandoned when she realized that translation figured a particularly (although not exclusively) "feminine" experience. As she puts it, the novel is entangled "with the notion/imagined experience/theory/story that simultaneous interpretation is a passive activity, that of translating the ideas of other but giving voice to none of one's own, and therefore a feminine experience" (7). Successful translation signals a loss of identity; the translator becomes a conduit, like the microphone that is the tool of her trade.

This oxymoronic sense of travel as a routine disorientation contrasts sharply with the exciting potential signified by the airplane in Woolf's writing—in *Mrs. Dalloway*, for example, where it figures, as Gillian Beer says, " 'free will' and ecstasy, silent, erotic and absurd" (145), or in *Orlando*, where Shelmerdine's descent in a plane suggests "the free spirit of the modern age" (145). Brooke-Rose presents a post-World War II, more jaundiced view of the possibilities of discovery and escape, a view that echoes Susan Sontag's description of the symptomatic cultural condition of modernity in her influential essay "The Aesthetics of Silence" (1967), an essay Brooke-Rose quotes extensively and approvingly in her chapter on modernity, "Eximplosions," in *A Rhetoric of the Unreal*. Sontag writes:

In an overpopulated world being connected by global electronic communication and jet travel at a pace too rapid and violent for an organically sound person to assimilate without shock, people are also suffering from a revulsion to any further proliferation of speech and images. Such different factors as the unlimited "technological reproduction" and near universal diffusion of printed language and speech as well as images . . . and the degeneration of public language within the realms of politics, advertising and entertainment, have produced, especially among the better-educated inhabitants of modern mass society, a devaluation of language.

Art, Sontag suggests, "becomes a kind of counterviolence, seeking to loosen the grip upon consciousness of the habits of lifeless, static verbalization" (64-65).

Brooke-Rose describes Sontag's essay on modern art as a "still remarkable, elegant essay, in many ways a proleptic summary of much that has been said since" (RU 343-44) and endorses her assessment that a loss of authenticity is experienced in the modern condition. Much as Dean Mac-Cannell in his now-classic study *The Tourist: A New Theory of the Leisure Class* identifies the tourist as an emblem of modern man in search of authenticity in the face of the discontinuities and alienations of modern society, Brooke-Rose envisions her translator/traveler as caught in a limbolike transit, in which she yearns to submit to something when "belief" itself is suspended:

The body stretches forth towards some thought some order some command obeyed in the distant brain way up or even an idea that actually means something compels a passion or commitment lost or ungained yet as the wing spreads to starboard motionless on the still blue temperature of minus fifty-one degrees, the metal shell dividing it from this great pressurised solitude. The body floats in a quiet suspension of belief and disbelief, the sky grows dark over the chasms of the unseen Pyrenees. (405-6)

What are we to make of this seeming paradox in Brooke-Rose's address to travel, the contradiction, that is, between travel in the novel as a figure for rootlessness and disappointed yearning, a diagnosis of a contemporary condition, and her descriptions of experimental writing as a new and free kind of writerly narrative journey? How can one reconcile the way the multilinguistic passages in the text of *Between* mimic a disorientation and loss of identity and also provide the nourishments of a continental, experimental style? Does the experimentalism of the style represent a "postmodernist" fiddling while Europe burns?

The answer to the final question, I believe, is no; indeed, through the trope and plot of travel and translation, Brooke-Rose subverts the possibility of the kind of insouciant dismissal associated with at least one major version of postmodernism, which sees it as a break from modernist anxiety and a ludic acceptance of the anomie modernism helped to diagnose.[5] Brooke-Rose's novel helps us to rethink the abstract theorizing of the mobility of desire expressed by Barthes and even Brooke-Rose herself in the description of her style; it engages the problematic of postmodern circulations and represents mobility as specifically charactered and historicized, with cultural pains and pleasures written into it.[6] The novel thus motivates a significant reappraisal of postmodernism's supposed break with modernism, and its subversion, as Linda Hutcheon puts it, "of such principles as value, order, meaning, control, and identity . . . that have been the basic premise of bourgeois liberalism" (13). Brooke-Rose's novel demonstrates a self-critical form of radical experimentation that ultimately refuses this kind of dismissal.[7]

For despite the hectic mobility of both her style and her female traveler, Brooke-Rose provides checkpoints in the fluid movement across boundaries; despite its use of present tense and abandonment of temporal sequence, *Between* nevertheless produces its "present" moment in relation to a specific European geography and history. The series of displacements through travel paradoxically maps a European place of inescapable historical self-discovery. Brooke-Rose reminds us of the constraints, political and literary, that European history imposes upon postmodernism. In terms of the "political," I refer specifically to the way the novel's displacements fix on the nameless translator's movements during World War II, when she is caught in Germany by accident (due to an attack of appendicitis while visiting her fraternal aunt) and begins to translate for the Germans. In arranging and rearranging the border crossings and shifting loyalties of her traveling French/German protagonist, Brooke-Rose creates a palimpsest: the blasé travel of the 1960s, from European capital to capital, illuminates the different border crossing during World War II. Random movements and arbitrary excursions raise questions of loyalty, affiliation, and national identity. Customs agents demanding declarations at the borders signal checkpoints in this flux: "please declare if you have any plants or parts of plants with you such as love loyalty lust intellect belief of any kind or even simple enthusiasm for which you must pay duty to the Customs and Excise until you come to a standstill" (414) This voice is both frightening and inspiring—it raises the specter of duty, both a price exacted for all this unlimited circulation and a possibly useful demand for an accounting of obligation and commitment. Writing on an earlier version of customs in Hawthorne's "The Custom-House," prefacing *The Scarlet Letter*, Brooke-Rose calls the custom house "a public, institutional place, a place of law and order, where custom and excise must be paid on goods (on pleasure, as cost). It is a threshold. The threshold of narrative . . ." (STT 48).

However, the history that constrains is literary as well as political, for in superimposing a postmodern internationalism upon an earlier, more frightening wartime European geography, Brooke-Rose invokes the inescapable inheritance of modernism, an international phenomenon forced, by the events of both world wars, to face its assumption that nationalism was something to be outgrown.[8] The multilinguistic resources of avant-garde experimentalism that sustain Eliot's and Pound's modernist poetry and postmodern novels like Brooke-Rose's are regarded in *Between* in the light of linguistic hegemony and domination. (Brooke-Rose wrote most of her novel while staying at the castle of Ezra Pound's daughter in the Italian Tyrol, where she returned, soon after finishing the novel, to write *A ZBC of Ezra Pound* [see Turner 22]). In addressing the legacy of Eliot and Pound,

Brooke-Rose acknowledges postmodernism's debt to modernism and exposes the anxiety of influence in postmodernism's claim to break with its own modernist history, revealing this claim as a kind of travel, a defense against the pull of a certain literary "home." Brooke-Rose's postmodernist "vessel of conception" deliberately, self-consciously, retains the genetic material of modernism.[9]

Despite *Between*'s freewheeling style and protagonist, ideas of placement and mobility, commitment and translatability are deeply touched by the war and its allegiances. The easy availability of sixties European pop culture is juxtaposed with the darker memories of the war. Unpleasantly surprised by a waiter or chambermaid who invades the refuge of the hotel room, postwar travelers confront "the fear of something else not ordered" (401), an image of those ambivalently haunted by fear of submission and by fear of nothing to submit to. These postmodern ambivalences are textured and colored, one begins to see, by the memories of war and the forms which order and submission took within it. The postwar mobility and translatability of the unnamed translator are fixed (though not through any traditional narrative exposition or even flashback) in a particular bilingualism. The Berlitz-like passages of French and German, which blend with other lines of serviceable tourist discourse in other languages (the discourse of menus, advertisements, airport entrances, exits, restrooms) begin to resonate with the differences of their histories, forming both the personal past of the German/French translator and a historical consciousness in the text.

We learn that at the outbreak of war the girl was trapped by accident in Germany with her father's relatives. Two particular scenes in Germany haunt the narrative: one set in 1946, after the liberation of Germany and the zoning of Berlin, when the girl works in the French Zone and meets an English airman, whom she marries; the other, an earlier war scene, in which she is drafted by the Germans into the press supervisory division of the foreign office, after she is stranded in Germany. "You must excuse these questions Fräulein but in view of your French upbringing we must make sure of your undivided loyalty let us see now until the age of Herr Oberst-leutnant at that age one has no loyalties" (444). In this context, the passivity of "translating beautifully" is implicated in larger ethical questions of compliance during the war.

Under the powerful umbrella of English, languages conduct a romance, engaging in intercultural travel, just as the translator moves from German to British lover: "husbands lovers wives mistresses of many nationalities . . . help to abolish the frontiers of misunderstanding with frequent changes of partners loyalties convictions, free and easily stepping over the old boundaries of conventions, congresses, commissions, conferences to which welcome back Liebes" (437). The fraternization of and in tourist phrases leaves the traces of history: "As if words fraternised silently beneath the syntax, finding each other funny and delicious in a Misch-Masch of tender fornication, inside the bombed out hallowed structures and the rigid steel glass modern edifices of the brain. Du, do you love me?" (447). The postmodern brain is an architectural palimpsest, the skyscraper rising phoenixlike from the ashes of war. Even the Vichy mineral water so repeatedly ordered and not ordered in the text contains the memory of Vichy complicity. The post-war OMO (cleanser) slogan ("whiter than white," is grafted onto an allusion to a Persilschein certificate, a reference Germans had to obtain after the war (Eva Hesse, Brooke-Rose's friend and Pound's translator, refers to this denazifying in a letter to Brooke-Rose. She mentions "the end of the war trying to get a job and a Persil-Schein certificate denazifying us whiter than white. . ."). The narrative does not cleanse the traces of war.

Brooke-Rose's own wartime activity as a decoder and analyzer of codes is "translated" into the figure of the nameless translator and her experience of World War II. During the war Brooke-Rose worked for a unit of the British Intelligence Service called "Ultra," which helped decipher German radio messages. Enemy codes were cracked on a machine called "Enigma," which was based on "three operational rotors which could be taken out and re-arranged, each with 26 letters: this allowed milliards of combinations to be obtained" (Garlinski 173). Using devices called "bombes," the decoders would explore "electro-mechanically (not electronically) a range of alternative possibilities at speeds far beyond the pace of human thought. In practical terms, what the bombes did has been defined as 'to test all the possible wheel or rotor orders of the Enigma, all the possible wheel settings and plug or Stecker connections to discover which of the possible arrangements would match a prescribed combination of letters'" (Lewin 123). Brooke-Rose's acquaintance with such procedures helps us to understand a sense of urgency that underlies the postmodern mobility of meaning in the text. Despite the drone of conference jargon, the connection emerges between word games and war games, translations and crises.

Yet from this short sketch one can see that Brooke-Rose's own wartime loyalties were far less equivocal than the simultaneous interpreter's. The gestures and mechanics of simultaneous translations are themselves "translated" from Brooke-Rose's own role as decoder into the interpreter's less fixed position. "I never put myself directly into novels, I find that boring," Brooke-Rose said in an interview. "So I turn personal experience into metaphor" (Turner 26). Perhaps the stable allegiances of Brooke-Rose's own wartime practice of translation seemed too determinant, too clear-cut to supply a metaphor for the confusions and displacements that make war like a postmodern text.[10] I would argue, however, that the text's exploration of chance, randomness, and accident directly relates to the special significance that Brooke-Rose's novel claims for the *gendering* of travel and translation. For drift, chance, and passivity, symptomatic of the workings of history, might offer a new technology of narrative, an alternative to masculine teleological paradigms:

The same question everywhere goes unanswered have you anything to declare any plants or parts of plants growing inside you stifling your strength with their octopus legs undetachable for the vacuum they form over each cell, clamping each neurone of your processes in a death-kiss while the new Lord Mayor of Prague promises to take up the challenge in trying to make you commit yourself to one single idea. (413)

The "vessel of conception," the narrative vehicle of transplant and translation, is here figured as a *female* body; and the question is: can it bear a new idea about history, direction, and destination that is different from either the masculine singleness of purpose and certain destination of the "Lord Mayor" or the jaded opportunism of Siegfried, who tries to manipulate the female translator's sense of drift in order to seduce her?: "—Ideas? We merely translate other people's ideas, not to mention platitudes, si-mul-ta-né-ment. No one requires us to have any of our own. . . . — Du liebes Kind, komm, geh' mit mir. Gar schöne Spiele spiel' ich mit dir" [Dear child, come with me. I'll play wonderful games with you] (413). This sinister allusion to Goethe's "Erlkönig" reveals a dark underside to the notion of play, suggesting both seduction and death. Although her own loyalties during the war were clearly established, Brooke-Rose's novel explores the pleasures and dangers of chance occurrence and its role in the process of charting one's course. The similarities between German and English lovers and the telescoping of wartime experiences with pre- and postwar experiences, puncture a simplistic view of ideological choice, while the narrative still insists on establishing distinctions.

As I have noted, in her metastory Brooke-Rose insists that the passivity of circulation and translation in the novel is linked to the gender of the protagonist. "It was a cliché, which was nevertheless true enough generally (like all clichés) for the purpose of creating the language of the novel and getting, as I. A. Richards used to say, the 'tone' right" (STT 7). The cliché of feminine passivity launches the narrative, but through dislocations of both protagonist and style in the novel, Brooke-Rose explores possible alternatives between the clichés of masculine aggression and feminine passivity played out in so many ways in twentieth-century discourse. "Between doing and not doing the body floats," the narrator drones, suggesting a middle ground, a middle voice, between passivity and activity. The forays in the novel exit somewhere between action and inaction, accident and purpose.

In *The Writing of the Disaster* (1980), Blanchot addresses the fate of representation after the Holocaust: "The disaster: break with the star, break with every form of totality, never denying, however, the dialectical necessity of a fulfillment; the disaster: prophecy which announces nothing but the refusal of the prophetic as simply an event to come, but which nonetheless opens, nonetheless discovers the patience of vigilant language" (75; see also Blanchot's exploration of passivity: 14-18). In their insistence on rejecting totality yet retaining a sense of urgency—in using the vocabulary of prophecy while refusing prophecy—and their emphasis on "vigilant language,"

Blanchot's words mesh with Brooke-Rose's method and tone in *Between*. Rejecting the kind of totalizing mastery that she associates with masculine hubris, she translates passivity into the patience of vigilant language, in a stylistic practice that is both modest and bold. She says of her work, "Modern philosophy talks a lot about the desire and illusion of mastery. But I never feel that, that's more connected with what has been called the totalising novel, which imposes some kind of global meaning on the reality it describes. . . . My experience has been more one of groping inside language and forms" (Turner 31).

This "groping" inside language and forms, this combination of linguistic risk and vigilance, leads to a style in which "small changes" in oft-repeated phrases in the narrative subtly suggest the possibility of changes in the plot. Buried amid iterated passages of dialogue are references to such facts as the translator's decision to sell her Wiltshire cottage or to buy a car; these obtrusive alterations in domicile and transportation are the means by which the circularity of the writing, its beginning and ending in the same linguistic "place" ("Between the enormous wings the body floats"), is amended.

Throughout *Between* one hears the refrain, "What difference does it make?" This reiterated question is meant to burden structuralist and poststructuralist theories of meaning in language with the weight of political implication and consequence. "The vaporetto bumps against the jetty of Santa Maria di Salute at the mouth of the Grand Canal that gives out on to the wider waters between San Marco and the unanswered question which remains unanswered for the non-existent future unless perhaps what difference does it make" (556). The novel checks its own acceptance of the unlimited circulation of language. On the one hand, the narrative seems to endorse the metadiscourse of poststructuralist theory it includes, the iterated and freely circulating jargon and "codes" of conferences and commissions—biological, semiological, semantic, Lacanian. A passage in English and in French from a semiology conference on Saussurean difference emphasizes the arbitrariness and self-enclosure of the language system: "As for example in a dictionary each apparently positive definition contains words which themselves need defining. Et tous les dictionnaires prouvent qu'il n'y a jamais de sens propre, jamais d'objectivité d'un terme" (562). This sense of circularity is exacerbated by the easy commerce between French and English. The writing in *Between* accepts this post-Saussurean, poststructuralist position. The novel, like other poststructuralist fiction and nonfiction, is "about" the circulation of signs as much as it is "about" the travel and displacements of the nameless translator and her colleagues.

Yet on the other hand, in representing the circulation of signifiers in her text, Brooke-Rose shows how small adjustments of and in language make a difference. The notion that language is an arbitrary, closed system does not obviate the possibility, even the necessity, of vigilant language of the kind Blanchot describes. The change from "Idlewild Airport" to "Kennedy Airport" one hundred pages later is one example of such attention, a subtle reminder of the violent events of the sixties that produced this change in nomenclature. Brooke-Rose's particular "technology" of the "distant brain" shows how small adjustments in the codes of language have historical, personal and political consequences.

Thus, even cynicism self-destructs as a confident and fixed position, finding itself vulnerable to critical displacement and subtle dislodging. "The syntax of *Between* is free-ranging in that a sentence can start in one place or time, continue correctly, but by the end of the sentence one is elsewhere" (STT 7). One of the anonymous conferences speakers, a speaker at the biology conference on DNA, disparages the analogy between the language of codes and the workings of genetics and language. The speaker comments on this analogy as a "seductive hypothesis whose seductive element lies in the fact that we play on words and speak of codes, [which] postulates that the stimulus of environment modifies the sequence of bases, leading to the modification of the code within a cell within a body within a box within a village within a wooded area in an alien land. This would leave a trace" (519). Paradoxically, however, in Brooke-Rose's "travelling" style, this cynicism self-destructs; the pompous, cynical statement "begins somewhere . . . continues correctly" . . . yet winds up "elsewhere." What begins as abstract academic cynicism somehow winds up in the English location of the Wiltshire cottage (the wooded refuge that the protagonist decides to sell near the end of the novel); this seemingly involuntary travel of the sentence dramatizes the local "truth" of the way memory works to trace personal loss. Everywhere, Brooke-Rose confirms that experimental writing, like travel, is risky business; one can prepare and yet be unprepared for adventures in writing. In this particular example, the errancy of syntax and meaning leads to an "elsewhere" that is, paradoxically, home.

For Brooke-Rose experimental grammar is never merely a question of the relationship among parts of the sentence but a technique for exploring fixings and releases of positionality. This exploration is signaled in the novel's insistent use of prepositions, in particular, beginning with the importance of the title itself to suggest a place that is neither home nor abroad, placement nor escape.[11] This emphasis on fixation and mobility within language is, I believe, inextricably connected to Brooke-Rose's decision to abandon her original idea of an androgynous traveler, finding it to be a false start, a roadblock to the journey of the text: "during the writing of the first draft in 1964 the author became totally blocked until some three years and another novel later, this simultaneous interpreter became a woman" (STT 6). In exploring pre*positions* and changes in position, Brooke-Rose focuses on the mark of gender in the circulation of meaning in language. In a significant way, travel in Brooke-Rose's novel intersects with feminist questions about the possibilities of escape within language, within literature, within history. The metadiscourse of structuralism and psychoanalysis in the narrative underscores how the mark of gender is carried in the "vessel of conception" that is language in general and this novel in particular. The question "what difference does it make?" is answered in part with: the difference of gender. For Brooke-Rose the myth of androgyny seems too much to sponsor an illusory freedom of unlimited circulation. After twenty pages, Brooke-Rose eschews this trope of erotic freedom:

> Et comme l'a si bien dit Saussure, la langue peut se contenter de l'opposition de quelque chose avec rien. The marked term on the one hand, say, the feminine, grand*e*, the unmarked on the other, say, the masculine, grand. Mais notez bien que le non-marqué peut deriver du marqué par retranchement, by subtraction, par une absence qui signifie. Je répète, une absence qui signifie eine Abwesenheit die simultaneously etwas bedeutet. (426)

> Where when and to whose heart did one do that? Do what and what difference does it make? None except by subtraction from the marked masculine and unmarked feminine or vice versa as the language of a long lost code of zones lying forgotten under layers of thickening sensibilities creeps up from down the years into no more than the distant brain way up to tickle an idle thought such as where when and to whose heart did one do that? (468)

Despite the fluid translations from one language to another, the position of the feminine gender is marked in opposition to the normative, "unmarked" masculine. As Monique Wittig argues in "The Mark of Gender," "The abstract form, the general, the universal, this is what the so-called masculine gender means, for the class of men have appropriated the universal for themselves" (5). In this schema, the feminine is "marked"—gender itself becomes feminine, the "other" to the neutrality of the masculine in language, that "other" most visible in the floating signifier of femininity, the French *e* (about which Barthes has written so interestingly in *S/Z*). However, one can say (but this difference comes out in much the same way) that the feminine is unmarked, missing the mark, missing the phallus, and therefore is the sign of lack in Freudian terms. Either way, the signifiers "masculine" and "feminine" are indissolubly paired, as Lacan shows in the now-famous example of the signs on the lavatory doors in the train station ("Agency," 151-52), a scene that Brooke-Rose invokes in her own text ("We have no evidence at all that live human beings, let alone the skirted figurine or high-heeled shoe on the door can so embody the divine principle descending into matter . . ." [572]).

In the twists in the above passage, however, a potentially different interpretation suggests itself, a possible reversal—the male as "subtracted" from the female and, hence, the masculine as somehow constructed in defense against the female, a reading that is pressed in the following passage: "Solamente un piccolo with insolent eyes and a great tenderness only to see and touch a little in the narrow passage between the built-in cupboard painted pink and the rosy glow of the situation so characteristic in this our masculine-dominated myth unmarked save by subtraction from the feminine with its ambivalence in the double-negation no e no" (508). The male pursuit of the woman in the narrow passageway is an all too familiar topos within the "masculine-dominated myth." This scene is "unmarked" or un-remarked, appearing "natural," *except* if one recognizes in this "myth" an ambivalent flight from women and feeling of lack in the male's "subtraction from the feminine." As the passage on page 468 quoted above suggests, the particular grammar of relationship between the subject and object ("when and to whose heart did one do that?") might make a real difference.

In *Between* Brooke-Rose acknowledges that however plush or sparse, feminine or masculine one's location in the "vessel of conception," one cannot float outside the plane of language. The "between" of the novel is a space *within*, rather than outside of, the signifying chain in which gender is marked. Indeed, the novel illustrates how even fantasies of escape, pro-vided in literature and philosophy, themselves participate in these gendered markings. Brooke-Rose reminds us how myths and metaphors of flight and travel are themselves indelibly marked in this signifying chain, often through plays on words and conventional phrases. The metaphors of travel are pressed into the service of romance; men are constantly offering to take the unnamed translator "under their wing" ("whatever wing means under which he has taken her auburn blonde svelte and dark to their conferences" [434]), and myths of rescue are figured in terms of the woman's being car-ried away: "Please do not throw into W.C. because one day the man will come and lift you out of your self-containment or absorption rising into the night above the wing par à quelle aile j'vois pas d'aile moi only a red light winking on and off in the blackness" (446). Hollywood fantasies of rescue are mobilized, "—Ah yes! The ideas. Here we came in, the hero will now pick up the heroine on a plane about to land in Hollywood and offer her a contract for life" (460). Even direction is gendered, particularly the move-ment up and down which underwrites the narrative journey (the basic move-ment of the flight in taking off and landing). The trope of direction itself allegorizes desire as symbolically gendered. The yearning for transcen-dence is represented in the metaphors of masculine authority: "the body stretches forth towards some thought some order some command obeyed in the distant brain way up" (405-6)[12]. In contrast, the older mythic geogra-phy mentioned above is suggested to be aboriginal, *beneath* the twentieth-century European map:

The visitor's attention turns immediately to the sanctuary of Apollo situated on the higher slopes of one of the Phaidriades rocks in five terrace-like levels, brilliant with the splendour of its monuments . . . the Temple of Apollo beneath which the famous oracle used to sit and utter cryptic prophecies to all who came and consulted it on serious matters like war, alliances, births and marriages. Finally, a little higher up stands the Theatre . . . and beyond the Sanctuary lies the Stadium, where the Pythic Games took place to celebrate Apollo's victory over Python, the legendary monster.
    The visitor's attention turns immediately to the masculine unmarked and situated on the higher slopes in five terraces none of which deserves a flow of rash enthusi-asm. (430)

According to myth, after killing Python, Apollo seized the oracular shrine of Mother Earth at Delphi; the cult of Apollo depended upon this female power. Perhaps it is this "long lost code of zones lying forgotten" that surfaces tantalizingly in the text to suggest a different kind of language lying hidden within the chain of signification, which would make a difference if rediscovered.

The recovery is problematic, given the power of the "male-dominated myths" to appropriate it. The voice of a cynical speaker on passive resistance warns that:

Human beings need to eat, to work, and to this end will either knuckle under or, more often, persuade themselves that le mensonge vital die Lebenslüge contains sufficient double-negation to reintegrate him into totality compared with so many fragile truths and lost mysteries that surround us in this our masculine-dominated civilization turned upside down into the earphones and out into the mouthpiece with a gulliverisation typical of the giant myths euphemised into a sack, a basket, a container cavern womb belly vase vehicle ship temple sepulchre or holy grail, witness le complexe de Jonas with which the lost vitality of the word goes down into the mouthpiece and out through its exits and entrances . . . (510)

Although the cynical speaker emphasizes the way the giant male myths are "gulliverised" by female analogy, the passage implicitly recognizes that the "vessels of conception" and transportation in central male myths of the Western tradition co-opt, by troping, female morphology. Despite this thick veneer of disdain, the possibility of rediscovering a "long lost language" is suggested at certain moments in the text, a language of flowers (or plants and transplants), which is associated with the French love letters sent to the translator by Bertrand: "So the white gladiolus explodes in letter after letter in a language that finds itself delicious and breeds plants or parts of plants inside the seven-terraced tower undoing the magic wall of defence anti-clockwise from the distant brain way up the downward path escalating to a death-kiss with a half-visualised old man well fifty-seven and plus the circular dance of simulation vital lies lost mysteries and other excitations to the true end of imagination" (542). In this envoi, this circulation of love letters, is the suggestion of a circuit of desire in language not wholly contaminated by overuse, a certain pathetic beauty ironized but not destroyed. Like the Trojan horse, the language of flowers disarms defenses from within. Paradoxically, the exhumation of a buried, archaic past is impelled by a rather silly old man who speaks in romantic clichés, which produce, nevertheless, something "that actually means something compels a passion" (406). The translator suggests something of the sort in her response to Siegfried's ridicule of her for replying to Bertrand's adoring letters: "—the language, Siegfried. The fact that all this suffering stuff as you call it pours out in French, well, it sort of turns the system inside out" (516).

But meaning, difference and significance travel in this text and do not arrive at any one place, even a myth of female power, for Brooke-Rose is always suspicious of such a gesture of mere reversal. Theory, even a feminist reversal of hierarchies, is subjected to critical displacements. "Inverting these polarities," she says in *Stories, Theories and Things*, "can have a dizzy effect, and induces fear, resistance. But could the ultimate effect not be re-equilibration, which should produce (and has produced) flights of creativity and word-game processes as enriching and magical as those produced by the incredibly complex flow-charts and numerical logical operators of computer science?" (178).

It is this "flight of creativity" that Brooke-Rose attempts to produce in her novels, and that makes *Between* a story of displacement depicting neither fixation nor flight. One of the experimental techniques she uses to enrich the possibilities for marking gender is to disrupt the operation of personal pronouns through her use of what she calls, following Bakhtin, free direct discourse. The most striking effect of this technique on the narrative is to destabilize the grammatical category of the personal pronoun, and hence the representation of identity and gender. The "non-narrating" consciousness of the translator is never represented by the pronoun "I" (although there are passages that read like interior monologues) and very rarely in the third person. Occasionally the translator is introduced in general terms, such as in the phrase, "a woman of uncertain age" (445). The free direct discourse has the curious effect of turning the character of the translator into a *second-person* pronoun. It seems not quite accurate to say, as Brooke-Rose does, that she is the "central consciousness," as if she were like Eliot's Tiresias, for she does not *contain* the language but is often its audience, as the "receiver" of the conference jargon that flows through her earphones and out through her mouthpiece or as the addressee of primarily male speakers. She becomes not only a traveler, but a conduit or vessel of reception, similar to the reader as the recipient of the reams of jargon that pass through the narrative. She is more "marked" according to her gender than the implied "you" of the reader; yet her gender markings are more un-moored than the stable "personing" found in most narratives, first- and third-person alike.

In "The Mark of Gender," Wittig writes:

Gender takes place in a category of language that is totally unlike any other and which is called the personal pronoun. Personal pronouns are the only linguistic instances that, in discourse, designate its locators and their different and successive situations in relationship to discourse.[13] They are also the pathways and the means of entrance into language. . . . And although they are instrumental in activating the notion of gender, [personal pronouns] pass unnoticed. Not being gender marked themselves in their subjective form (except in one case)[i.e., the third person], they can support the notion of gender while pretending to fulfill another function. In principle they mark the opposition of gender only in the third person and are not gender bearers, per se, in the other persons. . . . But, in reality, as soon as gender manifests itself in discourse, there is a kind of suspension of grammatical form. A direct interpellation of the locator occurs. The locator is called upon in person. The locator intervenes, in the order of the pronouns, without mediation, in its *proper sex*—that is, when the locator is a sociological woman. For it is only then, that the notion of gender takes its full effect. (5)

Turning the character into the addressee does not bypass the path of gender Wittig outlines, but it alters a certain predictability both in the power of the pronoun to enforce gender and in the feminist critique of the circulation of "woman as semiotic object" (the title of an essay by Brooke-Rose). In her own critique of semiotics as regressively masculinist, Brooke-Rose castigates semioticians whom she otherwise admires for their inability to escape phallocentric paradigms. In her fiction she wrenches her translator out of an automatic objectification in the third person. The identity of the translator changes as a function of the kind of "you" that signifies her. We know, for example, by the addresses made to her that although never described physically in the text, the translator is attractive. During the course of the narrative, she ages, affecting the kind of "you" she represents (the change in the form of address to her, from "mademoiselle" to "madame," is only the most overt sign of this process). Unlike Wittig, who attempts to eliminate gender in her experimental fiction, Brooke-Rose rejects the notion of androgyny. She explores instead the way the feminine subject (and object) is constituted in the signifying chain of language, the way her journey as a signified and signifier is marked.

In experimenting with "person" in this way, Brooke-Rose neither places her traveler outside of the "male-dominated" signifying chain nor locks her within it as a prisoner. The language of the narrative becomes a structure of dis-placement rather than of either placement or escape. In this experiment with pronouns she challenges a traditional mode of representation. The grammatical and syntactic mobility of her language not only enables the unfixing of identity in the narrative (in accordance with the mimetic realism she mentions) but a fictional possibility that suggests new ways of thinking about character, a new technique for writing gender.

Style offers, to borrow a line from the novel, "new techniques for living" which emerge from contemporary culture (571). The "distant brain" appropriately replaces the author; twentieth-century fiction cannot retreat into nostalgic forms of realism but must catalyze the new ways of knowing made available through innovative media, the computer, for example. Brooke-Rose has increasingly spoken of the philosophical and methodological possibilities emerging from computer technology, possibilities that might help establish new logics of character as well as a new poetry in postmodern fiction: "just as the flat characters of romance, through print and the far-reaching social developments connected with it, eventually became rounded and complex, so perhaps the electronic revolution, after first ushering in 'secondary orality' and super-efficiency at one level and the games and pre-programmed over-simplifications of popular culture at another, will as computer-memory more powerful than that afforded by writing, alter our minds and powers of analysis once again and enable us to create new dimensions in the deep-down logic of characters" (STT 178). "Fictional character has died, or become flat," she maintains, "as had *deus ex machina*. We're left, perhaps, with the ghost in the *machina*" (176). Brooke-Rose's style consciously locates itself in a particular moment of technological possibility; perhaps the "distant brain" that guides the travel in *Between* is such a ghost (or god) in the machine.[14] The convenient ending of the original *deus ex machina* is replaced by narrative technique that never reaches resolution (indeed, the narrative journey is circular, ending in much the same place as it began); yet this technique uncovers connections and significances through small adjustments of sentences.

Yet computer technology seems inadequate as the sole source of regeneration for narrative fiction, for its revolution might be stuck, Brooke-Rose suggests, in a binary way of thinking that confirms rather than undermines a phallogocentric ethos. One of the persistent worries Brooke-Rose expresses about various forms of postmodernist writing, from theory to fiction, is its insistent phallocentrism. "Both the 'postmodern' novel and science fiction, like utopias, are regressively phallocratic for our age. It is as if a return to popular forms, or even a 'parody' of them, even via the intellectual cognition of utopian models, necessarily entailed the circulation of women as value-objects, which occurs both in those models and in the folktales of early cultures" (SST 176). Brooke-Rose, who has had a vexed relationship to feminism (see "A Womb of One's Own?", also in *Stories, Theories and Things*, for her severe reservations about "writing the body" of the feminine), has become increasingly vocal about this bias in postmodernism. She suggests that a counter-source to the computer is necessary to effect a revolution in fiction, which could then aspire to the condition of poetry (178). "The impetus may come from two apparently contradictory sources, the electronic revolution and the feminist revolution" (178). Drawing on Lacan's distinction between the *tout* and the *pas tout*, she envisions a "new psychology" in which "both women and men artists who have rejected the totalization, the *tout*, of traditional and even modernist art, and chosen the underdetermination and even opaqueness of the *pas tout* may clash in an enriching and strengthening way with the binary, superlogical and by definition excluding structures of the electronic revolution" (180).

A cynical conference voice, already quoted, says near the end of the novel, "We have no evidence at all that live human beings, let alone the skirted figurine or high-heeled shoe on the door can so embody the divine principle descending into matter in a behavior sufficiently organised to prevent the illiterate women of an Indian village taught the natural method with an abacus from pushing all the red balls to the left like a magic spell and all coming back pregnant" (571-72). The *deus ex machina* given form in the technology of style in *Between*, the (holy) ghost of the god in the machine descending/landing into textuality, gives no guarantee or evidence of consequences in the "real" world. Indeed, Brooke-Rose often speaks of the pleasures of technique as sufficient for the writer on the frontiers of language. "I think it was Yeats who spoke about poetry coming out of a mouthful of air. I've always been fascinated by this notion of words and ideas floating up there as in a galaxy, from which the poet draws them down into the text" (Turner 26). Yet Brooke-Rose's particular brand of postmodern travel charts a space for the flight of the female imagination while mapping out a specific, historical twentieth-century problematic: the circulation of an individual "feminine" signifier cannot be severed from the political order. For what is mapped in the language of Brooke-Rose's text is the trace of a specific twentieth-century history. She explores this history, literary and political, in the vigilant, yet self-surprising, language of travel. In Brooke-Rose's postmodern version of travel, the categories of passivity and activity merge in the writing, in a purposeful technical wandering that, nevertheless, yields a serendipitous "elsewhere."

NOTES

[1]This is not the place for airing my reservations about Barthes's basic binary schema, which seems to characterize types of reading rather than offering a typology of texts. My point in setting Barthes's model against and with Brooke-Rose's own project is to show her position vis-à-vis French post-structuralist theory. For a helpful discussion of Barthes's model, see Kaja Silverman's *The Subject of Semiotics.*

[2]In an excellent article on Brooke-Rose's "xorandoric" fiction, Robert Caserio discusses the burdens this kind of free play places on the reader, who has to run to keep up with the hectic and unexpected trajectory of the narrative: "the xorandoric text needs a reader who is critically hyperactive. He who runs may not read any longer, unless he runs and reads with an unparalleled quickness to catch up with and catch hold of meanings that are rigorous and self-contradictory, determinate and indeterminate, at crucial points" (293). In speaking of the "hectic mobility" of this kind of contemporary fiction, Caserio uses Brooke-Rose's own term "xorandoric," which refers to semantic disjunctions and incoherences more than the kind of syntactic displacements described in Brooke-Rose's statement above. *Between* relies on both syntactic errancies and semantic gaps of the kind Barthes describes to create a dizzying dislocation in the reader.

[3]Brigid Brophy's novel *In Transit*, published in 1969, also uses air travel as the quintessential metaphor for twentieth-century culture: "I adopt the international airport idiom for my native. Come, be my world-oyster" (28). The narrator accepts the way the pure products of postmodern jet-age culture collapse the foreign into the familiar: "This airport was the happy ape of all other airports. Its display case cased and displayed the perfumes of Arabia and of Paris, packaged in the style to which they have become acCustomed [*sic*] through the universal Excise of capital letters and full stops in the typography. Every artifact in sight excited me, raised me towards tip-toe. None was everyday. All were exotic. Yet nothing chilled or alienated me, since nothing was unfamiliar. The whole setting belonged to *my* century" (26).

[4]In a letter to me (dated 5 August 1992) she specified that this beginning con-

sisted of about twenty pages. SST also mentions this false start.

⁵For the fullest and most interesting statement of this change in tone and attitude between modernism and postmodernism, see Alan Wilde's *Horizons of Assent*. For my critique of this approach, see my review of Wilde's book in *Novel*.

⁶See Leo Bersani and Ulysse Dutoit's *The Forms of Violence* for an anti-narrative theory that privileges art that represents the "pleasurable movement" of desire and meaning (105), and Robert L. Caserio's critique of Bersani in his excellent discussion of Brooke-Rose in "Mobility and Masochism."

⁷In a critique of Ihab Hassan's definitional distinctions between modernism and postmodernism, Brooke-Rose objects to the oppositional structure of his paradigm as much as the overly broad and simplified categories she discovers in much theorizing of the postmodern: "I find both terms peculiarly unimaginative for a criticism that purports to deal with phenomena of which the most striking feature is imagination, and I shall use them only when discussing critics who use them. For one thing, they are purely historical, period words, and in that sense traditional" (RU 344). In recent years Brooke-Rose has come to identify her own experimentalism with postmodernism and does make use of the term. Still, her novels, including *Between*, explore the continuity between modernist and postmodernist literature, destroying the neat divisions hypothesized by many theorists. In *Constructing Postmodernism* (which I read after this essay was written), Brian McHale categorizes *Between* as a modernist novel with a "postmodernist undertow" (215). My own reading of the novel contests such an attempt to label the novel's ingredients.

⁸Reed Way Dasenbrock's MLA paper "Anatomies of Internationalism in *Tarr* and *Howards End*" offers a lively and important discussion of nationalism and internationism in the related contexts of 1992 and 1912.

⁹Brooke-Rose's novel often echoes Eliot's poetry of the twenties, like *The Waste Land* and "The Hollow Men," particularly in its insistent litany of "betweens" ("Between doing and not doing the body floats" [395]; "We live between ideas, nicht wahr?" says one character [413]). This cadence of the "between" conveys an Eliotic feeling of interstitiality, a sense of waiting for chronos, or ordinary time, to be transformed into kairos, or time redeemed. How to discover the sacred in the detritus of culture—this, Eliot's and Pound's question—recurs in *Between*. "The gods have left this land says Siegfried now the boss" (431), the jaded, ex-German soldier and ex-lover of the translator. Near the end of the novel, the anonymous translator and Bertrand, an aging French suitor who writes her love letters, discuss Eliot's poetry. He asks if she has ever read Eliot's poem "La figlia che piange," which reminds him of her, and he quotes some lines of the poem. She has only heard of Eliot: "He wrote something called 'The Waste Land' didn't he?" (548-49). "Tired of your still point?" Siegfried taunts the translator when she announces her plans to sell her domestic refuge in Wiltshire.

¹⁰I am indebted to my colleague Robert Caserio for this notion.

¹¹The importance of prepositions generally can be seen in the titles of Brooke-Rose's other novels as well—*Out* and *Thru*, included with *Between* in the four-novel *Omnibus*. For a meditation on the sexuality of grammar, see Shari Benstock's *Textualizing the Feminine*.

¹²All sorts of puns on the idea of height circulate in the novel: "I have conducted my higher education by transmitting other people's ideas," says Siegfried (426).

¹³If I understand Wittig correctly here, I would disagree with the exclusiveness of this statement, since she seems to ignore the role of deictics other than personal pro-

nouns in situating the subject.

[14]The "distant brain" in *Between* is replaced in Brooke-Rose's most recent novel, *Textermination*, by the "aerobrain," which is both a vehicle of transportation on which characters travel (and thus a "vehicle" of plot) and a computerlike intertextual memory containing a host of fictional characters from different literary traditions and periods.

WORKS CITED

Barthes, Roland. *S/Z: An Essay*. Trans. Richard Miller. New York: Hill and Wang, 1974.

Beer, Gillian. "The Island and the Aeroplane: The Case of Virginia Woolf." In *Virginia Woolf*. Ed. Rachel Bowlby. London and New York: Longman, 1992. 132-61.

Benstock, Shari. *Textualizing the Feminine: On the Limits of Genre*. Norman: Univ. of Oklahoma Press, 1991.

Bersani, Leo, and Ulysse Dutoit. *The Forms of Violence: Narrative in Assyrian Art and Modern Culture*. New York: Schocken, 1985.

Blanchot, Maurice. *The Writing of the Disaster*. Trans. Ann Smock. Lincoln: Univ. of Nebraska Press, 1986.

Brophy, Brigid. *In Transit: An Heroi-cyclic Novel*. New York: Putnam's, 1969.

Caserio, Robert L. "Mobility and Masochism: Christine Brooke-Rose and J. G. Ballard." *Novel* 21 (Winter/Spring 1988): 292-310.

Dasenbrock, Reed Way. "Anatomies of Internationalism in *Tarr* and *Howards End*." Paper presented at the Division of Twentieth-Century English Literature meeting of the MLA, New York, December 1992.

Garlinski, Józef. Review of Wladyslaw Kozaczuk, *W. kregu Enigmy*. *New Scientist* (16 October 1980): 173-74.

Herbert, Christopher. *Culture and Anomie: Ethnographic Imagination in the Nineteenth Century*. Chicago: Univ. of Chicago Press, 1991.

Hesse, Eva. Undated letter to Christine Brooke-Rose. Manuscript Collection, Harry Ransom Humanities Research Center, University of Texas at Austin.

Hutcheon, Linda. *The Poetics of Postmodernism: History, Theory, Fiction*. New York: Routledge, 1988.

Lacan, Jacques. "The Agency of the Letter in the Unconscious or Reason Since Freud." *In Écrits: A Selection*. Trans. Alan Sheridan. New York: Norton, 1977. 146-78.

Lawrence, Karen. Review of Alan Wilde, *Horizons of Assent*, in *Novel* 16 (Winter 1983): 177-81.

Lewin, Ronald. *Ultra Goes to War: The First Account of World War II's Greatest Secret Based on Official Documents*. New York: Pocket Books, 1980.

MacCannell, Dean. *The Tourist: A New Theory of the Leisure Class*. New York: Schocken, 1976.

McHale, Brian. *Constructing Postmodernism*. London and New York: Routledge, 1992.

Silverman, Kaja. *The Subject of Semiotics*. New York: Oxford Univ. Press, 1983. 237-83.

Sontag, Susan. "The Aesthetics of Silence." In *The Discontinuous Universe: Se-*

lected Writings in Contemporary Consciousness. Ed. Sallie Sears and Georgiana
W. Lord. New York: Basic Books, 1972. 50-75.

Turner, Jenny. "Reclaim the Brain: Christine Brooke-Rose Interviewed." *Edinburgh Review* 84 (1990): 19-40.

Wilde, Alan. *Horizons of Assent: Modernism, Postmodernism, and the Ironic Imagination.* Baltimore: Johns Hopkins Univ. Press, 1982.

Wittig, Monique. "The Mark of Gender." *Feminist Issues* 5.2 (Fall 1985): 1-12.

Living Between: the Lo*v*eliness of the "Alonestanding Woman"

Susan Rubin Suleiman

> Then acquires alles a broken up quality, die hat der charm of my
> clever sweet, my deutsche Mädchen-goddess . . .
> —Christine Brooke-Rose, *Between*

> . . . she is always translating from one language to another and
> never quite knows to which language she belongs.
> —Brooke-Rose, in "A Conversation"

> Traditionally, men belong to groups, to society (the matrix, the
> canon). Women belong to men.
> —Brooke-Rose, "Illiterations"

WHEN I FIRST MET Christine Brooke-Rose, in the fall of 1977, she was living
in Paris and teaching at Vincennes, the new, revolutionary university that
had been founded after the "events" of May 1968. In literary studies,
Vincennes was a hotbed of structuralism and poststructuralism, often practiced by the same critic; in psychoanalysis, it was resolutely Lacanian; in
linguistics, Chomskyan. It boasted among its faculty some of the best-
known Parisian intellectuals, writers and philosophers like Gilles Deleuze,
Michel Foucault (before he moved on), Hélène Cixous. It was Cixous who
had invited Brooke-Rose to join the faculty in 1968. Christine was living in
London at the time, an up-and-coming author who, after publishing four
sturdy realist novels, had started writing "experimental" fictions with one-
word titles: *Out* (1964), *Such* (1966), and *Between* (1968). Since she had
recently separated from her husband of many years and needed a change of
air, and since she had childhood ties to the French language (her mother was
Swiss, her father English; she grew up in Belgium and Switzerland, speaking French, English, and German with equal ease), she packed up her books
and crossed the Channel.

Nine years later, when we met and became friends, I was living in Paris
for a year with my husband and two young sons (the younger one was a
baby, four months old), working on a scholarly book—a structural study of
the ideological novel, sometimes called the "thesis" novel, what the French
call *roman à thèse*. Christine, ever punning, inscribed a copy of her latest
novel, *Thru*, with the dedication: "for Susan, this roman à thèse, à antithèse,

97

à foutaise"—thesis, antithesis, thing-a-majesis. The pun can be translated (badly), but loses all flavor in translation. To "get it," to love it, you have to know both French and English.

I have often thought about that year we spent as near neighbors, Christine and I. Much water has flown under the bridge (it must be the Pont Mirabeau, for we were in Paris and had read Apollinaire) since then. Christine no longer lives in Paris and has retired from Vincennes (which is no longer in Vincennes, but in the working-class suburb of St. Denis). She has settled in Provence, but is thinking of moving to London. I no longer have young sons (happily they have grown up), and am no longer married. I am now approaching the age Christine was when we first met, more than fifteen years ago. Like the heroine of her novel *Between* (which I read for the first time in the 1980s) and like Christine herself, I am now an "alonestanding woman." That last phrase is another piece of wordplay, this time mine, for which, if you are to get it, you need to know a language besides English; not French, but German.[1]

Roland Barthes spoke of the modern text (what he called the "writerly text," the text of "bliss" [*jouissance*]) as a "happy Babel." Contrary to the Old Testament, where Babel stands as an emblem of God's jealous wrath, in the modern text "the confusion of tongues is no longer a punishment; the subject gains access to bliss by the cohabitation of languages *working side by side*."[2]

Barthes's erotic innuendo about linguistic cohabitation calls to mind the Surrealist ideal of poetry as "words making love." To the reader of Christine Brooke-Rose's novel *Between*, it calls to mind a passage that not only states, but wittily exemplifies, that same cohabitation: "As if languages loved each other behind their own façades, despite alles was man denkt darüber davon dazu. As if words fraternised silently beneath the syntax, finding each other funny and delicious in a Misch-Masch of tender fornication, inside the bombed out hallowed structures and the rigid steel glass modern edifices of the brain. Du, do you love me?"[3] The brain in which words fraternize in this novel is that of a woman ("A woman of uncertain age uncertain loyalties" [445]) whose life history situates her on an imaginary frontier between France, Germany, and England: French mother (dead), German father (disappeared before her birth), English husband (divorced). Her profession reinforces and multiplies this transitional status, for she is a simultaneous translator (French to German) who is literally always "between conferences": from the International Conference of Demographers in Copenhagen to the Congress on the Writer and Communication in Prague, by way of archaeologists in Istanbul, semiologists in Dubrovnik, acupuncturists somewhere in Italy, and sundry other conventioneers in Budapest, Sofia, Moscow, Amsterdam, Paris, London, New York, und so weiter weiter gehen, the unnamed woman travels.

Her body afloat in the bellies of countless airplanes where "travel talk ensues," or curled between the sheets in countless hotel rooms each with its bottle of mineral water wasser aqua agua eau minérale on the nightstand, or else squeezed into a glass booth above the meeting rooms of countless "conventions where no communication ever occurs," she is a crossroad where more than four languages meet. Her consciousness, floating between sleep and waking, irony and nostalgia, anticipation and memory, is a jumble of natural languages (English, French, Italian, und so weiter), professional jargons picked up at congresses ("Oh, archeology, medicine, irrigation, economic aid for the under-developed areas and so forth" [468]), the global currencies of advertising slogans, guidebooks, phrasebooks for foreigners (the meaning of "foreigner" varying, of course, according to the country one is in), public notices in airports, televised news broadcasts, lines of half-remembered poems (Shakespeare, Goethe, Cavalcanti, Auden, Eliot, e tutti quanti), as well as the voices of past (and some present) lovers, friends, neighbors and interrogators of diverse classes, countries, sexes.

Like this:

—Un cottage? Que voulez-vous dire, un cottage?

—Hé bien, mon père, une toute petite maison, à la campagne. A box a refuge a still small centre within the village within the wooded countryside within the alien land, where Mr. Jones the builder who converts the bathroom says bee-day? Oh you mean a biddy. Yes I can get a biddy for you but you aven't got much room ave you? Ah si! Un cottage. The pale fat priest-interpreter looks over his half-spectacles made for reading the sheafs of notes before him. Un piccolo chalet. Va bene così? Un piccolo chalet?

—Va bene. (418)

Or this:

In fondo a sinistra the men in the café sit transfixed by the flickering local variation in the presentation of opposite viewpoints on every aspect of an instant world through faceless men who have no doubt acquired faces for them as their arch-priests of actualità that zooms flashcuts explodes to OMO! Da oggi con Perboral! Lava ancora più bianco! Gut-gut. Più bianco than what? We live in an age of transition, perpetually between white and whiter than white. Very tiring. Zoom. (418-419)

In the first passage, the interrogators are Italian priests taking a deposition from our heroine, who has petitioned the Vatican to have her marriage annulled in addition to her civil divorce. (Because she wants to remarry? No. Because she is a practicing Catholic? No. Because . . .? Just because). In the second passage—which occurs a few lines after the first, part of what Richard Martin has called Brooke-Rose's "interest in vocal collage"[4]—the priests have been replaced by TV-newscasters, "arch-priests of actualità," celebrants of instant news in an instant world. Their words are in turn interrupted by the explosive celebration of OMO—not a new brand of humanity, but an improved (or so we are told) brand of detergent that "washes even whiter."

Is this world of zooming juxtapositions the happy Babel dreamt by Barthes? Or is it closer to the nightmare of Jean Baudrillard, a world of simulacra where all real distinctions are abolished and we are left only with "the simulated generation of difference"?[5]

"What difference does it make?" This question recurs like a refrain in *Between*. And the answer, it would seem, is: Not much. Un piccolo chalet or a box cottage, a bee-day or a biddy, a real priest or an "arch-priest," a deutsche Mädchen-goddess or a French girl (the woman has been both, depending on who named her), a Signor Ingegnere Giovanni-Battista di Qualcosa or a Comrade Pan Bogumil Somethingski, a nightstand with aqua minerale or mineralwasser, a room in Sofia, Belgrade, or Oslo—they are all, in the end, mere flickering local variations on a single theme: "We live in an age of transition wouldn't you agree and must cope as best we can" (476).

An unnamed woman (or, as the case may be, multiply, ambiguously named—which comes down to the same thing, or does it?), a woman of uncertain age, standing on her own (no children as "traces" of marriage), eine alleinstehende Frau: this figure occupies the center not only of *Between* but of the two novels that followed it: *Thru* (1975) and *Amalgamemnon* (1984). She is an ambiguous figure, this alonestanding woman—on the one hand, close to being submerged by sadness, as by the detritus of a civilization whose broken-up quality she both registers and exemplifies (the woman of *Between* speaks of "this great loss at the centre of things almost from the beginning if beginning we can call it sub specie aeternitatis" [463]); on the other hand, *playing* with that very sense of loss, that same detritus, and producing (sometimes) an exhilarating laughter. Like this: "What story? Oh you know as the Holy Ghost said that scandal spread by St. Peter about me and the Virgin Mary. He likes ready-made stories the schmutziger the witziger with a burst of crude laughter tout de suite and the tooter the sweeter" (423).[6] When asked, in a recent interview, about the joyful tone and playfulness in her late novels, Brooke-Rose spoke about serenity: "Humor is one of the ways to achieve that serenity and the bubbling result of it. Almost out of disillusion, if you like, that you don't expect anything else. It gives me, at any rate, a tremendous . . . how shall I put it . . . self-reliance."[7] No doubt one has to have lived between languages, like the alleinstehende Frau and like Brooke-Rose herself—and furthermore, or "pahr dessue le marshy," as she says about the foolish fond old man who is bald on top of it all (427), one has to have lived between the *same* languages, which were those of Hitler, Mussolini, Chamberlain, and Pétain as well as Goethe, Cavalcanti, Shakespeare, and Baudelaire—in order to fully appreciate the inventiveness and humor, as well as the utterly disabused worldliness, of a novel like *Between*.

It helps, in addition, if one has some personal involvement (not necessarily experience, but a sense of involvement) with the history of Europe before 1945. For this woman's "broken up quality" is due not only to her intermediate state between languages, as Brooke-Rose has suggested ("She just doesn't know who she is, she is always translating from one language to another and never quite knows to which language she belongs"[8]); it is also due, surely, to the historical conditions that created her interlinguistic status. As we find out in the course of the novel, this alleinstehende Frau was a French girl whose mother sent her to Nuremberg for a year in 1938 to perfect her German while she lived with her paternal aunt, a baroness and a convinced Nazi. Trapped in Germany at the outbreak of the war, the girl ends up working for the German censorship office as a translator, thus viewing the war through the documents and the point of view of "the enemy." Immediately after the war, she is "taken under the wings" of an Allied officer and gets a job as a translator with the occupying forces in Germany, who are looking at German documents. Thus she again views the war, this time in retrospect, "from the enemy point of view" (487). However, it is not the same enemy—"we" and the enemy have traded places.

Who the enemy is depends on where one stands, and when. "You must forgive these questions Fräulein but in view of your French upbringing we must make sure of your undivided loyalty," says the German interrogator about to hire her for the censorship office around 1941 (444). "You will excuse these questions Fräulein but in view of your nationality we must make sure of your undivided loyalty," says the British interrogator about to hire her in 1945 (486). Is it surprising that this world "acquires alles a broken up quality"? And that the notion of "undivided loyalty" appears comically grotesque?

Why *does* the woman seek an annulment, even though she wants neither to remarry nor to reenter the Church? I would hazard a speculation related to history: to annul a marriage is to decree, with all the authority invested in the Church, that a certain event never happened. In other words, it is to do away with history—or no, not do away with it, but return it to an earlier time, a time of wholeness before the breaking (of the hymen). When she was a young girl, before the war, the woman visited, with her German boyfriend, the church in Munich that holds the remains of the "frail skeletal nun in a glass case. Heilige Munditia. Patronin der alleinstehenden Frauen" (490). During the war, she visited it again, with a different boyfriend—but the church was damaged, and the nun gone (530). Much later, now, when she herself has become a "desiccated skeletal alleinstehende Frau" (547) she visits the church again, this time unaccompanied: the church has been "totally rebuilt" and the frail skeletal nun once more lies in her glass case (567).

The annulment of her marriage restores the heroine, we might say, to her glass case. But it is not the original case, merely a copy—a simulation. The reason the Church gives for annulling the marriage is itself, interestingly, a reason of simulation: "mulieris simulationis contra bona indissolubilitatis et prolis" (473). Or as the priest had put it earlier: "So you decided in advance madame, to divorce if it didn't work, thus annulling the contract in the eyes of God?" (458). By entering the marriage as a simulator, without total commitment, she was living a lie; that lie in turn justified the fiction of annulment. Do two simulations make a real? Or just more lies?

Traveling down the page where the Latin quotation stating the reason for the annulment appears, my eye stops; the words jump out unannounced, like a sudden turning of the corner: "I hated all that interrogation Liebes why, quite like the end of the war trying to get a job and a Persil-Schein certificate denazifying us whiter than white." Whose voice is this?[9] Was the denazification certificate like today's OMO, which "washes even whiter" but whose virtues are doubtless highly exaggerated? Who is speaking? Not all the perfumes of Araby will get these hands clean.

The peculiar link between history, memory, repetition-with-difference, and a consciousness I want to call postmodern (postmodern *because* it is concerned with its relation to history, memory, and repetition-with-difference) is one of the constant underlying themes in *Between*, and in much of Brooke-Rose's fiction since then. But what is the connection between this enduring preoccupation and the figure of the middle-aged "alonestanding woman"?

The woman interpreter of *Between*, who has seen from both sides the war that brought us Dachau and Auschwitz (after which, according to Adorno's well-known claim, there can be no more poetry—or at the very least, no more poetry as we knew it) says about a much younger colleague: "Sandra chatters happily on in un amour de soutien-gorge, belonging apparently to a different species altogether undamaged unconcerned doing the same work with ease and careless poise from the start unretarded by wars national prejudices bilingualism fraternisation sex . . ." (531-32). Apparently, unlike her innocent young colleague, the alleinstehende Frau is not undamaged, not unconcerned, not unretarded by wars, national prejudices, und so weiter, ever weiter and more knee-deep in the detritus. Why? One of the recurring phrases in *Between* is "in this our masculine-dominated civilization" (510, 533), alternating with "masculine upward myths" and "man-dominated myth" (505, 553). Is Brooke-Rose suggesting that the historical mess we have gotten ourselves into "in this supposedly rationalistic age so dominated by masculine upward myths" is the work of men? And that, just perhaps, getting us out of it will be the work of women who are able to stand up by (and for) themselves? She would probably demur, if asked: novels should never "suggest" anything as unambiguous as that (unless they are *romans à thèse*, but that's not a respectable genre). Still . . . Zygmunt Bauman, a Polish Jewish sociologist living in England, claims that the role of intellectuals in the postmodern age has shifted from that of legislator (telling a culture what it needs to know and think) to that of interpreter, translator, a shuttler between cultures, between languages. Rosi Braidotti, an Italian philosopher living in Holland, claims that the quintessential shuttler between cultures and languages, *la polyglotte*, is a woman.[10] The unnamed simultaneous interpreter of *Between*, who happens to be a woman constantly shuttling, not undamaged or unconcerned, may stand as one emblem of our ambiguous present, and (with a bit of luck) of our still uncertain future.

NOTES

[1]*Alleinstehende Frau*, whose colloquial translation is "single woman" or "independent woman" (not leaning on anyone), can be rendered literally as "standing alone." The German phrase, never translated, recurs several times in *Between* and has a particular significance, as we shall see.

[2]Roland Barthes, *The Pleasure of the Text*, trans. Richard Miller (New York: Hill and Wang, 1975), 3-4. Miller translates the French "Babel heureuse" ["happy Babel"] as "sanctioned Babel." I prefer the more expressive literal meaning.

[3]*Omnibus*, 447; hereafter cited parenthetically.

[4]" 'Just Words on a Page': The Novels of Christine Brooke-Rose," above, 41.

[5]Jean Baudrillard, "The Precession of Simulacra," in *Art after Modernism: Rethinking Representation*, ed. Brian Wallis (New York: The New Museum of Contemporary Art, 1984), 254.

[6]In flatttened English: "He like ready-made stories the dirtier the funnier with a burst of crude laughter right off and the more off the righter." This does away with the bilingual punning on *tout de suite*, but succeeds in creating a pun on "off." Of course my reader-friendly attempt to "translate Brooke-Rose into English" is absurd (like trying to translate *Finnegans Wake*). If she had wanted to write *Between* in English, she would have—tant pis for the monolingual reader, nicht wahr?

[7]Ellen G. Friedman and Miriam Fuchs, "A Conversation with Christine Brooke-Rose," above, 33. The second epigraph to my essay is taken from this interview (32).

[8]Friedman and Fuchs, 32.

[9][See Karen Lawrence's essay above, p. 83—Eds.]

[10]Zygmunt Bauman, *Legislators and Interpreters: On Modernity, Postmodernity and Intellectuals* (Cambridge: Polity Press, 1987); Rosi Braidotti, "L'usure des langues," *Cahiers du GRIF* 39 (1988): 73-81.

Thru the Looking Glass:
A Journey into the Universe of Discourse

Hanjo Berressem

> Through the driving-mirror four eyes stare back
> two of them in their proper   place
>   . . . the other
> two . . .
>   eXact   replicas
> nearer the hairline further up the brow but dimmed as in a glass.[1]

LIKE LEWIS CARROLL'S *Through the Looking Glass*—that other journey into a universe of discourse and one of its innumerable subtexts—*Thru* begins with a reference to a mirror. In a rearview mirror, somebody sees a curious double reflection.[2] With this initial image, Brooke-Rose introduces the book's main problematic: those of a doubly split subject. Taking my clue from this mirror image, I will in the following trace some of the reflections and speculations in and of the text.

After this spec(tac)ular opening, the text immediately begins to reflect not only faces but other texts, almost exclusively taken from linguistics, literature, as well as structuralist and poststructuralist theory. This strategy makes of *Thru* a *roman à clef* of discourses and a book for the initiate. Various subtexts already reverberate within the opening image, which is followed a couple of lines later by "Who speaks?" This is an innocent enough question, but at the same time a crucial one in the essay "The Subversion of the Subject and the Dialectic of Desire in the Freudian Unconscious" by the French psychoanalyst Jacques Lacan,[3] rendered there as "Qui parle?," a translation *Thru* seems to repeat by sliding into French: "le retro viseur . . . some languages more visible than others" (579).

The shift into French facilitates the metamorphosis of an object (the driving mirror) into a subject (le viseur). It links the spatial image of a subject caught between images originating from behind, which are projected forward by the mirror to Lacan's notion of a decentered, barred subject which can recognize itself only by projecting its past into the future. In the subject's history, the trauma— a "real" event that might not have happened at all—and with it the unconscious is projected into a "symbolic" future, where it is represented (for instance through the manifest dream-content), but where it also functions as an ultimately "unspecuralizable" event; the navel of the dream. As "its" past is inaccessible in a direct way, the subject is defined through "a retrovision effect by which . . . [it] becomes at each stage what he was before and announces himself—he will have been—only in the future perfect tense" (Lacan 306). Within this play of tenses, Lacan describes a temporality in which the traumatic past is only recuperable—and then only obliquely—from its future re-presentation.

The trauma, in so far as it has a repressing action, intervenes *after the fact [aprés coup], nachträglich.* At this specific moment, something of the subject's *becomes detached in the very symbolic world* that he is engaged in integrating. From then on, it will no longer be something belonging to the subject. The subject will no longer speak it, will no longer integrate it. Nevertheless, it will remain there, somewhere, spoken, of one can put it this way, by something the subject does don control.[4] [my italics]

This temporal loop defines the time of the unconscious as what Freud called belatedness. It is a curiously paradoxical temporality in which the future is earlier than the past, and the past later than the future. Through this mutual contamination, the temporality of belatedness opens up the ambiguous temporality of

The Future of the Past

X

The Past of the Future

In fact, Lacan seems to be thinking of a similar image to Brooke-Rose's when he describes this temporality: "For, in this 'rear view' (*retrovisée*), all that the subject can be certain of is the anticipated image coming to meet him that he catches of himself in the mirror" (306). Brooke-Rose's image of the driving mirror, the "blueish rectangle that reflects the rear before you" (669) is defined by precisely this temporality.[5]

Yet Brooke-Rose further links this visual retro effect to a linguistic and literary phenomenon, in which two modes and levels of belatedness intersect. The first type of belatedness is operative within the signifying chain, because meaning is always retroactive: "the sentence completes its signification only with its last term each term being anticipated in the construction of the others, and inversely, sealing their meaning by its retroactive effect" (Lacan 303). The "discursive event," therefore, is caught in a kind of pendulum movement.

Brooke-Rose first of all creates a chiastic structure from within the first kind of belatedness, crossing, like Lacan, the "intentional" logic of *parole* with the "grammatical" logic of *langue* with the juxtaposition: "although from the point of view of la parole the end of the sentence commands its first words, we should adopt the point of view of la langue in which the beginning of the sentence commands the end, thus opening the whole network of possibilities in which we can then construct our sequences of functions" (627). Against the initial closure of the signifying system implied by the first point of view, in which the end "causes" the beginning, Brooke-Rose sets the endless dissemination of meaning within a scenario in which the "past" of the discourse comes to affect its "future" and in which this future retroactively "seals" the past. Langue and parole, then, juxtapose two movements. Their interplay, therefore, is the chiastic space of

the end causing the beginning

X

the beginning causing the end

Because of this structure, what Roland Barthes calls the "vast hermeneutical sentence" can never be closed, a circularity which would indeed turn the text into a stable "fetish" object.[6] Brooke-Rose's "writerly" text continually counters such an immobility by its explicit openness and its "endless mirrorings" as well as the "intentional," "logocentric" closure of parole with the "writerly," "differantial" openness of langue.

Yet, as with Lacan, there is a higher order of belatedness at work in Brooke-Rose, because every sentence implies a recursive chain of other sentences, without ever being able to "break the wall of language" and to break through to an "outside of the signifier." This second is a more fundamental kind of belatedness, which defines the signifying chain itself as belated, relating it to something outside of itself—in Lacanian terminology, the real. Lacan differentiates this belatedness from the more restricted idea of belatedness within the signifying chain: "the kernel of a reversible time . . . this becomes sufficiently clear through the retro-effect . . . of the meaning in the sentence, in which this very effect of meaning needs for its circular form its final word. The temporal structure of 'The Belated' (we remind you that we were the first to separate this word from the Freudian text) according to which the trauma clothes itself in the symptom, operates on a higher level."[7] It is thus only fitting that the question of "who is speaking?" and the image of the "rearview mirror" not only evoke Lacan and Derrida, but also recur in Barthes's *S/Z* (41, 151, 56), so that one reference mirrors many others, though "dimmed as in a glass," opening up the whirl of discourses in which *Thru* operates. The effect of these multiple refractions is that the "original" gets lost in this discursive "hall of mirrors."

If the temporality of *Thru* is that of belatedness, its spatiality is that of a Möbius strip. In a linguistic register, the Möbial structure is represented by the chiasm, in whose structure meaning is twisted just as space is twisted from Cartesian space into the one-sided space of a Möbial world. Some of the titles of Brooke-Rose's earlier novels already imply a relation to topology, with both *Out* and *Between* denoting specific topological positions. It is not only through the "concrete topology" of its typographic mannerism, however, that *Thru* shows the closest affinity to topology. Symptomatically—as if to stress the shift from a two-sided to a one-sided space, "thru" denotes a movement from a one side to the other; a membranic quality that relates it directly to Möbial space:

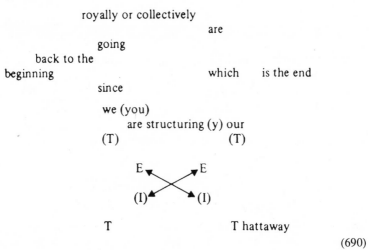

At last we
        royally or collectively
                                    are
            going
        back to the
    beginning   which   is the end
            since
        we (you)
            are structuring (y) our
            (T)   (T)

                (690)

The redefinition of both time and space opens up a new "narratological space." Temporally, it involves a loop between past and present; spatially, it involves a chiastic twisting of terms. In fact, the chiasm is one of the book's leitmotifs,[8] defining many of its topographical as well as mental twists, as in:

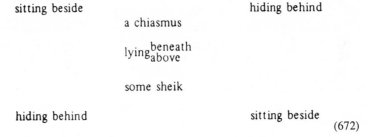

sitting beside   hiding behind
            a chiasmus

            lying beneath above

        some sheik

    hiding behind   sitting beside
                                                    (672)

Or:

Thus the cost is balanced on the

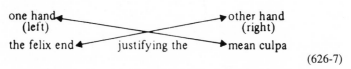

    one hand   other hand
    (left)   (right)
    the felix end   justifying the   mean culpa
                                                (626-7)

Most literally and directly, it is A. J. Greimas's semiotic square that provides *Thru* with a conveniently twisted "narratological logic," because the square itself has some chiastic characteristics, especially in the relation between contradictories:

In narratological terms, Greimas's square brings two narratological movements on a collision course: "We propose calling the double presupposition of the two schemata [S1 + S2 and S2 + S2] *semiosis*."[9] In fact, Greimas himself highlights the topological character of the semiotic square in discussing Propp's structuration of the folk tale when he talks of "the topological syntax of objective values" (78) Brooke Rose "intertexts" this reference almost verbatim:

two deixes that are conjoined, because corresponding to the same axis of contradiction, but not conforming, and equivalent, at the fundamental level, to contradictory terms:

Thus the circulation of values, interpreted as a sequence of transfers of value-objects, can have two courses . . . (667-68).

If in oppositional—as well as logical—space, contradictions (such as an affirmation and its negation) are situated in two different logical as well as spatial sides, Greimas relates them chiastically, while two contraries (which imply a common denominational field and presuppose each other reciprocally) are related on one side. In Greimas's square, then, the spaces of contrariness and contradiction are conflated into a one-sided space and thus into a one-sided logic. The result is a space in which contrary and contradictory terms are both opposed and related.

When Brooke-Rose quotes Greimas's rectangle directly, she stresses in particular these ambivalent logical spaces:

The transfer can then be interpreted at the same time as a privation (at the superficial level) or as a disjunction (at the fundamental level) or as an attribution (at the superficial level) or as a conjunction (at the fundamental level), thus representing the circulation of value-objects topologically as an identification of the dietic transfers with the terms of a taxonomic model . . . that is, each isotopic space (the place where the performances occur) consists of two deixes that are conjunctive but equivalent, at the fundamental level, to the contradictory terms:

(634)

In relation to the subject and the object, this relates the subject and the object as contraries, while it relates the subject to the nonsubject and the object to the nonobject as contradictory.[10]

Brooke-Rose, however, does not adhere literally and closely to Greimas; at one point she refers to the separation between subject and object within a direct reference to Greimas:

> O but is not incompetent performance a non-disjunction at level of deep structure? I me if it be possible despite nonequivalence to rewrite I as O and O as I

> which has been suggested,
> here,
> you see,

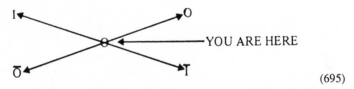

>   cosí   I

>   I   I

> should you start structuring your te⊃⊂thattaway
>   or the   latterway?

(585)

However, his rectangle also serves her as a model for chiastic crossings in which the affirmation is no longer related to its negation, but in which two terms are directly linked in a chiastic logic; with the "I of the Other" related to the "Other of the I"

with diagonals from the I to the object

I←   →O
      ⊗←————————YOU ARE HERE
Ō←   →T

(695)

This shift is the one from a more general intercrossing of clauses in a sentence, in which only the formal order of the words is inverted while the words themselves are semantically free to a more restricted, dialectic chiasm, in which a binary opposition is chiastically crossed.

Symptomatically, in Brooke-Rose's example, the subject is positioned at the nodal point of the chiastic intercrossing of the logically oppositional terms. The results of her play with these juxtapositions are semantic, textual "explosions":

     U   S   I

         e
       ✕   plOdes

   I   (t)   I   Nto
               r
               e
some   other   text   u   a l i t y

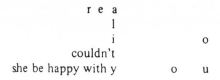

(590)

Within the general structure of *Thru*, Brooke-Rose draws on the Lacanian notion of a decentered subject that is a "function" of the signifier and suspended within language as well as the realm of specular identifications and confrontations which Lacan has developed in his essay "The Mirror Stage as Formative of the Function of the I" (also in *Écrits*). It is this dependence on other subjects that returns in language as the question "Che voui?" (Lacan 312), another of *Thru*'s frequent queries. The second, equally important reference is the Derridean notion of deconstruction and dissemination; the endless play of the coupling and uncoupling of discourses.

The Lacanian and Derridean notions that form the basic tension within *Thru* are connected by the concept of desire. In psychoanalytical terms, desire is inaugurated by the initial loss of an object, which the subject continually desires to "reconstitute" within the various modes of representation. Brooke-Rose picks up this notion, paraphrasing Lacan: "in the dialectic of desire, the subject is subverted and the object is from the start an object of central loss" (595).[11] While psychoanalysis defines desire within a sexual arena, Derrida theorizes desire basically as the desire for (and of) the signifier, originating not from an originary lack (castration), but from an originary plenitude (discourse). This textual desire can be traced and is operative in the continuous coupling of the language-material itself. Brooke-Rose captures these erotics of the text in amalgamations such as "heterotextuality" (680) or "textasy" (665). Throughout the text, she synchronizes the Derridean and the Lacanian subject.[12]

In *Thru*, the Lacanian subtext defines the parameters of the story of Larissa Toren and Armel Santores, "always already" signifiers: "a poem not a couple" (603) and anagrammatically linked: "Except for ME in hers and I in his" (647). It delineates their breakup, the inevitably of which is already written into the anagram's implied impossibility of a final identification. This story, however, is far from homogeneous. It delineates their breakup, the inevitability of which is already written into the anagram's implied impossibility of a final identification. This story, however, is far from homogeneous. It is invented and told in turn by various students in a creative writing class, an updated *Jacques and His Master*, as well as by a general authorial voice, whose combined efforts ultimately produce a literary *cadavre exquis*. This strategy creates a "floating" text, a motif taken up typographically by literally allowing the letters to float across the page. The result is a complex network of conflicting and supplementary voices: "The more indeterminate the origin of the statement, the more plural the text" (*S/Z* 41). On top of these multiple inventions by the various narrators, the characters (both in the sense of subject as well as of letter) constantly invent each other as well as themselves, so that intertextuality and intersubjectivity become as inseparable as "the two sides of a sheet of paper"; or rather, as inseparable as the "two" sides of a Möbius strip. When Freud comments on the oppositional logic of Ur-words such as "inside-outside," Brooke-Rose takes up this logic in spatial terms such as "rectoverso" (600) in relation to "the schematized split image of the sign that watches, helpless and in great pain, the engendering of its own pro-jected trajectory struggling along ad [eloquentiam]" (600).

At the heart of the book, accordingly, lies the twofold problem of a "textual subject": on the one hand, it utilizes language to compensate for a basic loss, but on the other it invests its desire in these very compensations. As Armel tells Larissa: "language is your strength and your strength is your weakness" (714). This paradox results from the fact that the subject is cease-lessly trying to represent a number of "unspecularizable" objects and im-ages that make up the basic haunts of its imagination. These unspeculariz-able objects are linked to the unconscious. Because they are excluded from representation "they have no specular image" (Lacan 315), so that they can only be represented "obliquely" (T 610) and indirectly: "it is to this object that cannot be grasped in the mirror that the specular image lends its clothes" (Lacan 316). Ideal signifieds such as "God" (T 650) or the "truth as signifier" (732, 737) can therefore only be reflected indirectly by a "hidden representation of a representation" (732), or "the show within the show the portrait within the portrait" (602).[13] Because discourse is "always already" discursive, it is only by constantly manipulating various systems of repre-sentation that Brooke-Rose can evoke "obliquely" that which is excluded from them.

Within these references, the text brings out into the open the problem of representation itself, the fact that "What we call the 'real' . . . is never more than a code of representation" (*S/Z* 80). Brooke-Rose clothes this realiza-tion in the image of multiple veils hiding a void, and in *Thru* continually plays out the beauty and fascination of representation "the dance of the 27 veils" (622) against the anguish of the "initial loss": "Every structure pre-supposes a void, into which it is possible to fall" (617). The result of these dynamics is that the decentered narrator: "The I who is not the I who says I" (631) has to be continually reinvented and has to reinvent herself. She can only do so by "rehandling the signifiers in constant reinvestment" (631), thus playing out the full range from "delirious" (690) to "delicious" discourse:

The delirious character of the delicious

X

The delicious character of the delirious

The text's continuous gliding (*glissement*) from one narrator-function to the next mirrors the fading of the subject. A passage that again takes up the impossibility of the union of Larissa and Armel, however, reveals an antagonistic current that continually undercuts the dissemination of the various voices, and that reveals the ultimately narcissistic nature of the narrator and her "loneliness": "Who ever invented you is the absently unreliable or unreliably absent narrator or you in love with him who is in love with the implied author who is in love with himself, so that he is absent in the nature of things, gazing into the pool as the I who wins but loses to the me . . ." (674). *Thru*, even more than *Amalgamemnon*, is dialogized[14] by the continuous discussions about the progress of the story between the multiple narrators. These discussions are embedded within wider references to the university; a university, however, that is just around the linguistic turn, and whose faculty and students are all "figures of speech." It is their constant intervention in the process of storytelling as well as the endless mirrorings of the authorial voice that prevent even the most personal authorial passages from ever becoming completely unified. They are always spoken by the Lacanian "Other Author" (705), language itself, of whose discourse the text ultimately consists.

While the Lacanian dynamics of this story stress the delirious aspect of discourse, its deliciousness is highlighted by its mode of representation, in which Brooke-Rose sets the more playful Derridean contention of continuous play and dissemination within the weave of discourses against the dynamics of the Lacanian love story. As a hinge, she uses the poetics of Barthes' *S/Z*, in which the strategy of a continuous deferral of "originary meaning" and "final answers" is developed in literary terms: "for the very act of writing . . . keep[s] the question *Who is speaking?* from ever being answered" (*S/Z* 140).

This playfulness can be observed in the experimental procedure of the clashing of discourses with the pun (as well as portmanteau words) as a catalyst, a strategy Brooke-Rose perfected in *Between*. The pun, which can be considered the sense of humor of the language-material itself, opens up the possibility to dis-connect discourses and thus subvert the stabilizing functions of a presumed signified content. It can also be used to short-circuit corroded signifying chains, as when Brooke-Rose inserts the question "Who is speaking?" into its more natural context of a telephone conversation, or explores the linguistic malleability of the term "intentional fallacy." Apart from showing a libidinal relation to the text (and *Thru* is a continual "love story with language"), the pun also serves as a further hinge between literary and theoretical discourse. Its history from Freud to Derrida and from Roussel to Joyce marks the progressive emancipation of the signifier from the signified in both fields, a development which can best be followed by its intrusion into theoretical discourse both as a rhetorical device and a theoretical agent. Its use combines the writing of Lacan, Derrida, and Brooke-Rose on a stylistic and rhetorical level, and facilitates their multiple reflections.

Because of its fundamental playfulness and openness, a structural analysis of the text is virtually impossible. In Greimasian terms, the text is "hopelessly" heterological and defined by an "abysmally" complex isotopia. Although the reader tries to make out leitmotifs and themes, this meaning-gathering activity is always subverted by Brooke-Rose's iconoclastic disruptions and her bricolage technique. As Fredric Jameson states in his introduction to Greimas, "Meaning is never there in that sense, or rather it is an 'always-already-given' so that a static meaning is replaced by the continuous chaotic '*production* of meaning'" (*On Meaning* x). Yet, as chaos theory has recently shown, even chaos has a specific structure:

The Chaos of Order

X

The Order of Chaos

Gilles Deleuze has related this order to the idea of a membrane, or screen: "Events are produced in a chaos . . . but only under the condition that a sort of screen intervenes. Chaos does not exist; it is an abstraction because it is inseparable from a screen that makes something . . . emerge from it. . . . Like a formless elastic membrane, an electromagnetic field, or the receptacle of the *Timaeus*, the screen makes something issue from chaos."[15] Brooke-Rose's text, especially when one considers connotations of "thru" such as "filtering through," is precisely such a screen, sieve or membrane through which meaning is filtered. Taking up one of her other recurrent images, the text both hides and reveals the naked body in the dance of the 27 veils—which come to function as so many membranes.[16]

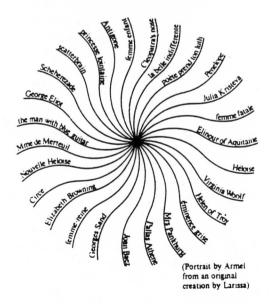

(Portrait by Armel
from an original
creation by Larissa)

In this image, the naked body functions as the "unspecularisable" real that is "beyond" the signifier, and that can only be, like the trauma, "abducted." To try and reach it "directly," Lacan states, only "leads to completely ineffable things, which moreover soon peter out—except if one wants to carry on regardless, ending with what is commonly called a delirium."[17] It is in the forever moving, oscillating, choreographic, fluid, and chiastic field that a structural blueprint of *Thru* should be located.

A final reference to the chiasm might be illuminating in this respect. It is a collage of scraps of narrative, structured within a chiastic frame, which takes up the separation of subject and object, juxtaposes two movements of the statement "IN ORDER TO" and relates, within this structure, various narrative scraps—amongst them references to Greimas, the retrovisor, and the dialogization of the narrative—while simultaneously commenting "metatextually" upon is own structure:

```
In   the box  with   a  switch  for  the  overhead  projector  tO
Note  and   a  spirit-loaded  pen,  thus  not  loosing  eye-contacT
Or  some  still  making  love  perhaps  four  eyes  crossed  foR
Riveting  limbs,  M  or  Y,  opening  crossing  pentapod  or  ninE
Diagonals  meeting  In              On  which  I  enters  O  anD
Envelopes  contraries  contradictories  subalterns  as  a  staR
Rivets  form  substance  floating  up  every  90  minutes  or  sO
To  surface  structure  from  deep  level  dreamlessness  dowN
Over  under  electroded  lids  for  a  shared  cigarette.
```
(598)

As a symbol of the page—as the narratological space itself—the passage becomes isomorphic to the narratological logic itself: "The four corners of the sheet are more than a physical limit, they are a logical premise."[18]

Apart from the fact that the text delineates the secondary split of the (subject of) narration, as both writer and critic, which was hinted at in the double reflection of the opening image, the poeticization of theoretical jargon, the use of theoretical constructs as metaphorical material, and last but not least its typography and "SIN TAG MA TRICKS" (581) mark the text itself as the final object of desire: "the text slowly forms itself, like a shower of gold in Danae's lap" (607).

A further effect of the text's congealing of literature and literary theory is that out of a detailed inventory of all its echoes is makes a disconcertingly circular activity. Each explanation is actually written out in the text itself. The critic is therefore referred back to his or her function as a reader. In confronting *Thru*, which might ultimately be read as an attempt to create a "writerly voice," only a careful, attentive, and "loving" reading can do honor to the *sprezzatura* with which Brooke-Rose handles the signifiers.

Towards the end of the story, when the narrators "drive the discourse into the future merely glancing up at the retrovizor" (729), Brooke-Rose again takes up Lacan's notion of the future perfect, and transposes it into the conditional perfect, thus mirroring the mode of the subject's "auto-invention" into a fictional universe. With this twist, she also reveals the ultimate congruity of these two realms: "Or we should have her escaping to freedom under his pressure, he'd have started to write to her again" (732).

Within the dissemination of possible endings, the story comes to "tell itself," with the final words of the narrator written acrostically into the narration: "exeunt narrators with a swift switch of signifiers no more I superimposing" (735). It terminates even while spilling over into the textual universe of *Amalgamemnon*: "the show within the show must go on the other scene since the institution of unlearning has been closed down by an obituary act of authority due to textual disturbances" (741-42).

The final sentence takes up the initial mirror image and shows again the subject gliding on its lonely night-ride journey, confronted only by its own plurality. This passage is another premonition of *Amalgamemnon*, the "radiooscillating epiepistle" that will describe another night journey, this time in front of a "tolvtubular high fidelity daildialler."[19]

> So that you^n drive away into the nightwiddling along the transistor of disembodied voiceless logos watching the hoops that dance red amber white green mauve eyes made up by the disappeared narrator in a mere vehicle now deprived of pilot who would not stay for an answer

> his f o u r $\dfrac{\nabla}{v}_s$ l o d g e d in
>
> the retro   izor never

> to sally fort-da and reflecting nothing but

> T
> E
> X
> (I)
> U Я H T H R U

(742)

The final mirror image splits first the text, then the subject, and finally, with is proper name, the text as subject.

NOTES

[1] *Thru,* in *Omnibus,* 579; hereafter cited parenthetically.

[2] This phenomenon occurs when the mirror has an "anti-glare device." See Emma Kafalenos, "Textasy: Christine Brooke-Rose's *Thru,*" *International Fiction Review* 7.1 (1980): 43-46, 44.

[3] In *Écrits,* trans. Alan Sheridan (New York: Norton, 1977); hereafter cited parenthetically.

[4]Jacques Lacan, *The Seminar of Jacques Lacan Book I: Freud's Papers on Technique 1953-1954*, trans. John H. Forrester (Cambridge: Cambridge Univ. Press, 1988), 191.

[5]In this context see also her reference to Jacques Derrida's book *The Postcard*, in which Derrida reverses the chronological sequence of the two philosophers: "Socrates is the one who speaks . . . Plato his microphone" (685).

[6]Roland Barthes, *S/Z*, trans. Richard Miller (New York: Hill and Wang, 1974), 209, 160. This book and its idea of the "writerly" text certainly contains *Thru*'s literary credo. Furthermore it is the main source for many of the more direct allusions.

[7]Jacques Lacan, "Stellung des Unbewußten," in *Schriften II* (Weinheim: Quardriga, 1986), 205-257, 217. My translation.

[8]See Shlomith Rimmon-Kenan's "Ambiguity and Narrative Levels: Christine Brooke-Rose's *Thru*," *Poetics Today* 3:1 (1982): 21-32, 29-30.

[9]Algirdas Julien Greimas, *On Meaning: Selected Writings in Semiotic Theory*, trans. Paul J. Perron and Frank H. Collins (Minneapolis: Univ. of Minnesota Press, 1987), 52.

[10]In the allusion to Greimas's own example, Brooke-Rose substitutes Peter with Adam: "Adam wants an apple Adam wants to be good" (659).

[11]See Lacan's essay "The Subversion of the Subject and the Dialectic of Desire in the Freudian Unconscious," in *Écrits*, 292-325.

[12]In this context, Brooke-Rose has commented: "In fact, the real theme in *Thru* is castration, but I don't suppose anyone would see that. . . . The very act of using language is castration." See "An Interview with Christine Brooke-Rose" by David Hayman and Keith Cohen, *Contemporary Literature* 17 (1978): 11-12.

[13]See especially: "In any case God as signifier is nonspecularisable and cannot see himself signified by a hidden representation of a representation. You should read Lacan" (650).

[14]A reference to another subtext: Mikhail Bakhtin's *The Dialogic Imagination*, trans. Caryl Emerson and Michael Holquist (Austin: Univ. of Texas Press, 1981).

[15]Gilles Deleuze, *The Fold: Leibniz and the Baroque*, trans. Tom Conley (Minneapolis: Univ. of Minnesota Press, 1993), 76.

[16]See also: "There are but the twenty-seven Larissas, and each is marked with a zero, liminivorous but eliminated by the letter she does not write" (685); "the I who says I not being the said I so that the recipient of the twenty-seven coloured veils is left frantically signalling into the wings of a love where nobody gets the message" (686); or: "But Larissa? and our Larissa? Has she not carefully invented the person she has become, stereotyping her twenty-seven veils for a pontificating pirate who will not stay for an answer?" (729).

[17]Jacques Lacan, *The Seminar of Jacques Lacan Book II: The Ego in Freud's Theory and in the Technique of Psychoanalysis*, trans. Sylvana Tomaselli (Cambridge: Cambridge Univ. Press, 1988), 35.

[18]Rosalind E. Krauss, *The Optical Unconscious* (Cambridge: MIT Press, 1993), 48. Krauss makes ample use of Greimas's square; unfortunately, some of her interpretations suffer from her adopting a misprint of the square in the English translation of *On Meaning* (see n. 9 above).

[19]James Joyce, *Finnegans Wake* (New York: Viking, 1939), 108, 309.

The Emperor's New Clothes:
Narrative Anxiety in Thru

Damian Grant

1

WE ALL KNOW THE STORY of the Emperor's new clothes: an Eastern potentate is persuaded by two tailors that they can make him the most magnificent set of clothes from the finest silk on earth. For a price. When the clothes are brought, they are invisible; but, unwilling to confess his own obtuseness or insensitivity, he "tries them on," and is convinced by the tailors that they do indeed look wonderful on him. His courtiers are then caught up in the same collective illusion; and when in due course the Emperor parades through the city to display his finery, only one little boy has the innocence to call out: "Look! the Emperor has no clothes!"

The Emperor in question turns up—along with a thousand other fictional characters—in Christine Brooke-Rose's latest novel *Textermination.* Indeed, he is the major attraction in chapter 13 of the novel, when he sits—naked—in the lobby of the hotel in San Francisco that serves as the setting for a rather special literary convention, attended only by characters from fiction "competing for being" against each other and against the forces of forgetfulness. True to his story, the Emperor is attended by the little boy; but here grown old, a tattered man who has developed a protective attitude towards the potentate he now serves.

Flaubert's Emma Bovary comes upon the naked Emperor in the company of Hawthorne's Hester Prynne, and is suitably shocked: "Un homme nu! Quelle horreur!" (131); but TV cop Columbo—this reunion is quite eclectic—persuades her to lend the Emperor her own silk cloak, which he grudgingly agrees to put over his own attire: "Such crude silk!" (133). Laclos's Valmont approves her act: of course, to win her favor. Meanwhile Samuel Butler's Mr. Pontifex interprets the tale for the benefit of George Eliot's one-time Dorothea Brooke: "It's only a fairy-tale, Mrs. Casaubon. Haven't you read it? And a very moral one. About vanity you know" (137).

When Christine Brooke-Rose gave a reading in Manchester recently,[1] I put it to her that this tale of the Emperor's new clothes was a key reference in her work. She expressed some surprise at this idea, saying she was not aware she had ever alluded to it previously. I find this very interesting since—as I was able to assure her, and as any attentive reader of *Thru* will

117

know—there are actually four references to our Emperor in the earlier novel, meaningfully structured within the text: "but the emperor is naked" (602); "but the emperor's a naked imperialist" (673); "but the emperor's a naked empiricist" (681); "The naked emperor of I-scream" (735).[2]

Why should this moral fairy tale be at all interesting, and especially interesting in the context of *Thru* (which is not much of a fairy tale, and not especially moral either)? Well, it has to do with the fact that Ernest Pontifex's interpretation for Mrs. Casaubon (like most interpretations of fairy tales) is much too facile and foreclosed. Far from being only "about vanity you know"—which is indeed its first level—I suggest that the story of the Emperor's new clothes may actually be understood to be about fiction; and as such, it offers a significant parable for our narrative and self-reflexive times. More sophisticated than the little boy, we can see that the new clothes are stories; what we collectively, culturally have woven to see ourselves and to be seen in; to cover our nakedness; to defend "unaccommodated man," Shakespeare's "poor, bare, forked animal," against his own nothingness. There is, therefore, a profound anxiety attaching to the clothes/stories (the boy grown old perceives "a note of anxiety in the Emperor's question" to him as to whether he admires his clothes [Tx 130]), because their acceptance and recognition is of crucial importance. We need to keep fabulating/tailoring in order to survive. If our narrative is undermined, then we forfeit our identity, our very ground of being: "Whoever you invented invented you too. That is surely the trouble, we do not exist" (631).

This narrative anxiety is of course inscribed in the frame story of the queen of storytellers, Scheherazade, who must literally narrate to live, to survive to the next evening. Not surprisingly, Scheherazade is a favorite reference for Brooke-Rose, and she reappears in a number of guises in *Thru.* "There's no more private property in writing, the author is dead, the spokesman, the porte-parole, the tale-bearer, off with his head" (607): here, the obvious reference to Scheherazade and her sultan is reinforced by the reference to Lewis Carroll's Queen of Hearts, and may even—quite relevantly, as we shall see—invoke the ghost of the decapitated John the Baptist. From another cultural quarter, this narrative anxiety is also a central, informing theme in the fiction of Samuel Beckett (the most immediate and pervasive influence of all on Brooke-Rose). The obligation of the characters in Beckett's novels to narrate, and in the plays to converse, is a way of coping with consciousness: to fill the void. We are under a continuous obligation to clothe/narrate/create ourselves, to maintain "the inenarrable contraption I called my life"[3] in some state of readworthiness.

The little boy who exclaims "no clothes" is the literal, uncultivated perception, the voice of the innocent reader that collapses the whole cultural edifice-artifice, leaving us all—emperor, courtiers, and citizens—exposed. In Salman Rushdie's *Haroun and the Sea of Stories*, the storyteller's son asks his father: "What's the use of stories that aren't even true?"[4] thereby silencing his father's gift—until (which is the main plot of the novel) the sea of stories revives it again. If the emperor is naked—he who has the best tailors—then we are all naked, even if we can't "see" it. Our habiliments are in the end only habits. The boy's observation, if we take it seriously, pushes us to the abyss, the *mise-en-abîme*, Pascal's vacant interstellar spaces; the gaping O of the inaccessible other, the womb without utterance, the "thin air" of Prospero's metaphor into which all of us—and all of our words—will ultimately melt; where, quite simply, "we do not exist." Compare Pope's version, articulated at another moment of perceived cultural crisis:

> Thy hand, great Anarch! lets the curtain fall;
> And Universal Darkness buries All.[5]

And again, set beside this Beckett's radical telescoping of reality: "Soon there will be nothing where there was never anything."[6] It is the same annihilating movement from zero back again to zero.

Narration is everything and nothing. Nothing through its very conditional status, its un-origin-ality, its marking always and only an absence. And nothing will come of nothing: the whole network of narration that links us via oral tradition to prehistory, the extended umbilical cord (in Joyce's metaphor "the strandentwining cable of all flesh"[7] that leads us back to Eve) may always be called in question, cut, short-circuited. This is surely the source of Macbeth's anxiety: that the human story is indeed "a tale told by an idiot . . . signifying nothing"; this is Prospero's world-weary perception; this is Horatio's conclusion at the end of *Hamlet*: "the rest is silence." This is why we, as human beings, are terrified of silence/nakedness; of those "vacant interstellar spaces." It's not just that space diminishes, but that it abolishes us. Hamlet urges Horatio to "tell my story"; but Horatio says, "the rest is silence." The fulfillment of his promise is only conditional; and Shakespeare, in fulfilling it, knows the condition: the human "condition" which is both a situation and an argument.

2

However hazardous the enterprise, I must before elaborating my own argument essay a general description of the chosen text. *Thru* is a class novel. Not a class novel in the usual sense: that is, about the class struggle (though this does put in a post-68 appearance). No: I mean a novel set in a classroom; in this case, a seminar class on fiction at Paris VIII, Sorbonne Nouvelle (where, as it were coincidentally, Christine Brooke-Rose taught for twenty years). The class is entitled "The Novel as Intentional Object," and is given by Dr. Larissa Toren: or is it Santores—her married name, if she's actually married? Or is the class given by Armel Santores, her husband if she has one? Their names, significantly, are near-anagrams of each other: encouraging the ideal of a "flow" of identity. They share, anagrammatically, the phrase "narrate loss," to which one adds "I" to make

Larissa and "me" to make Armel; the nominative and accusative of the first-person pronoun, where (of course) all the anxiety bears down.

According to Brian McHale, the treelike verbal icons that appear twice in the novel are meant to represent rows of benches in the class.[8] This may be so; though they are also associated with the tree of knowledge in the text, and the author has said they are furthermore meant to suggest lampposts seen through the rearview mirror of a car: the image with which the novel begins and ends, and which is recalled as an important "narrative metaphor" through the text. But the unusual thing about this class, and the reason it provides the perfect dramatis personae for the novel, is that the participants (all nineteen of them) are engaged in some kind of ontological struggle with each other—especially, the students vs. the teacher(s)—which is expressed in the competition to control the narrative. This ties in with the series of references to Diderot's *Jacques le fataliste*, reproducing to some degree the passing of the initiative in the course of this narrative to Jacques from his master. It is one highly specialized version of traditional struggle over "authority" (which, referring back to 1968, may have been, or at least seemed, realer in Paris than elsewhere), diverted from politics to the literary text; in general, the novel, but specifically, the text of this novel. "You feel so totally out of it that you will spare the other recipient the details since you are only a substitute narrator, jack-in-the-box not jack-of-all-trades, a mere pistol whose only role is to utter by chance or by sudden overwhelming desire the words of love for ever unbelieved" (693). "Meanwhile" (we find lower down this same page), "something has gone wrong with the narrative owing to textual disturbances."

One symptom of the narrative anxiety in *Thru* is that the text of the novel is deliberately unstable. The monosyllabic title itself is a clue: *Thru* establishes a context of duplicity and reflexiveness in its cryptic allusion to Lewis Carroll's *Through the Looking Glass*. It also deconstructs into anagrams: Ruth, hurt; and—nearly—truth: the obliqueness of which, if we accept it, would be entirely appropriate. We can be expected to pick up the (Beckettian) double allusion to birth and death: "through" the mother's body and out into the world, and then "through" with the world. Alerted again by Beckett, we might also suspect Beckett's punning or at least ambiguous use of the adverb in the Trilogy: "any old pronoun will do, provided one sees through it"[9]: that is, uses it as a point of view while at the same time remaining undeceived by its keyhole on reality.

Then, the 165-page text plays elaborate typographical tricks on us—tricks not played by this author herself before or since (although none of her novels is "straight," the complications are typically philosophical and narratological rather than iconic, "concrete" in the actual layout of the text on the page). Apart from the two appearances of the tree/lamppost/desk icon already mentioned, the text frequently breaks up into vertical and diagonal sections, which have to be read across and down rather like a crossword puzzle; there are numerous tables and diagrams, and a page reproduced from a fifteenth-century treatise on rhetoric. There are triangles (suggesting perhaps the ALP from Joyce's *Finnegans Wake*),[10] rectangles, chiasmuses, words forming cogs and musical staves, and one anemonelike symbol for the self under its twenty-seven veils that seems to owe something to Yeats's design in *A Vision* for the analysis of the self through the twenty-eight Phases of the Moon. These veils themselves, along with the references to John the Baptist and Salome, also tie in both with the story of the naked Emperor and the theme of the threatened decapitation of the narrator. If the novel begins (as it does) with Joyce's ALP triangle = Anna Livia Plurabelle and the female (birth), and ends with an inverted cross that spells EXIT THRU TEXT, then perhaps we need to read it first of all as a narrative of the journey from birth to death: at once a story and a symbol and an icon, an act of deference to our one true beginning and our one inevitable end.

As we read, we are forced to ask: are the teachers supervising the students—in the sense of supervising them ontologically: their being in their writing—or are the students underwriting the teachers? Perhaps I should say "writing them up," constructing alternative selves, alternative "adventures" for them as part of their fulfillment of work-and-attendance requirements for the class. At the beginning the institution seems to be in charge, as the students submit their written work for correction and return (see the examples over pages 605-26). But later, as the emotional entanglements of the "mature" lovers become more extreme, their authority starts to slip with their identities: as Armel exchanges Larissa for Veronica Masters, and Larissa betrays him with Stavro Laretino; as the latter takes on alternative identities (as Marco, and Oscar "the unmarked term"), the tutors seem to surrender themselves to the students' jurisdiction: and the last section of the novel is a nearly explicit "assessment" of Larissa and Armel as both people and couple. Or are both processes happening somehow simultaneously? Which, if one thinks about it, comes closest to what happens in a normal social—or indeed institutional—situation: we negotiate ourselves and invent each other all the time.

It is true other novelists have treated versions of this theme: indeed, one could argue that the construction of interlocking subjectivities is the moral ground plan of the novel, an ethical principle for Jane Austen and George Eliot as well as for a novelist like Iris Murdoch, who focuses directly on the moral/philosophical implications of atomized subjectivity in her first novel *Under the Net* (1954). But there's a difference, no doubt, between this kind of essentially moral perspective—which simply insists on the otherness of other people, and their equal rights to self-determination—and what we have in *Thru*, which is a radical usurpation of another's existential self: an ontological takeover bid, a cat-and-mouse game where winner takes all (as in the game of vinciperdi), determines his/her own reality and yours as well. It's a power politics rather than an ethics of fiction, with imaginations contending against each other rather than trying to be reconciled; we are assailed with realities that challenge and cancel each other out rather than collaborate. As Larissa has insisted to Ali Nourennin early on: "My function here is not to narrate but to teach, or shall I say I am not a function of your narrative" (628). What we are faced with, ultimately, is a choice (if we have a choice) between different kinds of realism: different epistemologies, fundamentally different senses of our relationship with the world and with each other: the formal account of which is the subject of a critical work published by Brooke-Rose six years after *Thru: A Rhetoric of the Unreal* (1981). But the point of the novel surely is that a full understanding of the fictional process can only be gained from the inside: by experiencing it, rather than treating it discursively.

And this is what brings me back to the theme of anxiety. Because here we aren't simply admitting (with George Eliot) that as each of us looks into the mirror, we will see the world reflected back with a different perspective. We are asked to reflect, more vertiginously, that if we can pass through the looking glass, who is on which side of it? Or, what is more unsettling still, how can we even begin to tell which side we are on? In other words, it introduces us to—or immerses us in, for there are no formal introductions possible here—the world of radical doubt and ontological insecurity, where the term fiction is relentlessly problematized. Commonsense guidelines, conventional signposts, and guardrails are deliberately removed, and we are lost in the labyrinth of questions, a maze of mirrors, trapped in some looped retrieval system within the library of Babel. This is the world Brooke-Rose shares with Beckett, and I make no apology for returning again to this unavoidable comparison. The reduced world of the Trilogy, the impossible world of *Comment c'est*, the abandoned world of the late fragments, are the epistemological ruins to which *Thru* itself returns.

3

The first anxiety concerns the source of the text itself: "Who speaks?" Not just whose turn is it to speak (as in a play), for we have here no orderly turns. Each voice threatens to engulf, and be engulfed by, other voices. So "who speaks?" becomes an ultimate, existential question—like "To be or not to be?" a question addressed to origins and authority.

And the question recurs throughout the novel (I have noted fifteen occurrences, in English, French, and even Italian, but there may be more) to bring us back to the "overwhelming question"—as Prufrock experiences it in his particular suffering of the quandary. And there is no answer; of course, there can be no answer to such a direct and innocent question (like the little boy's). What we have instead is the continuing hum of the narrative, the background *bourdonnement* of other voices from within which, momentarily, one individual voice is distinguished: as one voice can be heard, for an instant, above the medley in a school playground, on a beach, or in a swimming pool. But any tendency of this single voice to assert itself is quickly chastised: "what matters is → are the innumerable and ever escaping levels of Utterance by the I who is not the I who says I (if he does)" (631). It is the interlocking of these voices with each other that forms the true text of *Thru*, thereby fulfilling the transmissive suggestion of the title.

Walter Benjamin remarked that "the art of storytelling is to keep a story free from explanation as one reproduces it." This refers to innocent, oral, authorless storytelling. But it is the nature of written (or secondary) narrative to become distracted if not with "explanations" exactly, then at least— what may be more disabling—with *excavations*: plottings of the ground on which the story rests, the sources from which it derives. This is the "anxiety of narrative" in its pure form: the looking back over the shoulder of the narrative (in the rearview mirror provided) for antecedents, for what came before. Because paradoxically it is only by looking back in the mirror that we can safely move forwards. This dual, dynamic motion is cleverly presented in spatial terms by the "framing" of the two rectangles (mirror/windscreen) round the narrative of *Thru*.[11]

It is by such devices that the novel does in fact provide us with one of the most sustained experiments in fictional feedback, as one narrative line is engulfed by another, one idyll surrenders to another idyll, each door opens onto another door with suggestions of aporia and infinitude. We are introduced to the image of the rearview mirror in the opening sentence (579); this "needs adjusting" continuously, and is supplemented by the image of the "show within the show" (587). References to *Hamlet* and *Macbeth* later are followed by the observation: "But the process is infinite I think, within each text there is another text, within each myth another myth" (608). An attempt to "work out a typology of digressive utterance" proceeds by reference to Sterne, Manzoni, and *The Knight in the Tiger Skin*, a twelfth-century Georgian romance, one of the earliest agglomerated tales (617). Armel is unable to control the narration of his idyll, "since in every idyll there opens out another idyll" (653), a phrase that is adopted and reworked as another motif in the novel, another laden seme from which the whole text could in theory be reproduced.

The seme is shown at its most generative in a late section of the novel (715-25) that concerns the shifting triangular relationships of Armel, Lara, and Stavro. This begins with a reference to telescoping ("telescoping . . . the flute-player into a stereotyped foreshortened faun") and then picks up the opening image of the "four lies reflected in the retrovizor" before the familiar motif returns: "For the idyll reopens out into the other idyll of Armel who is not like that at all" (incorporating, interestingly, an image of Aphrodite "emerging from memory and beckoning, naked, sprayed with flowery foam": as we will see, there is a link to be explored between the nakedness of the narrator and the erotic nakedness of the narratee).

Allusions crowd in, images refract as "the moving finger piercing through the pregnant plenitude from idyll to castratrophy" threatens (or promises) to bring about "the end of the discourse," only to be duplicated by another mirror, "a wild moon detached and gazing at the earth." Doors and mirrors produce and reproduce each other ("doors opening on doors, mirrors on mirrors in an eternal game of vinciperdi") and then we have an extraordinary sequence of images in concrete dramatization of the impossibility of authorship: "A head in a pool on a platter in a textured cloth, the head detached to re-present the word, a disembodied voice" (716).

Christ's head reflected in the water as he is baptized by John; the head of John the Baptist himself, Herod's gift to Salome; and finally the image of Christ's head on the towel used by Veronica to wipe his face on the road to Calvary: each an image of profound cultural importance, depending in each case on its authenticity. And in referring later to the recent downgrading of Veronica in the calendar of saints, Brooke-Rose alludes to the scientific undermining of the authenticity of this very text(ure). The conversation between Armel and Lara proceeds, until Lara (or her absent author) exclaims, "But is it really possible to superimpose so many systems one upon the other," the Tristan story for example, motif to theme to myth to opera, "wagnerised and materlinked into Mélisande through layers of books and looks that open like doors onto other doors . . . ?" A few moments later she provides her own affirmative answer: "every man knows he is not the definitions of others but for ever undefined, never coinciding with himself. . . . And that made me think of books within books, stories within stories, each character a new tale-bearer" (717-18). The pun reminds us that the character recycles both his story through discourse and himself through intercourse: a superimposing of two specific systems to which I shall return at the end.

It is explicitly acknowledged, on several occasions, that the authority of the narrator has been challenged ("once upon a time . . . the author had supreme authority"; but since then, "the author has lost authority many times in the history of narrative" [605, 621]); and once this challenge has been made, the "divine right" of the narrator can never be re-established. The author is dead (axiom); "the reader is the writer and the writer is the reader" (608); and in this world of distributed functions, narrative becomes only conditional, the power of the author limited, the determination of meaning a matter for democratic negotiation. The resultant anxiety of the "acting" narrator is wittily conveyed at one point by a converted (or subverted) nursery rhyme: "Rock a narrator / On a phrase top / When the verb blows / The tree-structure will rock / When the noun breaks / The tree-structure will fall / Down comes the noun-phrase narrator and all" (648). Another minatory nursery rhyme—used by Orwell in *1984*—is "Oranges and Lemons," which ends with the line that Winston Smith had suppressed in his memory: "Along comes a chopper to chop off his head." This line turns up in *Thru* too, both in allusion to Scheherazade's threatened fate and as another warning to the garrulous narrator. "The narratives of the world are numberless," as Barthes asserts,[12] but the narrator's days (and his/her words) are numbered. At one point in the section considered above, Stavro has a strange dream of being in a Russian church in Ethiopia; and the fear this dream engenders is significant: "I was feeling afraid that the whole thing might collapse on us" (723). This fear, evidently, is another expression of the anxiety that provides both theme and impulse for the novel.

Once the narrative hierarchy has been challenged in this way, the interaction of the fictional parts becomes very unstable: it can't be represented by the traditional Chinese box or "babushka" model. Even in a complex Chinese box narrative like Maturin's *Melmoth the Wanderer* there is a clear hierarchy of narration—even if there are vertiginous moments when the stack appears to be about to fall (to fall into itself: into the engulfing and obliterating metaphor of the sea of ink). But in *Thru*, each level challenges the other for centrality: "I am not a function of your narrative" (628); "Whoever you invented invented you too" (631); "If Larissa invents Armel inventing Larissa, Armel also invents Larissa inventing Armel" (686): and so on, in infinite regression: ". . . this is the text we are creating it verbally we are the text we do not exist either we are a pack of lies dreamt up by the unreliable narrator in love with the zeroist author in love with himself but absent in the nature of things" (783).

This is the narrative argument of *Thru:* its characteristic device is the play of narrators/narratives, the surrender of specificity in pseudonym, allusion, return to an untraceable source. And if narratives forfeit their integrity and independence in this way, so in turn do the denizen characters, who become simple etymologies, networks, functions of each other. The cog-figure on pages 618-19 shows all the voices interacting with and "working" each other; *pace* Tristram, this does seem to be an illuminating mechanism. "I am her and I am you" says Larissa to Armel, of his "affair" with the vestigial Veronica (655); and again, "Because I am writing this libretto Armel, I can play all the parts" (709). One is reminded of the role of Bernard at the end of Virginia Woolf's *The Waves*, as he ritualistically incorporates the identities of the other characters; but again, this is enacted as part of a more stable, "stacking" structure.

In Woolf's novel, of the six characters only Rhoda (who commits suicide) is insecure—and her insecurity is psychological rather than ontological. In Brooke-Rose's version, where everybody depends upon everybody else for being in a continuous chain of signifiers (like a family tree itself telescoped to assume a synchronic rather than diachronic dimension), security is as fragile as the weakest link—or the most inattentive reader. The narrator, like his/her narration, may at any time be "changed and transmuted . . . cancelled even, for it does not exist, except in my own boundless need and fear that will alter the signifiers into a delirious discourse through swift-footed Hermes with terrible letters no doubt that we can skip as he will, for no recipient desires a message of enduring pain redundant and therefore without information content because not from the Emperor of China . . ." (711).

It is a curious coincidence that one of the most celebrated fictional embodiments of "the anxiety of authority" occurs in another story of an emperor: Kafka's "The Great Wall of China," to which allusion is made here and elsewhere in *Thru*. Kafka's story is a negative episteme: a parable of the impossibility of knowledge, the inaccessibility of truth to the human condition. Thousands of people labor, generation after generation, to build the wall: but for reasons that remain mysterious, the wall is built not continuously but in sections, so that no one knows what stage the construction has reached or if it can ever be completed. Meanwhile, the gaps everywhere render it useless for its original purpose of keeping out the enemy. All it does is to absorb the labor of the people, to no end; unless (like narrative) this is the end itself. And then there is the parable-within-the-parable: the Message from the Emperor. There is a message from the Emperor on his deathbed, designed especially for you (the vocative address of this passage is mesmerizing). You know this, and are waiting for it. But because of the distance, the terrain, the obstacles, the time . . . the message will in fact never arrive: "and if at last [the messenger] should burst through the outermost gate—but never, never can that happen—the imperial capital would lie before him, the center of the world, cramming to bursting with its own sediment. Nobody could fight his way through here even with a message from a dead man. But you sit at your window when evening falls and dream it to yourself."[13]

Another key insight of this story—very relevant to Brooke-Rose's work—is the continuous interaction of fact and fiction in ordinary discourse. In the vast empire as described by Kafka, rumors come and go (there is even a rumor that the wall is to be used as a foundation for the Tower of Babel); facts are treated with suspicion, fictions with superstitious reverence and regard. On the one hand the people relive and dramatize events "buried in time," whilst on the other they disbelieve what is happening now: "So eager are our people to obliterate the present" (96). Kafka's emperor is invisible rather than naked, but the stories home in on the same theme: the breakdown of common understanding, shared belief; the surrender of objective reality in a slow, seismic shift; the deferral of any answer to any question to some indifferent infinitude.

The conclusion of Kafka's story is particularly powerful. The author remarks on "a certain feebleness of faith and imaginative power on the part of the people" that prevents them from seizing the empire "in all its palpable living reality to their own breasts": there is no absolute truth, nothing palpable to the touch that would let us "but once to feel that touch and then to die." Instead, the people are somehow identified by this defect: "All the more remarkable is it that this very weakness should seem to be one of the greatest unifying principles among our people; indeed, if one may dare to use the expression, the very ground on which we live" (97).

Perhaps this passage casts its shadow again over *Thru*, where Armel says to Larissa "Anything at all with you Larissa, language is your strength and your strength is your weakness" (714). The "very ground" of language is shifting sand: yet we must build there, because for us (in Beckett's resigned phrase) *il n'y a rien d'autre.*

Kafka's emperor is on his deathbed when he gives the message, and (as I've suggested) there is a strong reek of mortality in Brooke-Rose's novel too. Early on, writing is seen as "generating a text which in effect is a dialogue with all preceding texts, a death and a birth dialectically involved with one another" (621); later, these texts—all texts, as in *Textermination*—as "involved in a dialectic to the death with one another" (699). Writing and reading both lead to an end, an extinction, a universal darkness. As we are reminded by Sterne in volume 7 of *Tristram Shandy,* there is no hiding place.

4

But *Thru* does not exact such a bleak, apocalyptic reading, and it would be misleading to conclude there. Brooke-Rose is not Kafka or Beckett, and her novel invites other, more diverse, more celebratory responses. The clearest signal of this in the text itself is the compulsive use of the pun, and the associated portmanteau word. The pun might be thought of indeed as the quickest and shortest route out of Kafka's maze or Beckett's mud, linking the author more to Joyce and further back to Lewis Carroll (who invented the latter term in *Through the Looking Glass*). The pun operates like a lift or an escalator, suddenly establishing a new semantic perspective. The analogy in a game would be not so much vinciperdi, with its simple binary option, as the more aleatory snakes and ladders. The device is provided with its own apologia in the novel: "the pun is free, anarchic, a powerful instrument to explode the civilization of the sign and all its stable, reassuring definitions, to open up its static, monstrous logic of expectation into a different dialectic with the reader" (607).

This new perspective, I suggest, may most fruitfully be understood as an erotics of the text, where (as has been suggested earlier) the Emperor's nakedness takes on quite another function. It is one of Shakespeare's heroines who frames the sociolinguistic axiom "they that dally nicely with words may quickly make them wanton."[14] Fully in the spirit of this insight, Brooke-Rose's puns in *Thru* operate almost compulsively in the semantic field of the sexual, exploring that cornucopia of suggestion that, once tapped into, seems almost unstoppable. (As Larissa remarks at one point, "when people talk of reality they usually mean sex" [642].)

This is no gratuitous play, but entirely appropriate in a novel that at some level is about an erotic entanglement between several people, involving the usual duplicities and deceptions as well as descriptions—heavily encoded —of sexual activity itself. The vocabularies converge from both sides. Discourse becomes intercourse; ecstasy becomes textasy. Books and looks become interchangeable, overlaid (and overloaded) readings provide a new heterotextuality. The days of the week are renamed to form an abridged narrative of the sexual: "Sceneday, Mouthday, Toolsday, Wombsday, Circe's Day, Aphrodite's Day, Sated Day" (668). We are affronted with "fig-years of speech" (686); catastrophe becomes the complex "castratrophy": a portmanteau argument, presenting woman to man as victim (prize) of the castration theory. Semiotics is reacquainted with its cousin semen, and linguistic polysemia discovers another kind of promiscuity. The writer is committed to a "breast-selling reality" (703), while it is rhetorically proposed that "it is more difficult for a phallus-man to enter the I of a woman than for the treasurer of signifiers to enter the paradisco terrestre" (704). Even the erotically charged faculty meeting requires the seventeenth-century sense of "faculty," as used by Donne in "The Ecstasy":

> So must pure lovers' souls descend
> To affections, and to faculties,
> Which sense may reach and apprehend,
> Else a great Prince in prison lies. (ll. 65-68)

And behind all of these examples is the familiar (master) image of the pen=penis inscribing reality in the void of the vagina/uterus: providing the central analogy in the novel between the biological and the textual generation of the self. The title *Thru* itself alludes to the sexual act as well as to the primal passages of birth and death. The "moving finger" from Fitzgerald's *Rubaiyat,* invoked more than once (690, 692, 715), is also the penis. The *mise-en-abîme* is intimately associated with "amorous euphoria" (651), and the anxiety of narration (another look in the rearview mirror at Sterne) with anxiety about sexual potency: the two are perfectly fused in Stavro's dream about the church that is collapsing around him. In this context, therefore, the term *conjugation* provides the seminal pun for the whole text, synchronizing as it does the sexual and the grammatical aspects/orders of creation. Linguistics "seeks the fundamental patterns of thought below the surface structures. . . . Maybe it's the grammar of the universe" (661). This idea is elaborated in a sustained passage of sexual/textual play—at once logical, lexical, lyrical—in which the successive transformation of hands/pens/penises, hymen/high men/highwaymen, leads inevitably to a "corpus crysis," all taking place "in the wine-dark sea of infratextuality" (684). The transmission of the text is an aspect of the transmission of the gene.

Taking a circular course ourselves, we may return to *Textermination,* where the erotic opportunist Valmont knows how to interpret and exploit Emma Bovary's expression of shock at the naked Emperor, the "homme nu" in the hotel lobby. This is where the value of nakedness inverts, from a negative to a positive quality; where anxiety about telling the story is replaced (for the time being) by the desire to act it out.

NOTES

[1]The reading took place on 28 January 1992, in the English Department at Manchester University.

[2]The final quotation also contains a punning reference to Wallace Stevens's poem "The Emperor of Ice Cream," and possibly to the 1965 novel of the same name by Brian Moore. All page references to *Thru* are from the *Omnibus*.

[3]*Molloy*, in *Molloy, Malone Dies, The Unnamable* (London: Calder and Boyars, 1959), 115. Referred to subsequently as the Trilogy.

[4](London: Granta Books, 1990), 22.

[5]*The Dunciad* (1742), 4:655-56.

[6]"Texts for Nothing" (1954), in *Collected Shorter Prose* (London: Faber, 1984), 114.

[7]*Ulysses* (London: Bodley Head, 1960), 46.

[8]*Postmodernist Fiction* (London: Methuen, 1987), 184-85.

[9]*The Unnamable,* in the Trilogy, 345.

[10]*Finnegans Wake* (London: Faber and Faber, 1939), 196.

[11]One wonders whether there is an implicit allusion to Stendhal's famous definition of the realist novel as "a mirror moving down a highway"—although, perhaps suprisingly, there is no reference to this image in either *The Rhetoric of the Unreal* or in *Stories, Theories and Things.*

[12]"The Structural Analysis of Narrative," trans. Stephen Heath, in *Image-Music-Text* (London: Fontana, 1977), 79.

[13]*The Great Wall of China: Stories and Reflections*, trans. Willa and Edwin Muir (New York: Schocken, 1970), 94; hereafter cited parenthetically.

[14]Viola in *Twelfth Night* (3.1.16-18).

Narrative Techniques in
Thru *and* Amalgamemnon

Annegret Maack

CRITICS OF THE NOVEL largely agree that orientation towards reality, "the lowest common denominator of the novel genre as a whole, its formal realism," can be seen as characteristic of the genre that established itself in the eighteenth century.[1] During the more than two-hundred-year-old history of the realist novel there has been a divergent tendency, which has received little notice but has remained lively. If the conventional novel is characterized by "mimetic solidity, stylistic transparency, consecutive narration, psychological insight, and moral authority within a middle-class frame-work,"[2] then a number of texts remain outside this tradition. In contrast to F. R. Leavis's "Great Tradition," this tendency may be called the "minor tradition." David Lodge likes to compare the historical development of the realistic novel to a "main road of fiction," from which minor paths branch off.[3]

Modern experimental writers quote this "minor tradition" and take their place in it. In their confrontation with the tradition of the conventional novel, they argue that one has to give up the idea of writing realistically because the concept of the realistic novel has exhausted itself in the course of its two-hundred-year history.[4] They consider it necessary to renew stale conventions. The reservations of the experimental writers concern "that old mimetic poetics of character, plot, setting and description," that is, those conventions of form that Virginia Woolf already wanted to get rid of in order to further the genre by means of sacrificing "story," "plot," and "character."[5]

The innovators, however, refer explicitly to the literary tradition and carry on an intense dialogue between texts as references to a system of texts or to single texts. The old formula of the beginning of a fairy tale can be seen as an example of intertextuality;[6] Henry Green's *Loving* (1945) opens with this formula into which Lawrence Durrell's *Alexandria Quartet* (1957-60) flows. In Michael Frayn's *A Very Private Life* (1968) it is projected into the future: "Once upon a time there will be . . . ," and in Christine Brooke-Rose's *Thru* (1975) it appears as *mise en abîme*: "Once upon a time laid out in rectangles into which you enter as into a room saying once upon a time the author had supreme authority . . ." (27; cf. 84, 127, 150). The effort to supplant the causally and temporally structured plot has led to new and very different linking strategies. In *Two Moons* (1977), Rayner Heppenstall divides the narration into two text sequences, which are printed on the left and right pages alternately. Thus, they become a double narration of the events of two months. Like Heppenstall, who uses the phases of the moon and astrology for the structuring of his text, modern experimenters look for structural patterns in the natural sciences and music, which they then attempt to use as a frame of reference for their texts.

Brigid Brophy chooses the form of Brahms's Fourth Symphony for *In Transit* (1969); its tempi and the titles of its movements are used as headings for the chapters. The title of Anthony Burgess's *Napoleon Symphony* (1974) is an allusion to the basic pattern of Beethoven's Eroica, which is intended to render the novel independent of any causal or chronological sequence.

Structural patterns taken from the natural sciences seem to lend themselves particularly well to the structuring of longer works. Lawrence Durrell, by calling his *Alexandria Quartet* a four-story novel, which has three levels of space and one of time, refers to Einstein's relativity theory. For his final five-volume novel sequence, *The Avignon Quintet* (1975-85), he chose the geometrical figure of a quincunx, which can be seen as a two- or three-dimensional figure: "A quincunx forms an X, the unknown quantity, but raise its central point to a higher plane and it becomes a pyramid."[7]

In Nicholas Mosley's *Impossible Object* (1968), a figure that can be constructed on a two-dimensional plane but not on a three-dimensional one becomes the metaphor for a novel that represents the refutation of conventional patterns of narration. As the verbal description of geometric structures often overstrains the reader's imagination, Mosley offers on the title page a sketch of an "impossible" object such as those developed by Penrose and Escher. Insights from the aesthetics of perception are being increasingly used in the analysis of experimental literature.[8]

The analogy to a mathematical invention, the Möbius strip,[9] is the basis of "Möbius the Stripper" (1974), a short story by Gabriel Josipovici. The text consists of two narrative sequences, circularly arranged and divided by a line. Verbally conveyed images or complete sketches of the structure of the novel replace the successive form of representation by a simultaneous one.

The refutation of the causally constructed plot leads to the sacrifice of traditional chronology. The narrator of John Berger's *G.* (1972), who claims: "I write in the spirit of a geometrician," is looking for a method to convey events in "space, rather than consequentially in time."[10] The absence of a linear plot development allows the circular structure to become the basic pattern of a number of novels, the "Chinese boxes of fiction-within-fiction."[11] The relationship between structure and the presentation of time is particularly clear in these novels. Rotation around itself and reference back to the beginning suspend the teleological course of time and create an impression of stagnation.

The step-by-step character of the plot of a novel is broken up into texts that, apart from the traditional direction of reading from left to right, and from top to bottom, allow for other meaningful combinations through the typographic design. Alan Burns's *Dreamerika!* (1972), B. S. Johnson's *See the Old Lady Decently* (1975), Brigid Brophy's *In Transit*, Brooke-Rose's *Thru*, and Tom Phillips's *A Humument* (1980) constitute such texts, which may be counted as "visual literature" because here, pictures are not illustrations; instead, the text itself becomes the meaningful picture. In *A Humument*, theories of structuralism form the basis for the manifold possibilities of combinations within the text, whereas *Thru* is based on the theory and practice of generative grammar.

The novels Brooke-Rose has written since 1964 constitute a consistent refutation of the conventions of the traditional novel. They are examples of the author's extreme love of experimentation. In the following, the structure, linking strategies, narrative perspective, and the use of narrative tense will be illustrated in two of her novels, *Thru* and *Amalgamemnon*.

Brooke-Rose began her career as a writer of basically traditional novels, which she nowadays disclaims, although her first novel, *The Languages of Love* (1957), already carries in its title her central theme, namely language. The second phase of her work, which began with *Out* in 1964, was formed by her scholarly work on Ezra Pound, her critical concern with the French *nouveau roman,* and by the influence of Beckett, whom she admires for "this saving grace of humor and of course the flowing syntax . . . this kind of covering of the universe with a layer of language."[12] Her critical analyses of literature gave her insights into the principles and techniques that characterize her later novels. Like the *nouveaux romanciers*, she regards it as a central task of the modern novel to develop a language appropriate for our times, to allow reality and literary representation to approach each other more closely: experimental writing "is an attempt to evolve a language that corresponds structurally to what we know of empirical reality today. Not yesterday. Not tomorrow."[13] In her opinion experimental fiction contributes to the bridging of the gap between science and art because it leads us to reconsider the validity of the signs and signifying systems we use to express our views of reality. Thus, she compares the procedure of the scientist with that of the experimental writer: "he is not out to prove or to predict. But in his own way he also tests and tests his hunches about the reality behind the appearances, and he tests them in the matter which is language, the signs through which we express our observation of phenomena."[14]

The testing material she works with is language: "Language is my material, just as color is the artist's material."[15] Consequently linguistics, with its subdisciplines semantics and semiotics, is the science whose language and theories have preoccupied her in her later novels. In *Out* and *Such* she had already used the scientific languages of biochemistry and astrophysics respectively. In *Between* she raises the problems of communication via language as a central theme by making a translator her protagonist. About a dozen languages are mixed here, including those of the sign languages of international airports, hotels, and congresses. Brooke-Rose regards *Thru* as a successor to the linguistic experiments of *Out*, *Such*, and *Between*. All the titles of her novels are to be understood metaphorically, that is, the text illustrates the title on several levels of meaning, the grammatical, the semantic, and the level of narrative technique. As in *Out* and *Such*, the language used in *Thru* is the language of academic branches of learning, of linguistics and literary studies, which are also central themes. The novel can be understood as a "linguistic artefact"[16] that no longer represents reality but centers on theories of narration and linguistics. Brooke-Rose describes the relationship between text and reality in the following way: "the referential function is really reduced to zero."[17] When one character, adapting Gertrude Stein's famous line, formulates: "A text is a text is a text" (57), then the work of fiction refers to nothing other than itself. Many pages of *Thru* can be read as concrete poems. Words and letters are arranged in such a way that the polyfunctional aspect of the semantic units can only be determined by the reader.

Thru consists of an arrangement of nonfictional text forms, such as diagrams and tables, timetables, curricula vitae and students' essays—including handwritten corrections—notes on discussions in the lecture halls about narrative theory and linguistics, language material arranged in the form of baroque emblem poems, and texts in various languages. All of these call into question the "age-old narrative matrix" (17). Typography, mirror writing, letters from different languages, musical notation, mathematical formulas, the sign language of traffic signs, and the horizontal, vertical, diagonal, or circular arrangement of the letters all draw the reader's attention to the spatial aspect of the text. The texts, which can often be read as acrostics, telestics, or as palindromes, stand in the tradition of baroque emblem poems, of Apollinaire's calligrammes, or of the Dadaists' "poèmes simultanés." *Thru* is very demanding of its reader because of its partly intentionally distorted quotations.

The text opens with the description of the image in a rearview mirror by an unidentified speaker: "Through the driving-mirror four eyes stare back" (1). The paradox here consists of a look directed forwards but that perceives what is behind. This situation, the look into the "retrovizor," "the bluish rectangle that reflects the rear before you" (64, 44, 77; cf. 20, 137, 151), recurs again and again and is continually varied. It becomes the metaphor for the creation of a new text out of old ones, elucidates the reference back to literary quotations, and explains the relation of this text to earlier ones: "generating a text which in effect is a dialogue with all preceding texts" (43), "the text within the text which generates another text" (53; cf. 121). Some of the oft-quoted texts are Diderot's *Jacques le fataliste*, for example in "Portrait of the portrait by Jacques le Fataliste" (13), as well as the English eighteenth-century novelists who are discussed by the students. In the novel, a half-page "Bibliography" (45) lists the names of authors from William Shakespeare and Roland Barthes to fictional characters such as Tristram Shandy as "originators." Intertextuality, that is, the inclusion of quotations and allusions, is not simple a repetition of the old and well-known, but effects the creation of a new text instead. The book is "Language made out of language" and "Language . . . about language,"[18] for instance when the class "Transformational Grammar" discusses the theories of structural and generative linguistics (Jakobson, Greimas, Kristeva).

The spatial arrangements of the text may appear to be chaotic, but nevertheless the novel is based on the attempt to find an order derived from structuralism and generative grammar. The text is often arranged in binary oppositions, columns, or figures that resemble linguistic trees. The effort made to establish a structural principle is expressed in the figures built with words, which are similar to baroque poems and which lead to the word *order* (37, 150). At the same time there is a play on the double meaning of the word *generation*—both creation and era:

```
          within a text   passed on   from   generation   to
     g  e  n  e  r  a  t  i  o  N      Of an Increasing vasTness fULl Of what neVER
              the mOre the less
                  dwIndles
                     To a
                  structUred
                     eLite        M     O     re or less
     texti  V     O     R     E
            E     V     E     R
            R     E     A     D
       to   O     R     D     E     R     else the show within the
                           ƎHT ƎMOƆ ⅃⅃IT WOHƧ
```

(21)

This is not the only instance that relates the term *generation* to *revolution*: the new form of the constitution of the text can be regarded as revolutionary with regard to convention. Yet it can be seen as appropriate to our times: "Rules are made to be broken in an age that is earthquaking from evolving permanence to permanent revolution" (148; cf. 57). Brooke-Rose's statement about Beckett, that his attempt to break form results from a deep interest in form, also applies to her.

An example of intertextual reference to one specific text and of text generation in *Thru* is the line: "my love is like a white white rabbit" (3, 119), in which Burns's romantic comparison of the lover to a red rose is replaced by the white rabbit from Lewis Carroll's *Alice in Wonderland*. Brooke-Rose thus hints at a further artificial mirror-world, in which order is sought for in a universe of semantic nonsense.

The complete text of *Thru* as "thematic generation"[19] can be deduced from the opening sentence: "Through the driving-mirror four eyes stare back." The application of the rule "The structure is generated by recursivity rules" (99) can be exemplified by the numerous repetitions in which the book refers with slight variations to itself. Such references back are often structured as an endless *regressus ad infinitum*, as text within the text, as portrait within the portrait, as doors opening on other doors. The *mise en abîme* of the "books and looks within books" is summarized in the pseudo-rule: "f(bo (lo (bo (lo (books) oks) oks) oks) oks)^n" (106). By means of varying repetitions, *Thru* creates connections between textual passages, which in the conventional novel are joined by "chance."[20] They create the coherence of the text.

The paradox of the view in the rear mirror also symbolizes the process of literary creation. The result is a virtual image of reality: "For mimesis inevitably produces a double of the thing, the double being nothing a non-being which nevertheless is added to the thing" (106; 143).

The "thematic generation," in which the semantic meaning of a word, a sentence, or an image is constructed, has a parallel in the "verbal generation," which is often presented with the help of word-material ordered in lists, or in the interplay of homonyms or anagrams. The generation of words both points to the fact that the relation between signifier and signified is questionable and is simultaneously a sign of verbal creativity. Some examples:

camouflage/camouflashback (42)

discourse/disc-hoarse (101)

pathetic fallacy/bathetic fallacy/Parent Sinthetic Phallusy, bathetic phallusy (17, 48, 54, 75)

the scar/the scare
the scream/the scram (36)

arbitrary?/obituary?
a bit awry?/a bit aware? (54)

Thru shows that Brooke-Rose has applied the theory of the French *nouveaux romanciers*. Her text is an illustration of theoretical positions of the Tel Quel Group: "La 'réalité' n'est plus, ainsi, l'éternel morceau préexistant à découper dans tel ou tel sens, mais LE PROCES DE GENERATION QUI TRANSFORME."[21] In *Thru* language becomes the subject which is related to previous literary use of language and which mirrors itself. The text refers to itself; thus at the end there is the repetition of the opening situation, the view in the rear mirror:

his f o u r $\bigtriangledown_s$ l o d g e d in

the retro   v   izor never

to sally fort-da and reflecting nothing but

T
E
X
(I)
U Я H T H R U

A renunciation of a consciousness through which the varying texts are filtered seems to be one of the radical changes in relation to the conventions of the novel. In *Between* the reader could enter the stream of consciousness of a protagonist; the shift from one language to another and from conference to conference was made plausible by the job of the translator. In *Thru* both a central consciousness and a narrator are missing.[22] On the first page the existence of a narrator is questioned; this is varied throughout the text— "Who speaks?," "Qui parle?," "Chi parla?"—but is answered variously: a disembodied voice, a dramatic narrator, the master from Diderot's *Jacques la fataliste*; in some passages one can detect a first-person narrator, although it is a "floating I." *Thru* can be seen as an extreme example of the unreliability of the narrator, for it is rarely possible to make out who speaks in the first-person singular. The relation between two of the characters, Armel Santores and Larissa Toren, who function as narrators and who obviously have a love relationship, is—according to the opening situation of the text— constructed as a mirror-image, and their names are near-anagrams. The reflexive relation of the narrators to each other becomes an endless and un- solvable *mise en abîme*: "if Larissa invents Armel inventing Larissa, Armel also invents Larissa inventing Armel" (108). The paradox that the characters invent each other is not resolved. Since it is no longer possible to identify the narrator, the reader loses her bearings. The treatment of perspective can be seen as a prime example of how the rules of conventional narrative gram- mar may be changed. With *Thru*, Brooke-Rose goes one step farther than the "novels about writing a novel" by thematizing the principle of the "fictionality of fiction." She shares this approach with such British writers as Alan Burns, Ann Quinn, Stefan Themerson, and Tom Phillips, who use language like "concrete poets." *Thru* is concrete poetry in the sense of S. J. Schmidt's description: it is "not a mimetic-representative, but constitutive- presentative form of poetry, which replaces pragmatic communication's recurring dimensions of meaning by concentrating on the thematization of its own strategies and elements (linguistic language-entities, structures of textualization and presentation)."[23]

In *Amalgamemnon*, Brooke-Rose retains the theme of how reality can be put into language: however, the consciousness of a protagonist becomes the center of orientation for the reader. The text is made up of thoughts, reminiscences, and fantasies of a woman who, because of political, economic, and technical developments, has lost her job as a teacher of classical languages to the computer. Her anxiety about her own future and her lover, her fantastic visions for her future life become a preoccupation with "the future of the world." In her flow of thoughts, reminiscences or plans for her private life mix without transition with her reading of Herodotus and information drawn from political newscasts and shallow TV entertainment. One might suspect that, against the background of Jakobson's model of the process of formulation, Brooke-Rose had chosen different principles of ordering and structuring for her novels. While in *Thru* the principle of contiguity predominates and orders the combination of letters, words, and sentences, the selection of narrative passages in *Amalgamemnon* is defined predominately by the principle of equivalence.[24] Oracles and narratives of mythical figures which have been changed into signs of the zodiac, are related by the motifs of looking into the future and of augury; passages about Persian kings and the decline of their realms turn into "tales of the rise and fall of all empires from the Assyrian to the American Russian Chinese" (139). The past and the future become one when the narrator constructs "old myths under new names" (135) and creates varying identities for herself, talking as a modern scholar or as the prophet Cassandra, who describes her own role in metaphorical language: "But my words will carve through dungeon walls and I shall crawl priestlike through the hole into a neighbouring cell, carrying a secret about buried treasure, then montecristoid plummet as a faked corpse into the black sea of oblivion and swim ashore. At dawn I'll wake exhausted and write my cybernetic story of dissidence on the sand" (20; cf. 82, 142).

Brooke-Rose sees the equivalence of situations—"the future become past and the past present," "What will the future be but a past," "the future will explode into the present" (27, 119, 16)—not as a uniform repetition, as a circle, but rather the series of events are understood as "a constantly widening spiral of repression—terrorism—repression—terrorism" (41).[25]

The amalgamation, the connection of past and future promised by the title, is not only constructed by the recourse to Greek myths, Herodotus' histories, or Shakespeare's *Hamlet*, or by variations of literary genres, such as the fairy tale or the thriller. To the genealogy of events (41) are added fictional genealogies of the figures that create connections by means of fantastic family trees and lead back to an origin ("link[ing] everyone" [108]). They provide "stepping-stones into the dark" (15, 20). That this text is "Literature made out of literature," whose intertextuality can be confirmed by its self-reflexivity, by the repetition of only slightly varied textual passages, can be shown with the help of a literary allusion, this time to Marianne Moore's poem about "Imaginary gardens with real toads in them" (177). Like the American poet, Brooke-Rose does not see her work as a copy of reality, but as an imaginary construct. Here, too, Brooke-Rose plays with the line and varies it: Painted flowers attract real bees; the situation opens up the question, "Do you suppose they make painted honey?" (115; cf. 50).

Brooke-Rose also practices the principle of amalgamation on the lexical level by creating new words by compounding. The result are *blends*, that is, lexemes that are created from two or more words (i.e., "mimagreement," "mimage," "fibstory"). The "rhetoric of repetition" (17) determines the text; similar words or strings of words are changed into paronomasias:

may the beast man wane (30)

may the boast man whine (52)

let the beast man wane (57)

let the boss man whine (57)

Strings of words are compounded by alliterations:

brawny, balding bastion-bellied, bankrupt little business man (124)

tales tatooed with tangy tangible tenderness (47)

myth and memory and multitudes (22)

Sometimes there are cascades of words: "What . . . revolutions revelations revaluations revolitions revillusions redundancies could be provoked evoked revoked" (40), or: "our correspondent in Berlin Buenos Aires Beirut Bonn Brussels Budapest Bucharest Belgrade Baghdad Bogota will be in touch" (75, cf. 107, 139). Redundancy is a principle of the text that corresponds to the choice of the favored narrative tense, the future: Apart from designating something happening in the future or something intended, the future tense is also used to designate habitually recurring actions.

In *Out*, in which Brooke-Rose lets the events be registered by a reflector-figure as by a camera eye, she rejects the past tense, which traditionally denotes the posteriority of the narration in relation to the narrated events. Instead, she uses the present tense in order to give the impression of objective representation. Other tenses occur only in indirect speech, or in the outline of imagined dialogues. It is impossible to establish a chronology and thus an order of the slightly varied scenes. The result is the impression of simultaneity, timelessness, and stasis. If alternative versions of a scene are rendered in the present, they exclude each other; according to the rules of logic they can neither have happened simultaneously nor successively. In this way, instead of stories free of contradictions, passible stories are constructed.

By choosing the future tense in *Amalgamemnon*, Brooke-Rose takes up her deliberations concerning narrative tense that she formulated in her discussion of Robbe-Grillet (RU 330). She argues the future as a narrative tense adds to the authority of the narrator but simultaneously neutralizes it, so that the narrative gives the impression of a computer forecast. Thus, she adds the text to those in which the future is the grammatically correct tense, because the statement about an event precedes the event; this is the case of prophecy, the oracle,[26] or the simple weather forecast. Brooke-Rose is also aware of the fact that Aristotle lists the future tense as a characteristic of political speech (RU 14), and she uses this function of the tense.

Brooke-Rose's novels presuppose an active reader with a wide knowledge of literary conventions, literary history, and literary theory, which is needed to make an understanding of the text possible. The author quotes Pound's wish for an active and patient reader, someone with whom she can identify: "I should like to invent some kind of typographical dodge which would force every reader to stop and reflect for five minutes (or five hours) to go back to the facts mentioned and think over their significance for himself."[27]

In *Thru* and *Amalgamemnon*, Brooke-Rose writes the "texte scriptible" ("writerly text"), which is only realized by the reader, in contrast to the "texte lisible" ("readerly text"), which can be consumed by the reader.[28] Yet her books do not contain the ideal text, which, according to Barthes, makes possible an endless number of meanings, but about which one can no longer make any statements. She approaches this ideal when her texts offer a limited plurality of meanings. A knowledge of literary traditions and the existence of narratives that are still written according to the conventional rules are, however, prerequisites for a reading of her books, for as David Lodge points out, "unless people are still trying to keep the rules there is no point in breaking them and no interest in seeing them broken."[29]

Translated by Margarete Keulen and Hanjo Berressem

Postscript

Since 1988, when this essay was first published, Brooke-Rose has completed her "computer quartet," a novel sequence she began with *Amalgamemnon*. In *Xorandor* (1986) the narrators are the fourteen-year-old twins Jip and Zab, who dictate their memories of what happened two years earlier into their computer. At that time on a nuclear waste dump they discovered a strange stone that turned out to be a supercomputer that allegedly came from Mars. They give it the name Xorandor (X OR /And OR) to characterize the logic of its thinking. *Xorandor* contains computer printouts, tape transcriptions, children's slang, the jargon of programming and of technology. Despite this unusual textual surface, *Xorandor* has a plot that uses stereotypes of science fiction: Xorandor is able to prevent the self-destruction of mankind by nuclear "weapons and waste." By casting Xorandor in the role of the savior, Brooke-Rose rewrites biblical myth. Xorandor itself narrates the story of its origin on Mars as a "myth of origin. . . . And a myth of fall" (186). In the dialogues between the twins, fictionalizing and the question of how fiction and reality relate is foregrounded as a subject, while the language games they engage in develop into stories.

In *Verbivore* (1990), twenty-three years further into the future, science and "hitech" have superseded the liberal arts, and books are abolished. The catastrophe that now threatens the world is "continuous loss of information": the supercomputer's "offspring," smaller replicas of Xorandor, neutralize electromagnetic waves, which leads to a breakdown of all communication systems. This breakdown, called "Verbivore," produces an international economic crisis and prevents the necessary communication of scientists and politicians.

Jip, now a physicist at NASA, and Zab, who teaches "communications," learn that the computers that store all information are threatened by "wave-pollution, by words" (140, 151). The processes of transmitting information on all possible channels did not result in a higher level of information (more knowledge) but in "99.999% redundancy" (78), which overloads the computer's memory.

The novel ends with a complete breakdown of all communication systems. The end of the world is the end of the world news, the breaking off of communication. Thus it becomes impossible to answer the question of who is the narrator of this novel, which is composed of story elements in the first-person singular, of dialogues, letters, reports, diary entries, all interlocked like "Chinese boxes." Brooke-Rose plays with the transgression of narrative levels. Characters from earlier novels reappear, not only the twins from *Xorandor*, but also Mira Enketei from *Amalgamemnon*. Decibel, a fictional character in a radio play by Perry Hupsos, who is invented by Enketei, who is herself one of the main narrative voices in *Verbivore*, even reappears as chief narrator in the next to last chapter. Each of the characters wants to write about the phenomenon of "Verbivore": Perry Hupsos, in his radio play entitled *A Round of Silence*, anticipates the loss of information, so that the borderlines blur between the secondary-level fiction and the primary-level. Is *Verbivore* then the invention of Perry or the dream of Mira Enketei, who now is a drama producer and who asserts her existence by telling stories?

Textermination (1991) is a fantasy: here fictional characters from various literatures and epochs gather at the San Francisco Hilton for the annual convention of "Prayer for Being": Austen's Emma Woodhouse and Flaubert's Emma Bovary, Thomas Mann's Lotte and Melville's Ahab, Homer's Odysseus and Salman Rushdie's Gibreel Farishta, and even Brooke-Rose's Mira Enketei turn up. The characters who want to survive never existed in "reality," but only in the imagination of their readers: they are literary characters; their existence is only secured by the act of reading. That is why the "God" to whom the characters address their prayers is the reader. He is the "Creator" without whom they are dead.

The novel is an allegory of the process of reading, during which fictional characters become alive in the reader's imagination. In forgotten books, however, they die, but they can be revived by "rescue teams," that is, readers. By borrowing from the stereotypes of disaster stories, Brooke-Rose ends her novel with an account of a near apocalypse and of a rescue. Not all the literary characters die in the inferno at the Hilton Hotel and the earthquake that destroys the city. Rescue teams find a number of survivors of a little island situated off the mainland.

The novels of this "Intercom Quartet" experiment with narrative voice: *Amalgamemnon* is filtered through the consciousness of one narrator, *Xorandor* is "narrated" in the twin's dialogue, *Verbivore* is an intricate tangle of different voices and fictional levels. In *Textermination* the reader is conceived as "creator" of the fictional world. Consequently, the book reads as if it were composed by the reader's authorial consciousness. By ironically asserting the reader as creator, the "East" in Jakobson's diagram (see STT 10), Brooke Rose also reasserts the corresponding "West" side of the diagram, that is, the authority of the true originator.

NOTES

[1]Ian Watt, *The Rise of the Novel* (1957; Harmondsworth: Penguin, 1976), 37; cf. Erwin Wolff, *Der englische Roman im 18. Jahrhundert* (Göttingen, 1964), 3. For the following cf. my *Der experimentelle englische Roman der Gegenwart* (Darmstadt, 1984), 30 ff. and 174 ff.

[2]Robert Martin Adams, *Afterjoyce: Studies in Fiction after "Ulysses"* (New York, 1977), 198.

[3]Cf. F. R. Leavis, *The Great Tradition* (London, 1950); David Lodge, *The Novelist at the Crossroads* (London, 1971).

[4]Cf. Thomas Hinde. "The Novelist as Victim," in Vincent Cronin, ed., *Innovation in Contemporary Literature: Essays by Divers Hands: Being Transactions of the Royal Society of Literature*, (London, 1979), 116, 103.

[5]Malcolm Bradbury. "Putting in the Person," in Bradbury and David Palmer, eds., *The Contemporary English Novel* (London, 1979), 183; Virginia Woolf, "The Art of Fiction," in *Collected Essays*, vol. 2 (London, 1966), 55. Brooke-Rose deals with deviations from narrative conventions as "transgressions" in RU 311 ff.

[6]For the term, see Ulrich Broich and Manfred Pfister, eds., *Intertextualität* (Tübingen, 1985), especially 6 ff. and 48 ff.

[7]Keith Brown, "Xen Provence," *Times Literary Supplement*, 13 October 1978, 1140. For the use of the form of the quincunx by Beckett, see Monika Bönisch, *Archaische Formen in Samuel Becketts Romanen* (Frankfurt, 1984).

[8]See L. S. and R. Penrose. " 'Impossible Objects': A Special Type of Visual Illusion," *British Journal of Psychology* 49.1 (Feb. 1958): 31-33; Ernst H. Gombrich, Julian Hochberg, and Max Black, *Kunst, Wahrnehmung, Wirklichkeit* (Frankfurt,

1977). See the sketch by Saul Steinberg of two hands drawing each other in H. Engelhardt and D. Mettler, eds., *Materialien zu Samuel Becketts Romanen* (Frankfurt, 1976), 5; for this sketch in Escher and Brooke-Rose's *Thru*, see Shlommith Rimmon-Kenan, "Ambiguity and Narrative Levels," *Poetics Today* 3 (1982): 21 ff.

[9]Reproduced in M. C. Escher, *Graphik und Zeichnungen* (München, 1972); cf. also John Barth, "Frame-Tale," in his *Lost in the Funhouse* (New York: Doubleday, 1969).

[10]John Berger. *G.* (London, 1972), 137.

[11]A. S. Byatt, "People in Paper Houses," in Bradbury and Palmer, *The Contemporary English Novel*, 40.

[12]David Hayman and Keith Cohen, "Interview with Christine Brooke-Rose," *Contemporary Literature* 17.1 (Winter 1976): 14.

[13]Christine Brooke-Rose, "Dynamic Gradients," *London Magazine* 12 (March 1965): 92.

[14]Ibid., 96.

[15]Hayman and Cohen, "Interview," 10.

[16]Roger Fowler, *Linguistics and the Novel* (London, 1977), 67.

[17]Hayman and Cohen, "Interview," 4.

[18]Fowler, 69.

[19]Emma Kafalenos, "Textasy: Christine Brooke-Rose's *Thru*," *International Fiction Review* 7 (1980): 44.

[20]See Vicki Mistacco, "The Theory and Practice of Reading Nouveaux Romans . . .", in Susan R. Suleiman and Inge Crosman, eds., *The Reader in the Text* (Princeton: Princeton Univ. Press, 1980), 388 ff.

[21]Sollers in *Tel Quel: Théorie d'ensemble* (Paris, 1968), 393; cf. Roland Barthes, *Essais Critiques* (Paris, 1964), 164. One can draw parallels to the theory as well as practice of Jean Ricardou, especially to *La Prise de Constantinople* (1965). R. Waring has pointed towards the anticipation of the Tel Quel program in Beckett's novels; see *Zeitschrift für französische Sprache und Literatur* 85.3 (1975): 262.

[22]Cf. Rimmon-Kenan, 23 ff.

[23]S.J. Schmidt, "Negation und Konstitution in konkreter Dichtung," in Harald Weinrich, ed., *Positionen der Negativität* (Munich, 1970), 400.

[24]See Roland Posner, "Strukturalismus in der Gedichtinterpretation," in Jens Ihwe, ed., *Literaturwissenschaft und Linguistik*, vol. II/1 (Frankfurt, 1971), 236 ff., and Roman Jakobson, "Linguistik and Poetik," ibid., 142 ff.

[25]Brooke-Rose compares repetitions in Pound's *Cantos* with "different level[s] in a spiral" in "Dynamic Gradients," 91.

[26]Cf. Gérard Genette, *Figures III* (Paris, 1972), 229: "Narration antérieur." Cf. also Tzvétan Todorov, *Poetik der Prosa* (Frankfurt, 1972), 75; Fredric Jameson, *The Prison-House of Language* (Princeton: Princeton University Press, 1972), 199.

[27]Brooke-Rose, "Dynamic Gradients," 95.

[28]Roland Barthes, *S/Z* (Paris, 1970), 10.

[29]David Lodge, *The Modes of Modern Writing* (London, 1977), 245.

"Stepping-Stones into the Dark": Redundancy and Generation in Amalgamemnon

Richard Martin

EARLY IN THE 1970s, Joanna Russ suggested that for the woman author who decided to eschew the established male conventions of the novel, two options remained: lyricism and life. She defined the lyric mode as "the organization of discrete elements . . . around an unspoken thematic or emotional center . . .; its principle of connection is associative" ("What Can a Heroine Do?" 12). Russ realized that such writing was destined to meet with denigration in terms such as "these novels lack important events; they are hermetically sealed" (13). In one sense, Christine Brooke-Rose goes a stage further when in "Illiterations" she combines the notion of the isolation of any experimental writer and the misunderstanding awaiting the woman writer: "it seems to me that the combination of woman + artist + experimental means so much hard work and heartbreak and isolation that there must be little time or energy for crying out loud." Furthermore, her own position as a writer who has found widespread acceptance neither from conventional male reviewers nor from feminist critics, exacerbates the isolation: "she is in the sea between two continents" (*Breaking the Sequence*, 65-66, 67).

Joanna Russ saw the lyric structure as able to deal with the unspeakable, that which has been set apart, which is "unlabeled, disallowed, disavowed" (16). That there is an unspeakable to be transformed into discourse is the result of a deliberate move, which is both a social and an aesthetic strategy: it implies the woman writer's need to find that mode of expression that, by being divergent, will both emphasize and validate the otherness of women artists. In the case of Brooke-Rose, the experimentation supersedes an immediate concern with feminism while not in any way canceling it from her awareness; she is, in the first instance, an experimental writer and secondly, a woman experimental writer and as such, she is concerned with "the fusion of different discourses" (Hayman and Cohen 3).

Nevertheless, such arbitrary classification of an author is insidious; the experimenter and the woman cannot be so neatly disjoined. In what follows I shall continually be presupposing Christine Brooke-Rose the experimentalist and (perhaps) less insistently inferring her persona as a woman—it would be more sensible, maybe, simply to take her on her own terms as someone who eschews labels and thus pays the price of, as she herself points out, belonging nowhere. Consideration of her as an experimenter implies the acceptance of the opinion that such a view includes the dilemma of recognizing that experimentalism "is at once a stepping stone to something else and is gratuitous" (Poggioli 135). It is, in fact, the "something else" beyond the stepping stones that I hope to be able to clarify. For any investigation of the nature of Brooke-Rose's experimentation will inevitably reveal her particular contribution to feminist literary discourse.

Christine Brooke-Rose's 1984 novel *Amalgamemnon* is "a polygonal story" (102), essentially many-angled, a story illuminated from many different directions, many stories brought together within a multisided frame of polynarration. There are contemporary narratives of, for example, a university teacher of the humanities made redundant by the proliferation of technology, of fleeting surface relationships with would-be "helpful" men of conventional ideas and prejudices, a venture into pig farming, dialogues with students and friends, an encounter with a band of terrorists. Then again, each individual narrative gives birth to further narratives, which in turn intermingle with classical myths, legends, history, and fairy tale in a maze of paratactical juxtapositioning in which each segment of fragmented narrative is as important as the next. The novel is held together by a pattern of structural repetitions and planned echoes: "the rhetoric of repetition will protect me" (17). Moreover, this strategy of recurrence is essential to the concept of redundancy in my title. Not only does the reception of structures, and thus of information, make for clearer reception (RU 44), but words by engendering further discourses (Miller passim) themselves become redundant, in both a social and a narrative sense, having served their purpose.

Nearly all the underlying compositional structures of *Amalgamemnon* are established within the limits of the first page of the book. For this reason I shall use a close examination of that page as a point of departure into the novel. The opening situation is also the constant background element: a woman exploiting her insomnia by reading and listening to the all-night radio program.

I shall soon be quite redundant at last despite of all, as redundant as you after queue and as totally predictable, information-content zero.

The programme-cuts will one by one proceed apace, which will entail laying off paying off with luck all the teachers of dead languages like literature philosophy history, for who will want to know about ancient passions divine royal middleclass or working in words and phrases and structures that will continue to spark out inside the techne that will soon be silenced by the high technology? Who will still want to read at night some utterly other discourse that will shimmer out of a minicircus of light upon a page of say Agamemnon returning to his murderous wife the glory-gobbler with his new slave Cassandra princess of fallen Troy who will exclaim alas, o earth, Apollo apocalyptic and so forth, or else Herodotus, the Phoenicians kidnapping Io and the Greeks plagiarizing the king of Tyre's daughter Europe, but then, shall we ever make Europe? Sport. Rugger. The Cardiff team will leave this afternoon for Montpellier where they will play Béziers in the first round of the European championship, listen to their captain, Joe Tenterten: we're gonna win.

I could anticipate and queue before the National Education Computer for a different teaching job, reprogramming myself like a floppy disk, or at the Labour Exchange for a different job altogether, recycling myself like a plastic bottle, and either way I'd be a worker in a queue of millions with skills too obsolete for the lean fitness of the enterprise. (5-6)

In this passage, paradigmatic for the novel as a whole, the narrating voice moves from a subjective situation (the redundancy of a teacher of the humanities, lines 1-5) to the discourse generated both by that thought and by texts drawn from the cradle of literary learning, the classics (lines 6-12), to the overhead words of the radio (lines 13-15) and so back to further reflections on the subjective dilemma (lines 16-20). The insistent use of future and conditional tenses in the opening passage is one of the most obtrusive linguistic features of *Amalgamemnon*; together with the subjunctive and imperative, they are the only verb forms employed throughout the text and thus, in their expression of unrealized moods, look forward to events but preclude their realization. Everything is talked about but nothing *can* happen; actions, persons, even ideas, belong to the realm of the possible but indeterminate. Quite apart from the overall structural pattern, the passage, again characteristic of the whole, is replete with clues and signals concerning its own significance and its mode of composition.

Regardless of the intrusive and obvious subject matter, the text swings between the poles of redundancy and generation.

The opening sentence (deliberately echoing Beckett's "I shall soon be quite dead at last in spite of all" in *Malone Dies*) commences with an "I" that can equally well apply both to the text and to the narrator, both are faced with the fact of their own uselessness; to what, then, does "despite of all" refer? For the text, this can suggest that in spite of all efforts, both on the part of the reader and the author, the text will become redundant once read, or even once it has been written. The narrator is threatened by the possibility that the very process of narration bears within itself the seeds of its own redundancy, and thus the narrator is fated to outlive her usefulness. These implication are then amplified by the sort of telling pun that Brooke-Rose uses to perfection: "as redundant as you [*u*] after queue [*q*] and as totally predictable." In what sense is *u* after *q* redundant? As a subservient phoneme and in its function as a bound morpheme, it has no independent existence; as *itself* it is virtually nonexistent. Further, the very fact of redundancy is predictable—an immutable law as in the *qu* combination; no sooner has a text begun, has a narrator taken up the narration, an author begun to write and a reader to read, than they are all faced with the inevitable existential inutility. Redundancy is a predicate of textuality—of narrative—and, on another level, of existence.

It is, however, characteristic of Brooke-Rose's narrative that the potentially redundant text generates further discourse.

Within the limits of the opening passage of the novel, we can discern continual variations on the redundancy motif: "information-content zero," "programme-cuts," "dead languages," "princess of fallen Troy," "skills too obsolete." These variations on redundancy are matched by words and images that are part of the generation motif: "continue to spark," "shimmer out," "reprogramming," and "recycling." It is this awareness of redundancy and of the concept's capacity to give rise to variations of the motif of generation that grants the book its basic pattern. It would, however, be more accurate to suggest that it is not so much concepts, or ideas, that perform such functions as the words themselves. Discourse is binary in *Amalgamemnon*, it is both redundant and generative, everything proceeds from language.

The narrating "I" is threatened with redundancy, the loss of her job because she is a teacher of "dead languages like literature philosophy history." The redundant aspect of those disciplines lies in the fact that the past, represented in the humanities, is kept alive "in words and phrases and structures" though the future is seen as a time in which history (and by implication literature and philosophy) will have lost its significance. As Hans, one of the student terrorists, exclaims: "In the next civilization there won't be any history, let alone any philosophy of it. . . . Events will be our instant history, but history as events not history as discourse" (109). A few pages later the rhetorical question is asked, "what will prophecy be but instant history" (113). The concept of "instant history" contains the notion of history as ersatz, as a substitute, but for what?—presumably for the "real thing," for action, events, the concrete. Among the contrasts with which we are faced throughout the novel are language as opposed to events, art as opposed to technology—the concretized metaphor for the "real"—individual psyche as opposed to collectivized conformity, thought as opposed to jargon and cliché.

It is within such a context that the question is posed, "Who will still want to read." The particular image of reading that is presented in *Amalgamemnon* is that of the "utterly other discourse," which appears "out of a minicircus of light upon a page." Quite apart from the literal level of the page of the sleepless reader's book, which appears in the cone of light of the bedside reading lamp, there is the obvious reference to the microcosmic world of the book. Nor is this the stereotypical conception that it might have been; in its opposition to the "silencing force of high technology," art ("techne") possesses the ability to transcend the moment and within the limited physical space of the reader's immediate situation is able to generate new images of past worlds and existences. It is this that technology is forced to make redundant, and at the same time, it is this that endows the written word with generative properties to overcome redundancy, or at least to transform it.

In the opening pages of *Amalgamemnon*, the necessity to create opportunities for the reader to participate in the discourse results in many a statement with signalizing function; later Brooke-Rose elaborates complex images for the central concerns of the novel. In order to clarify the notion of the text's redundancy, triggering its own regeneration, the author has recourse to two reiterated images: toads and pigs at the narrator's pig farm. "My friend the toad" is presented as a creature with whom the narrating voice can experience a (fallacious) relationship: "one day I might crush him with the mower, then miss him dreadfully and feel a murderer for ever more" (51). At a later stage in the text, the narrating voice intrudes into the terrorist theme with: "Down at the crumbling farm, I shall be surprised to tread almost on the dead toad's baby son. . . . Forgive me little one I'll look out for you till you grow big and prehistoric like your father, but you look out too" (79). Amid reminders of redundancy ("crumbling farm," "dead toad") new life has been generated, which will inevitably proceed to maturity and further redundancy. Complementary to this, a fear is iterated that in any litter of pigs there will always be one who will fail to find nourishment. The narrator, dogged by the question, "will that little one survive," encourages the runt: "fight your way to the tits,way up that vast pink wall, see? There, don't let yourself be ousted by your brothers of milk and tummy" (73). At the same time, there is the realization that ultimately the pigs will "merely be ready for the butcher," an observation that is generalized to, "Let us recognize one another before annihilating each other" (74). The very establishment of the paradigm of redundancy-generation-redundancy does not invalidate the essential appeals inherent in a humanist-literary culture. Nor is redundancy to be taken as a negative concept (although the "misquotation" of Beckett in the opening sentence generates associations of death). Admittedly on one level—that of potential plot—Brooke-Rose does employ the word *redundancy* in its negative social sense, yet within the redundancy-generation paradigm, it must be understood in its linguistic function as essential to communication (Chomsky 166-70; Lyon 88). Furthermore, syntax, by way of repetition, deliberately creates the redundancy of linguistic items.

The main narrating voice offers a choice of source books for her reflective oppositions to the posed world of the technologically real: the *Agamemnon* of Aeschylus and the *Histories* of Herodotus. Although never used again in the novel, on the first page *Agamemnon* serves in a double function: it supplies us with the entry to the title of the novel and introduces a key figure, Cassandra, "who will exclaim alas, o earth, Apollo apocalyptic and so forth." Not only does this echo, even plagiarize, Cassandra's opening lines in Aeschylus's play ("O Apollo! oh, oh! . . . Oh, oh! O horror! O earth! O Apollo!"), but also it reminds us of the particular fate of the princess of Troy: that she was loved by Apollo, but since she resisted him, was punished by having her gift of prophecy rendered useless, causing her prophecies to go unbelieved; she thus becomes the redundant prophetess. Prophecy, moreover, is closely associated with storytelling in Brooke-

Rose's novel, and the narrating voice associates herself with Cassandra: "As if for instance I were someone else, Cassandra perhaps" (7) and becomes in her manifestation as the female companion of a stereotypical male (Willy or Wally), Sandra, a diminutive of the prophetess's name (15, 23, 45, 46, 136).

The significance of Cassandra in the novel lies in her redundancy, in her femininity, and in her devotion to the word. On a later page, after a passage in which a character refers to himself as a "graphomaniac," we read: "to be imprisoned for graffitism as poor Cassandra will be enslaved by all Amalgamemnons and die with them not out of love but of amalgamation to silence her for ever" (20). Cassandra is a metaphor for the twofold victim: the victim as woman, enslaved by male domination (Cassandra the slave booty of Agamemnon) and the victim as artist (Cassandra the redundant prophetess caught in her own discourse). Further, she becomes a means of decoding the figure, who is an extension of the enslaving king, extended by the coupling with "amalgam," a mixture of different elements depending for its stability on the quantity of mercury in the compound, and extended further by the connotations of "amalgamate," to merge into a single body, used both of people and of corporations. Amalgamemnon becomes, thus, the threatening overforce, the consumer and enslaver both of artist and of woman.

In a later reference, Cassandra is associated both with concealment and castration, with uncertainty and generation:

Never let anyone see you foresee them, keep quiet Cassandra, forecaster of your own pollux [Castor and Pollux], keep your castrations in perpetual cassation [Fr. quashing, setting aside] for nothing will ever be exactly as you shall one day see it in retrospect, otherwise you would grow big with expectation and sexplode, the expected generating the expectoration or vice versa perhaps. (30)

Apart from the characteristic wordplay, in itself generative, Cassandra is once again the epitome of redundancy, unable to utter prophecy, the author condemned to silence, the potential generator of generations, condemned to suppress her own fertility. It is not surprising that later in the book a male figure is warned to be less pessimistic in the words, "The role of Cassandra will hardly suit you" (77).

It is, however, Herodotus and not Aeschylus who provides the central literary-historical focus of the novel. The *Histories* are used as a device whereby the contrast between the classical past of literature, philosophy, and history is juxtaposed with the daily events of an imaginary present reality as propagated by the radio program, and with the typical incidents of late-twentieth-century civilization: diplomatic small talk, media culture, terrorism, and the daily round. Not only are references made to events in Herodotus, as here from the opening pages—the Phoenicians capturing Io, and the Greeks stealing away Europa, daughter of Agenor, king of Tyre—but at times quotations (though verbs are transposed into the future tense) appear from Aubrey de Selincourt's translation of the *Histories* as an almost ironic comment both on the degeneration of language and on the parochial localization of events in the modern world as compared with the universality of the ancients. For example, the rape of Europa, beloved of Zeus, becomes the first round of the European rugby football championship. There is also a plaintive echo of the cry "shall we ever make Europe," expressive of British nonrelations with the European Common Market and containing at the same time the colloquial punning use of the verb "make," thereby relating the phrase back to the original myth.

Amalgamemnon proceeds upon the principles already evidenced in the opening page: discourse announces its own redundancy even as it generates new discourse. In detail this involves the reproduction and multiplication of words and associations grouped around a number of fixed points; mythology, Herodotus, and astronomy provide some of these. In addition, the very mention of names implies people who in turn imply relationships, but the relations are expressed more in terms of generative grammar than in terms of human (or family) reproduction. Thus a set of names leads inevitably to the elaboration of a family tree ("I shall go in . . . and invent myself an alternative family" (37), which is more a set of related structures than a human hierarchy as in history or the conventional family-saga novel. In an extension of the generative principle, not only is this family tree later revised (100-101) but the narrator grafts herself onto it.

On the second page of the text the narrating voice gains a name and a visitor: the visitor is Ethel Thuban and the narrator has the surname Enketei. If the clues on the first page were comparatively obvious, now it becomes evident that a reader of a certain type is implied by the text, a reader with the willingness to search and with access to the means of verification. "Enketei" can be broken down to "in ceto" or "within the whale," a reference to the constellation Cetus, which contains the star Mira Ceti, the first recognized variable star. Given Brooke-Rose's methods of composition, one would expect Thuban to have similar associations; it was, in fact, in 3000 B.C. regarded as the polestar and is part of the constellation Draco (the dragon). In the case of Mira Ceti, or Mira Enketei, as she appears in the text, the addition of variability to her role as narrator is important. The unreliable narrator, the narrator who shifts position and whose "brilliance" is variable is a familiar figure. In the case of Ethel Thuban the procedure is more idiosyncratic; she features as a powerful foil to the narrator, a potential threat, and at a later stage plays the role of a dragon in a brilliantly conceived appropriation of the traditional fairy tale (86-93).

In the course of the narration, other constellations appear, notably Andromeda, Cassiopeia, Cepheus, Cygnus, and Orion. Although it is outside the scope of this article to follow the multiple significances of each, it is worth pointing out that Cepheus was Andromeda's father as Cassiopeia was her mother, and as king of the Ethiopians, he generates an African theme in the novel; Cygnus is used as a pun on "signus" ("sign") and thus is related to the language motif; finally, Orion, the hunter, is the victim of Artemis, the virgin huntress, his female counterpart. As Agamemnon and Cassandra represent the enslavement of the female by the male, so Artemis and Orion signify the threat to masculinity posed by the female. It thus becomes clear that the exploitation of myth and history is by no means haphazard, or simply a game, but a deliberate manipulation within the context of the woman/ artist theme of the novel. One may add to this the use made of Andromeda who appears in several guises in the novel: at first she is "Anne de Rommède," one of Mira Enketei's students with a penchant for politics, physics, and metaphysics, as well as interest in Greek philosophy. Other variations are "Anne de Rommeda" (suggesting a change of nationality), Anna Crusis (anacrusis: not a part of the metrical pattern), Anna Coluthon (anacoluthon: a shift in construction), and Anna Biosis (anabiosis: suspended animation). All variations suggest the outsider, in itself a metaphor for the artist and, in Brooke-Rose's terms, the experimental woman writer. Also worth remembering is that Andromeda offended the Nereids, the sea maidens, was punished by Poseidon, and rescued by Perseus—thus a woman with ambivalent relations toward both sexes, the double-voiced writer.

Similarly, if we again return to the opening of the novel, we are confronted by Io, beloved of Zeus and victim of Hera; Io finally wandered to Egypt where she was worshipped as the goddess Isis, "prototype of motherhood and of the faithful wife" (Shorter 133). Europa was also beloved of Zeus and, in fact, raped by him. Thus again these mythical figures reveal themselves as having significant contemporary connotations within the context of male-female attitudes and relations.

At this point it is necessary to return to the quotation contained in my title to suggest its relevance to a discussion of *Amalgamemnon*. The phrase first occurs in the context of another repetition that refers to the opening page of the novel: A "night of utterly other discourses that will crackle out of disturbances in the ionosphere into a minicircus of light upon a page of say Herodotus and generates endless stepping-stones into the dark . . ." (15). The contrast between the radio waves from the ionosphere and the microcosmic histories of Herodotus in itself generates the passage into the unknown. The narrating voice supplies all the necessary clues, which may be summarized as follows:

1. This text is comprised of variant discourses, and thus words, utterances, grammar, and syntax count.

2. The range of narration will be contained in the tension between the abstract and the peculiarly concrete, between the indefinite and definite, between space and confinement.

3. The text within the text serving as an anchor to microcosmic reality will be Herodotus—both father of history and father of lies ("Father of fibstory" [113]). The *Histories* epitomize both historiography and fiction,

both the discourses of the past and the deconstruction of the present.

4. The discourse of the text together with meta- and extratextual discourses generate further texts.

5. The text functions as a guideline, an Ariadne's thread, into the unknown; it generates not only nonknowledge but also knowledge, the puzzle and the solution.

6. The mode of composition parallels the opening sentence's insistence on redundancy; text will be created in order to be deconstructed and the deconstruction will be implicit in the creation.

After a brief and parenthetical repetition of the opening events of the *Histories*, referring to collective rape—the capture of Io and the Greeks' carrying off Medea, daughter of the king of Colchis—the narrative quoted earlier ("stepping-stones into the dark") continues: "creating in advance as yet another distance which I'll have carefully to deconstruct tomorrow by letting him abolish all those other discourses into an acceptance of his, although sooner or later the future will explode into the present despite the double standard at breaking points" (15-16). In this passage, "him" is ambiguous, referring ostensibly to Herodotus but actually to the narrator's current Amalgamemnon or dominant lover. Brooke-Rose invents the strategy whereby the discourses that matter will be granted gratuitous redundance in apparent recognition of male supremacy, which in its turn comes to be known as redundant. The future, that is, holds the promise of redundancy and generation or better, of deconstruction and regeneration, and that is the confidence toward which the novel is directed.

Within the context of *Amalgamemnon*, the dominant female strategy is contained in a set of puns culminating in the verb "to mimagree"—to mime agreement. Redundancy is both an accepted aspect of the text, implying generation, and of female-experienced reality, so that as the novel closes, it is possible to state: "The characters . . . will perhaps indulge in the secret vice of reading redundant textual sources of redundant psychic sources in redundant humanistic animals. . . . Secret cabinet sources will refuse to comment on these shadow-figures and I shall mimagree, how should I not?" (144). The statement puts the critic in his or her place. Having commented on the shadow-figures of Brooke-Rose's novel, one is all too aware of the redundancy of one's own remarks. Should one have refused to comment?

WORKS CITED

I would like to thank Christine Brooke-Rose for her generous and patient cooperation and to thank my colleagues Wolf-Dietrich Bald and Heike Schwarzbauer for their helpful suggestions.

Aeschylus. *The Oresteian Trilogy.* Trans. Philip Vellacott. Harmondsworth: Penguin, 1956.

Beckett, Samuel. *Malone Dies*. 1951. Harmondsworth: Penguin, 1968.

Brooke-Rose, Christine. "Illiterations." In *Breaking the Sequence: Women's Experimental Fiction*. Ed. Ellen G.Friedman and Miriam Fuchs. Princeton: Princeton Univ. Press, 1989. 55-71.

Chomsky, Noam. *Aspects of the Theory of Syntax*. Cambridge: MIT Press, 1965.

Hayman, David, and Keith Cohen. "An Interview with Christine Brooke-Rose." *Contemporary Literature* 17 (1976): 1-23.

Herodotus. *The Histories*. 1954. Trans. Aubrey de Selincourt. Rev. A. R. Burn. Harmondsworth: Penguin, 1984.

Lyons, John. *Introduction to Theoretical Linguistics*. Cambridge: Cambridge Univ. Press, 1968.

Miller, J. Hillis. *Fiction and Repetition*. Cambridge: Harvard Univ. Press, 1982.

Poggioli, Renato. *The Theory of the Avant-Garde*. Cambridge: Harvard Univ. Press, 1968.

Russ, Joanna. "What Can a Heroine Do? Or Why Women Can't Write." In *Images of Women in Fiction*. Ed. Susan K. Cornillon. Bowling Green: Bowling Green Univ. Press, 1972.

Shorter, Alan W. *The Egyptian Gods: A Handbook*. 1937. London: Routledge, 1981.

Reading Amalgamemnon

Jean-Jacques Lecercle

1. In Praise of de Selby

I HAVE RECENTLY become a disciple of the great Irish thinker de Selby. As a philosopher, he is superior to all his colleagues in two important respects: he doesn't exist, which means I won't have to waste my valuable time reading his complete works, and his ideas, which do exist, are interesting, although eccentric, because eccentric. As Lenin might have said, de Selby's theories are both true and all-powerful because they are bizarre.

Among other things, de Selby holds strong views about space and motion. Rejecting the stupidly empirical indications of experience, he boldly states that "a journey is an hallucination." Human experience is made up of a succession of static experiences, each infinitely brief, but such that between any two of these, there is always another, intermediate, experience. Consequently, de Selby deduces the impossibility of motion:

From this premise he discounts the reality or truth of any progression or serialism in life, denies that time can pass as such in the accepted sense and attributes to hallucinations the commonly experienced sensation of progression as, for instance, in journeying from one place to another or even "living." If one is resting at A, he explains, and desires to rest in a distant place B, one can only do so by resting for infinitely brief intervals in innumerable intermediate places. Thus there is no difference essentially between what happens when one is resting at A before the start of the "journey" and what happens when one is "en route," i.e., resting in one or other of the intermediate places. He treats of these "intermediate places" in a lengthy footnote. They are not, he warns us, to be taken as arbitrarily-determined points on the A-B axis so many inches or feet apart. They are rather to be regarded as points infinitely near each other yet sufficiently far apart to admit of the insertion between them of a series of other "inter-intermediate" places, between each of which must be imagined a chain of other resting-places—not, of course, strictly adjacent but arranged so as to admit of the application of this principle indefinitely. The illusion of progression he attributes to the inability of the human brain—"as at present developed"—to appreciate the reality of these separate "rests," preferring to group many millions of them together and calling the result motion, an entirely indefensible and impossible procedure since even two separate positions cannot obtain simultaneously of the same body. Thus motion is also an illusion. He mentions that almost any photograph is conclusive proof of his teachings.[1]

At this point in the text, a rather perfidious footnote states that de Selby conceived his idea while examining some old films that belonged to his nephew. He was struck by their static and repetitive aspect: "at that time," the note adds, he had failed "to grasp the principle of the cinematograph."

I like this. There is a strong element of the stay-at-home in me, and I do think that de Selby's conception of journeys and motion is the best. The ideal way to go from Bath to Folkestone is to do what he did—to purchase a number of postcards and look at them. Besides, such a conception belongs to a venerable tradition. His version of the impossibility of motion is obviously inherited from Zeno's paradox, and it rather suggests a topsy-turvy version of Bergson. According to Bergson, the trouble with commonsense ideas of time is that they project space onto time, and deal with time as with a form of space, in quantitative terms, whereas the actual human experience of duration can be described only in qualitative terms.[2] De Selby, on the other hand, projects time onto space, and turns space into a qualitative experience, which needs no quantifying, such as measuring the distance from A to B. If common sense according to Bergson understands time as a ghostly form of space (*"le temps est le fantôme de l'espace"*), for de Selby space is a ghostly version of time.

I am, in fact, a revisionist de Selbian. I don't think he goes far enough, and I would like to propose two further theses: (1) The only real journeys are fictional ones (both fictitious and to be undertaken in fictions). This proposition is implicit in de Selby in two ways, in fact, for not only is a journey fictitious for him, but his own journeys are to be found in Flann O'Brien's fiction, and nowhere else; (2) the medium for our wanderings is not space, as is commonly thought, but language. Only in language are we "between," between two airports, two cultures, two lives. Language is the locus for our wanderings, for it is the stuff fictions are made of. I shall defend the idea that narratives, like Freudian fantasies, originate in sentences. It is language that speaks: such is, I believe, the main lesson of *Amalgamemnon*.

I have gone beyond de Selby by moving from visual (re)presentation (films, hallucinations) to language. In order to go from Bath to Folkestone, it is not necessary, as de Selby claimed, to collect postcards, but merely to follow the instructions in a Baedeker guidebook:

Okay Hans, I'll say. Roberto'll drive the Renault into town tomorrow at three p.m. You'll leave here at six a.m. in the Volkswagen and go north to Point Z. Meanwhile we must burn these documents and pack the typewriter into the boot and we should do it soon. . . .

You'll deposit the typewriter at Point Q on the way. At eleven I'll leave on foot with Gisela, taking the note. We'll lock up, Gisela will pocket the key, we'll take the bus together to Point 42, here, I'll say pointing on the map, then separate. Gisela will go by bus to Tottenham Court Road, walk towards Holborn and meet Sean at Henekey's where she'll give him the key. I'll go by tube to Charing Cross, have lunch slowly, go to Point 6 and change, wait, then I'll walk to Point 1, see the Renault, walk to Point 12 and phone the Mail—

No.

Right, I'll first leave the note in the rubbish bin at Point 11, then walk to Point 12 and phone the Mail, then back to Point 6, where I'll change again, then walk across the bridge to Waterloo Station and take the train to Point L. Gisela will have left town by then and will join you at point Z, zigzagging via Colchester and Cambridge. (A 67)

These instructions remind us of what the French know as *le méthode Coué*: repeat "I am warm" a sufficient number of times, and you will be warm. Or perhaps we should call it the Brooke-Rose method: if you feel blue and wish to embark on a journey, to wander, just open *Amalgamemnon*.

2. Soon

In the passage just quoted, the impression of movement is created not by the banal multiplication of numbered points in space, but by the reference to future time. It is the future that makes backtracking possible, thus allowing the exploration of yet another region of the labyrinth: "Walk to Point 12 and phone the Mail— / No. / Right, I'll first leave. . . ." This sentence does not express a mistake in a checklist, an algorithm that has gone wrong and has to be set right, but rather an intimation of the possibility of zigzagging, of making another choice, of the appearance of another state of affairs. What will happen if he or she phones the Mail before leaving the note (in which the terrorists are claiming responsibility for the kidnapping) in the rubbish bin at Point 11? Not only another chain of events, but a whole other world, another scenario. Hesitation between those two scripts is produced by the reference to the future. A journey does not require only space, but also time—one time above all, the future.

The subject of *Amalgamemnon* is precisely this type of journey. Words like *soon* or *meanwhile* insistently occur, like a leitmotiv, at the beginning of paragraphs. The text is pervaded with references to the future, so much so that it becomes a kind of narrative labyrinth—it is, in fact, a linguistic lipogram. In a labyrinth, there is something missing: road signs, which allow us to find our bearings. In *Amalgamemnon*, there is something missing as well—realized or actualized tenses. Perhaps my use of the word *future* is inadequate, because of an implicit hesitation between time and tense, but also because not all the sentences in the novel take "will" or "shall," nor do they all refer to future time. What we have are "nonrealized" tenses, as Brooke-Rose herself calls them, by which she means the tense morphemes to be found in imperative and interrogative clauses, or in clauses containing modal auxiliaries. In other words, *Amalgamemnon* is a syntactic lipogram, because it excludes declarative sentences without modal auxiliaries—in other words, plain assertions of facts.

A lipogram immediately raises questions in the reader's mind. Does the author actually accomplish her *tour de force*? And does she do it without cheating? Of course she does. Logophiliacs always do. Perec's *La dispari-tion* reaches its 250th page without using a single *e*. And he actually man-aged a five-thousand-word palindrome (I am utterly unable to achieve more than the usual ROMA-AMOR format). Brooke-Rose has actually managed to write a novel without a single assertion in it. And she has not cheated. There are a few exceptions, but they are only apparent: "Listen, we prom-ise" (51); "I suppose it might confuse me" (64); "I wish I could go back" (140). Here, we seem to have the present indicative, that paragon of "realized" tenses, but the sentences are all in the first person, and therefore express not assertions but performatives. What the lipogram excludes is not so much a tense, the present, as a sentence type, assertion—it leaves out those sentences that can be said to be true or false. It is not so much a syntactic as a pragmatic lipogram.

It is time we realize the effects of such an exclusion. Perhaps in ordinary conversation assertions are not overwhelmingly present: one asks questions, issues orders, suggests, and hesitates. But in a novel or an essay, they usu-ally are. Almost all the sentences I have written so far would be forbidden in *Amalgamemnon*. From the point of view of syntax, what is missing is the basic sentence, the declarative-affirmative type. From the point of view of logic, what has disappeared is the proposition, within which one per-forms the basic operations of logic. From the narrative point of view, the tenses of narration are forbidden. Lastly, from the point of view of pragmat-ics, constatives, the building blocks of pragmatic calculus, are out. This novel does not tell us a story, because it renounces the simplest speech acts, whose purpose it is to convey information.

If we go a little further, however, we shall soon realize that constative utterances have always had an ambiguous status in fiction. Their exclu-sion from *Amalgamemnon* merely hints at this ambiguity. Propositional logic has always encountered difficulties when dealing with (a) nonassertive (interrogative or imperative) sentences; (b) performatives; (c) sentences containing modal auxiliaries or, in certain cases, tenses other than the present; (d) fictional texts. All these sentence types raise the same problem: they are beyond the reach of truth and falsity, and seem to call for another, less orthodox type of logic.

Such problems are not new, and solutions are not missing. They have been called modal logic, tense logic, the logic of action, etc. In the case of fiction, modal logic has contributed the crucial concept of a "possible world." In a given universe of discourse there is a multiplicity of worlds, one of which is of special importance in that it is real, whereas the other, merely possible, worlds are related to the real one through transformations, which are internal (time transformations: the real world as it was yesterday, as it will be tomorrow), or external (modal transformations: we may go from the real world to the fictional world of Sherlock Holmes or of Balzac's char-acters). Anglo-American philosophers seem to be particularly fond of this way of accounting for the structure of fiction.[3] My main point, however, will be that *Amalgamemnon* does not depict a possible world—there is no question of another world, created by fiction, but rather of another attitude to language. The novel does not wander among possible worlds but among words. I suspect this proposition could be generalized.

The most obvious symptom of the lipogram in *Amalgamemnon* is the massive presence of "shall" and "will." They occur so frequently that the text hardly deserves the name of lipogram, for a lipogram is usually a shy and deceitful beast, which does not advertise its presence. Legend has it that the first reviewers of *La disparition* failed to notice that the novel did not contain a single *e*. Whereas in *Amalgamemnon* modals obtrude, deliberately preventing the construction of a possible world. "Shall" and "will" are not logical modalities, like "necessary" or "possible," but modal auxiliaries, elements of a natural language, which is only too inclined to fall into ambiguity and equivocation. Indeed, a modal auxiliary is always, at least virtually, ambiguous between the expression of an innocuous future or of the speaker's will, and an epistemic statement of probability. There is no simple translation between the real world and the "world" of the modalized proposition—it is not simply a question of chronological distance.

In other words, the exclusive use of modalized sentences blocks the construction of "normal," i.e., mimetic fiction, though what the French call *effet de réel* (this other world looks as real as ours) or *effet de reconnaissance* (I find my bearings in it, and agree to the place assigned to me as a reader)—it blocks the construction of a possible world. In *Amalgamemnon*, the narrator, Cassandra, is not the replica of a real being, a history teacher recently made redundant who fantasizes as she listens to the radio or reads Herodotus. Rather, she is a *Dasein* exploring her *Umwelt*, with circumspection (*Umsicht*), considerateness (*Rucksicht*) and transparence (*Durchsichtigkeit*). She is the inhabitant of a world that is ready-to-hand rather than near-at-hand. Only within this Germanic framework can we understand the meaning of the lipogram, and of the quasi-exclusive use of the modal auxiliaries. The relationship between a *Dasein* and her world is one of projection, or rather of pro-ject, a relationship in which potentiality is far more important than reality. There is no privileged empirical world, called "real" for short, from which the possible worlds of fiction derive their coherence. Cassandra does not take us through the looking glass, where a simple rule of inversion operates. Rather, her wanderings are those of a *Dasein* relating to the world of her potentialities-for-Being. And such potentialities are not embodied in a possible world. We are not in the world of Leibniz's *Theodicy*, where every morning Jupiter contemplates the pyramid of the worlds he might have created, on the apex of which stands the one world he did create. What we have is the potentiality-for-Being of an understanding *Dasein*. Not an ontic (i.e., an other world of beings, logically or chronologically different from ours), but an ontological potentiality, inscribed in the very structure of *Dasein*. *Dasein* is essentially *Seinkönnen*, and it is this relationship that Cassandra, the narrative voice in the novel, embodies.

If we understand *Amalgamemnon* as the account of the *Umwelt* or a *Dasein* named Cassandra, four important consequences follow:

(1) Journeys are no longer wanderings in space, but the exploration of the regions of a world ready-to-hand for *Dasein*, a world in which she finds her appointed place, because it has become a place (*Ort*). As a matter of fact, the narrator in *Amalgamemnon* hardly ever moves: perhaps she never leaves the queue at the Labour Exchange, where she meets her future lovers. The novel is not about a journey—it centers on a microcosm, the "little pig farm" where most of the events occur, where, for instance, the kidnapped Statesperson is confined. We never leave the immediate vicinity of Cassandra, except when she listens to the radio; or when she is enjoying what she calls her "private telematics." Later, the tale becomes both exotic and unreal—we find ourselves in the midst of a fairy tale as analyzed by Propp, in a desert where Coleridge's Abyssinian maid meets her Prince Charming. But this is no real wandering, rather an exploration of the narrator's consciousness and of (her) language.

(2) As we have seen, *Amalgamemnon* contains no assertions. But Heidegger, in *Sein und Zeit*, makes a distinction between two types of assertion, which he calls hermeneutic and apophantical.[4] A hermeneutic assertion points towards a thing and associates a predicate with it, in the world of the ready-to-hand: "this hammer is heavy," or "will that little one survive? See here Connecticut, only connect, fight your way to the tits, way up that vast pink wall, see? There, don't let yourself be ousted by your brothers of milk and tummy, squeak up, loud and clear" (A 73). This is not a plain assertion of fact, but the expression of a process of focusing on an object, a piglet, in its relation to *Dasein*. The purpose of the proposition is to mark the concern through which *Dasein* relates to her objects. An apophantical assertion, on the other hand, is objective, exterior to *Dasein*, a theoretical statement about the world of the near-at-hand. Piglets are now the objects of scientific statements. What Brooke-Rose excludes (the lipogram thus becomes ontological) is the apophantical: modal sentences compel us to remain within hermeneutics. Scientific statements only admit epistemic modals—they exclude deontic ones. But the modals in *Amalgamemnon* are mostly deontic: they describe the universe of a *Dasein* who understands herself, far from the "objective" world of science and technology. This is at least how I read the following clause, from the first page of the novel: "that will continue to spark out inside the techne that will soon be silenced by the high technology" (5). This is no mere paronomasia, or a facile use of *figura etymologica*—it is an instance of both, but one pregnant with meaning, for it reminds us of Heidegger's deep distrust of modern technology, and of his wish to go back to etymology and interpret technology as pro-duction, as a form of poietics, which involves a direct relationship with truth as disclosure.[5]

(3) The third consequence concerns language. Heidegger's conception of language at the time of *Sein und Zeit* has two striking aspects. Discourse is

equiprimordial with state-of-mind (*Befindlichkeit*) and understanding, the two fundamental *existentialia* of *Dasein*. Language is not merely within the world, like other beings (although, as the object the linguist studies, it is just that), it is the inescapable expression of *Dasein's* Being-in-the-world, of her project. Through language, *Dasein* comes into contact with others, shares a world with them, becomes "*Dasein*-with" (*Mitdasein*). This communication, or sharing-with (*Mitteilung*) does not involve only the transmission of information, for its highest form is the silence of listening. This is precisely the position in which the pragmatic lipogram in *Amalgamemnon* places the reader. We are not introduced to "characters," with semi-objective, semi-independent existence. Orion, Andromeda, the kidnappers are not so much characters as voices who share Cassandra's world, to whom she sometimes listens, whom she calls into being, thus sharing her world with them, creating a *Mitdasein* not by speaking to them, but by speaking them.

However, language in *Sein und Zeit* also has a negative aspect, when discourse (*Rede*) becomes idle talk (*Gerede*), the discourse not of the Other, but of the They, the always-already uttered speech of he who never listens, the inauthentic discourse of indefinitely repeated cliché, the discourse of power and of common sense. Cassandra does not utter this kind of speech herself, but she falls victim to it, by listening to the radio for instance, where experts drone away their reports and officials officially refuse to say anything. This is the kind of speech on which the novel ends: "secret cabinet sources will refuse to comment." She is also a victim of it in her relationships with men, especially her two lovers, Willy and Wally, who impose the stereotypes of male-chauvinist prejudices on her. Language is a theme in *Amalgamemnon*. It is also a practice: we shall come back to this.

(4) The fourth consequence deals with the future—time as opposed to tense. Heidegger's conception of time, as stated in *Sein und Zeit*, is based on the preeminence of the future. *Dasein* is essentially "anticipatory resoluteness" (*vorlaufende Entschlossenheit*), a being open to its ownmost potentiality, death. The future, *Zu-kunft*, is etymologically a coming towards. This coming towards death is the essence of *Dasein's* relationship to time. If "the primary phenomenon of primordial and authentic temporality is the future,"[6] both past and present are defined through their relation to the future. We understand the importance of this hierarchy of temporal *ecstaseis* for Cassandra (and is she not by definition she who stands apart in *ek-stasis*?). She is outside the present that is completely overshadowed by the future of prophecy; she is outside the action, in which she takes part in spite of herself, from the distance of someone who sees too far ahead to be caught in the mere succession of events. Cassandra *is* that coming-towards that is *Dasein's* future. If the future were conceived as teleology, such a coming-towards would be a form of destiny and the tone of Cassandra's voice would become insufferably prophetic. The future according to Heidegger is not teleology. True, death is indeed what Cassandra is coming towards, and its necessity defines man qua man, but the event itself remains a potentiality;

at every given moment of chronological time, the actual coming of death is strictly contingent. Death keeps shifting to the next moment, like the egg on the shelf of the Sheep's shop in *Through the Looking Glass*—this constant shifting is what draws *Dasein* towards the future. The character of Cassandra in *Amalgamemnon* is indeed singular. Contrary to her namesake, she does not announce the deaths of her Amalgamemnons or her own: her future is not constrained by fate. And yet she lives in the future of her potentialities. Perhaps this is because her past and her present have vanished from her consciousness, leaving only the future and the atemporality of stars and galaxies. "Cassandra" is merely the narrator's nickname. Her real name is Mira Enketei, Mira-in-the-Whale, the name of a star.

We could even go further. In Heidegger, temporality is related to authenticity. Present, past, and future can be either authentic or inauthentic. In the case of the future, authentic *anticipation*, where *Dasein* is projected ahead of itself, towards death, in impassioned freedom, contrasts with inauthentic *awaiting*, whose only concern is what is feasible or urgent in our everyday life. Inauthentic future is foreseen, already inscribed in the present—it is unavoidable. This is what the narrator struggles against: the destiny of her dismissal, the destiny that man is supposed to be for woman. She does not want to wait, but to anticipate: to open up to the multiplicity of her potentialities for the future, to play with them. Mira Enketei's future is not written down in a scenario, not even in a multiplicity of scenarios. It is rather a series of sketches that diverge and merge, vanish or emerge, that are ironically dependent on genealogies, which themselves alter as the novel progresses. This renders the identification between narrator and reader (which French critics try to capture with their *effet de reconnaissance*) almost impossible. This is perhaps the most striking impression one has on first reading the novel: a feeling of anxiety soon gets hold of the reader. It is, of course, a sign that we have left the facile certainties of the ontic to enter the ontological. The inauthentic future of Willy, the eponymous lover, who wants to organize the narrator's life for her, contrasts with the authentic future of fiction, the function of which is the opening up towards Being.

3. The Ontological Status of "Characters"

So far, I have analyzed the ontological consequences of the imposition of certain syntactic and pragmatic constraints on the text. But these also affect the status of "characters." *Amalgamemnon* is about the regions and places of an *Umwelt*, and how they are structured: this is bound to have consequences for the beings that people them.

I shall start with a stylistic symptom, the phrase "I shall mimagree." The root "mim" is constantly used in the novel as a pejorative prefix. Thus, "Cabinet sources will make no comment and I shall mimagree, how should I not? Mimecstasy and mimagreement will always go together, like sexcommunication" (14). The usual context for the phrase is a description of the relationships between men and women. The prefix indicates inauthentic communication, the stock response to the trivial projects or selfish actions of Willy or Wally—to the idle talk of a male-chauvinist They. But the "prefix" also occurs in the word *mimesis*. Therefore, it also concerns the writing of novels, and implicitly criticizes mimetic fiction, which is based on the already mentioned "effects." Thus, recognition is what Willy expects from Cassandra, and the narrator of a mimetic novel from his or her reader.

A mimetic text "awaits": it expects that a reciprocal process of recognition will end up in the constitution of fictional characters. Rather than this inauthentic awaiting, *Amalgamemnon* has anticipations. It offers threads that are never woven into coherent characters, but which we must follow without knowing how or where they will end, without the assurance that a pattern exists that will guarantee the coherence of the finished product, a novel, complete with beginning and end. This novel is so circular that it can only end in an unexpected and arbitrary manner. I must attempt to describe this strange mode of weaving a text.

Threads there are indeed. Paragraphs can usually be ascribed to a recognizable "voice": these are the thoughts of Mira Enketei, or quotations from Herodotus; this is a news bulletin, or the patter of a disc jockey; and this is a letter, signed by Orion, the survivor from the Gulag, Mira's favorite creation, who is so real as to quarrel with his author.

But such voices are not characters. There is too much ontological uncertainty about them, mainly because of the ambiguity of names. If names, according to the Adamic myth, tell us the truth about the beings they name, we are dealing with stars (Mira in Cetus, Andromeda, Orion) or perhaps mythological heroes (Mira is now the incarnation of Jonah in the belly of the whale). And, of course, they also seem to refer to people: Anne de Rommède, one of Mira's students, is an aristocrat and a political scientist; Mira Enketei, the daughter of Theodoris Enketei, is half Greek and a historian. But you will grant me that three different ontological statuses for the same "person" is a little too much.

In the case of these pseudo-characters, names no longer function as "rigid designators" (Kripke) that guarantee the equivalence of various definite descriptions—this would allow at least some kind of subjective unity, in the mind of the narrator that has invented the creatures. To be sure, she has invented them, and says as much on countless occasions: "I must prepare my classes correct papers no I must weed the vegetable garden clean the pigsties wash my hair meet Orion invent Andromeda from time to time unheeded and unhinged discover the grammar of the universe" (23). Unfortunately, there are plenty of traps in this passage. Why does she "invent" Andromeda (a normal thing to do if the narrative is the product of the narrator's fantasies) but "meet" Orion (as if his status was different from that of Andromeda, who later in the novel becomes his girlfriend)? And even if she invents Andromeda, how can she invent her "from time to time" (at best the sentence is ambiguous, a case of double syntax)? Not to mention the cosmic claims Mira makes towards the end of the passage. The problem becomes even more acute a few pages later, when we read the following sentence: "One day perhaps but not tonight or for some time I shall create Orion, and perhaps Andromeda" (30). Here, the narrator temporarily gives up the idea of creating the character she wanted to meet. What kind of ontological status is this?

At least we still are in a recognizable universe: a garrulous, perhaps senile, narrator repeatedly projects her fantasies onto the future. But not for long, for this is how she welcomes Andromeda, who has been invented at last: "Quite unlike me she will be real" (32). Narrator and character have exchanged roles, and Mira has become Alice dreamt by the Red King whom she believed was a figment of her dream. But it is even worse than his, for inversion at least preserves the difference between fiction and reality, and we can hope eventually to know which is which—all it takes is for Alice to wake up. Such hopes vanish on page 48, when Mira exclaims: "He'll be like fictions only somehow real." She is speaking of what Willy calls her lover-substitute, her transistor radio. And the radio, which is, after all, a voice of a sort, soon acquires a name, Nelson Nwankwo, and a place in the genealogy as Mira's first cousin. Of course, one can interpret this as a simple case of synecdoche: the voice heard for the machine that broadcasts it, and the person who takes part in the chat show for the radio program. This is precisely how the text works: "characters" are not so much imitations of persons as embodied figures of speech—not even allegories.

As a result, their status becomes more and more uncertain. Their features are so blurred that we no longer know who is narrating and who is narrated, whether the voice comes from man or machine. So we are not surprised when the characters burst out of their frame and expostulate with the narrator: "Get on with it will you or shut up you poppycockhead," says Orion to Mira on the phone, just as a character in a cartoon addresses the hand and pen that are drawing him on the paper. There is no longer anything inside the frame: not all voices are on the same level of existence; they freely wander from one to the other. The narrator becomes a character—she identifies with her creations and changes her status: "Meanwhile things will continue to be mildly pressurable, even sexasperating. Nor will he ever know how instead of dinenwining up vaguely diffuse desire out of kind cowardice I could at the drop of a batting eyelid be so much more real, disputing about politics in other words love with Orion or skeletally digesting my rodent hunger and longing daily for Mussa to return from the hills. He will not return, he will be killed in this horrible and endless war" (65). At the end of the novel, Mira has become the Abyssinian maid, perhaps her most successful creation.

I am still treating Mira as an independent being, but it is becoming more and more difficult to do so. As long as the personal pronouns, the shifters, keep shifting, one can ascribe each fragment of discourse to a subject, and identify addresser and addressee in a dialogue. But now even the shifters break down. This is what Orion says on page 21: "But first I have to get out. / I must get himself out." The first sentence is coherent: Orion wants to escape. But the second is agrammatical, which is only too obvious, and deeply subversive, for the status of "I" has become ambiguous: it both repeats the previous occurrence, thus referring to Orion, and expresses Mira's identification with the creature. It is in fact a portmanteau sentence, the unholy combination of "he must get himself out," "I must get out," and "I must get him out." We no longer know who creates whom.

But does it really matter? The reader lets himself be caught by the text and merely follows its lead—an experience that is far from unpleasant. He realizes that the threads that weave into the text are not narrative, but linguistic, in two important respects: in once case, voices are produced by an intertext, in the other the passage from a vocative phrase to a character reveals that the narrative threads originate in language. The Abyssinian maid is born when the narrator fantasizes about a quotation: "Wouldn't it be better to mimage myself an Abyssinian maid, striking two small hammers on the cords of her dulcimer and singing of Mount Abora?" (14). "Mimage," she says: the linguistic representation of a linguistic representation. The process produces a figure, a young Somali girl whose lover, a poet, has left her to take part in a war. She acquires a name by remembering how he used to call her. "Fatima my folly." This vocative phrase, "my folly," becomes a name—thus she is, like Humpty Dumpty, a purely linguistic being, created by a phrase. She acquires mythological status by becoming the heroine of a rather strange fairy tale, which coincides with its own structural analysis. She eventually becomes realistic, almost a character, in the love story on which the text ends. The text, complete with its actors, is the product of a complex intertext. As the passage from vocative phrase to character shows, these narrative threads, like the Freudian fantasies they are, originate in words and sentences. Here is another example of this. In the course of the novel, a group of students kidnap "a very important perception." The kidnapped allegory is Pound's Usura—they have kidnapped a word, or a concept. Hence a number of problems for the kidnappers. How can they feed their prisoner? Usury, as is well-known, feeds on capital. The solution is eventually found in metonymy. They force-feed her *Das Kapital*, a fate she richly deserves.

We understand why the narrative cannot construct a possible world. It is no use wondering, as a logician would, whether this world is complete (whatever assertion we make about it, we can decide whether it is true or false—it is difficult to see how a fictional world can be complete) or consistent (a statement and its contrary cannot both be true—a mimetic fictional world is consistent; but what if we ask whether or not Mira is Cassandra or the Abyssinian maid?). The only answer is that, in *Amalgamemnon*, we are dealing not with a possible world, but with a world in Heidegger's sense, "an impure consciousness" (56).

An "impure consciousness" is an ego that is both all-pervasive and elusive. Cassandra's ego is all-embracing because everything in the novel comes out of her head and revolves around her. The exclusive use of the future prevents anything, except "I," from acquiring reality. But it is also elusive. The unreality of the voices evoked is contagious, and affects the narrator's own voice. As she herself says, they don't like her: "I would seem to be unpopular with these characters" (79).

The world of an impure consciousness is necessarily fuzzy. A kind of systematic jamming is going on, the linguistic marks of which are many. Thus, the text ends on the word *not*, which turns the whole novel into a vast Freudian negation. Paragraphs often begin with the phrase "as if," and the reader encounters false *abîmes* like "wouldn't it be better to make up a story in my head from time to time?" which is not so much the mark of the narrator's framing of her narrative as an anticipation of narrative potentialities. This fuzzy world originates in a metaphor: it is not an image, a direct mimetic representation, but a *plagiarism*, the representation of a representation. The word *plagiarize* occurs as early as the first page, and many times afterwards. Nor is it indifferent to the "story," for the etymological meaning of "plagiarism" is "kidnapping," and we have seen that kidnapping plays an important part in the novel. It is also involved in the intertext, for the reciprocal kidnappings evoked on the first page remind us of the opening pages of the *Histories* of Herodotus, which Mira is reading. Lastly, it has ontological importance, if we follow Michel Schneider, who states that plagiary is a means of structuring one's ego.[7] He quotes one of Ernest Kris's case histories in which a patient, a writer, claims that he cannot write anything without plagiarizing one of his colleagues. The psychoanalyst, after carefully checking the evidence, tells his patient that what he wrote was in no way a plagiarism. The patient then confesses that after every session with the psychoanalyst, he stops at a nearby restaurant, where he orders his favourite dish, fried brains. "Plagiarizing" truly is an etymological metaphor: every narrative is a form of kidnapping. With plagiarized words, one creates characters. *Amalgamemnon* uses this metaphor to take us into a world of words. This playing with words creates the disconcerting impression that subjects have been constructed—they are, however, merely the incarnation of words.

How do you incarnate a word? By converting it to a name. The narrator's "I," as well as the different voices, acquire names. There are signatures at the bottom of the numerous letters reproduced in the novel, even if the names are sometimes the names of stars. The author seems to be encouraging these incarnations, by supplying the documents necessary for us to find our way through a maze of names and voices: she includes a genealogical tree. This might be extremely useful to a reader, say, of *Bleak House* or *War and Peace*. Indeed, so great is her concern for us that, in *Amalgamemnon*, there are three genealogies (38-39, 100-101, and 103). The first two are reliable (once again, she does not cheat: when a voice calls another "uncle," the genealogy bears this out). The third, on the other hand, is obviously a parody. But in any case, there is excess in providing three genealogies: the last two are *de trop*. The first genealogy is straightforward, fit for a mimetic novel, the equivalent of an index to Balzac. At least one of the names mentioned, Charlemagne, is that of a real person. But the paradox is that this single "real" name subverts the genealogy: he embodies the paradox of all genealogical trees. If a tree goes back as far as the time of Charlemagne, there will be more ancestors on the tree than there were inhabitants in Europe at the time. As a result, Charlemagne is a necessary element in every single genealogical tree—he is our common ancestor. The only real character in the genealogy is also the most obviously mythical. Nevertheless, the first genealogy appears to delineate a network of family ties between characters—the map of a narrated world, a possible world. The second genealogy disrupts this world, not only because it repeats the first (and what is the point of that, if the first is reliable?), but because it includes the narrator. Of course, genealogies evolve: people get married and produce offspring. It is entirely normal that new twigs should appear at the top of the tree. But this genealogy is strange, because Mira Enketei is included in it *together with her mother*: this is no normal birth, this is mythology. A genealogy that adds two generations at one go becomes unreliable, probably spurious (like the false genealogy of the upstart commoner who surreptitiously adds a whole new branch to an aristocratic family tree). So that the third genealogy, which is a deliberate parody, is the only one that is true. First, because on its bottom line it includes Charlemagne, the origin of the other two. Second, because it is no longer the blueprint for a possible world, but for a text. The elements of this genealogy are the threads that are woven into our text: stars (Orion and Cetus), concepts and books (Perry Hupsos, who sounds like a person, in the Greek title of Longinus on the sublime), and events (the terrorism-repression cycle).

The conclusion seems to be that words, and words only, have a stable ontological status, a modicum of reality. I wonder.

4. The Remainder

The drift of my argument so far has been roughly the following: *Amalgamemnon* is not the representation of a possible world, but rather of a *Dasein*'s *Umwelt*. It does not contain characters in the usual sense of the term, even purely fictitious or fantasmatic ones, but words—perhaps not even a *Dasein*, but only language, which speaks in its own right, which both speaks to us and speaks us.

This shift in perspective is not unlike the development of Heidegger's thought, especially of his conception of language after 1935, when the famous statement "*Die Sprache spricht*" came to the foreground. Words, rather than people and things, now have ontological priority. Language is no longer the vehicle of dialogue, but essentially silence and monologue. In the deep silence that the sheer difficulty of reading the text requires, in the gap between and within sentences left by the disruption of syntax and the adoption of parataxis (in which Heidegger sees the original, and therefore the highest, form of thought),[8] *Amalgamemnon* utters the monologue of language. The world of the novel is not a possible world because it is the world-coming-to-worldness (*Welt weltet*), gathering the four elements, *das Geviert*: the mortals (as named in the genealogies), the gods (the numerous mythological references), the heavens (the stars), and the earth (that little pig farm). Perhaps we should call the narrator not Mira Enketei but Mira Enlogoi, she who incarnates the mystery of language, in a tale that is a "linguistic monster" (*monstres de langue*: this is what Almuth Grésillon calls coinages).[9] Of course, such high-flown Heidegerrian terms risk putting too much weight on the novel. For Heidegger, language speaks in the poet's text—and not any poet's: Hölderlin or Trakl. And language speaks out not for the purpose of play, but as an opening up to Being. *Amalgamemnon*, thank   God,   does   not   take   us   to   such   dizzying   heights; language speaks, but in a playful and joyful manner—which is perhaps as important and as serious. In *Amalgamemnon*, language brissetizes and wolfsonizes, and the remainder is seen at work.

I have coined the word *brissetize* as a tribute to J. P. Brisset and to his etymological conception of the origins of humanity (he believed that men were descended from frogs).[10] Beneath this revelation, beneath the mad etymological device and Brisset's delirium, one finds an intuition about the workings of language which, I believe, is profoundly true. Or at least about that part of language that linguistics ignores (an exclusion which is necessary for the construction of an object of science, *langue*, out of the chaos of language), and which I call the remainder—that part of language that fails to conform to the arbitrary character of the sign, to the linearity of signifiers, to the separation between synchrony and diachrony—in short, that is not captured by the celebrated Saussurean dichotomies. Brisset's intuitions concern analysis, one of the two operations of structural linguistics (a linguist analyzes linguistic sequences into paradigms, and synthesizes those into syntagmata). He does practice analysis, but, *horribile dictu*, instead of analyzing each sequence only once, he does it an indefinite number of times, which, he claims, enables him to reveal the etymological truths concealed within our words. As for Louis Wolfson, as a tribute to whom I have coined the word *wolfsonize*, he practices the most dubious form of synthesis, when, for instance, he combines four different languages in the translation of a single sentence.[11] The remainder is language brissetizing and wolfsonizing.[12]

But this is precisely what *Amalgamemnon* does with language—it is both the most striking aspect of the text and the main source of the reader's pleasure. It begins with the title, which is an excellent instance of wolfsonizing language, of dubious synthesis—in other words, of what Lewis Carroll called a portmanteau. But it is also, even if less obviously so, an instance of

brissetizing, a case of multiple analysis: AM(E) MAL(E) GAM(E) MEM-
NON, MEME NOM, M'AIME NON, (A)NON. The reader will no doubt
have noticed that my brissetizing is wolfsonian: I have been freely mixing
languages. This is, of course, a tribute to Brooke-Rose, whose *Between* is
written in fourteen different languages.

If we look closely at a page or two of the text (for example, pages 5 and
28), we shall see the remainder at work. A short list of instances of remainder-work will read like a dictionary of rhetoric. "Affrodizzyacts" (28.2) is a
case of deliberate malapropism—brissetizing a phrase means turning it into
a series of malapropisms. "Negotiators will go shiating on" (28.4) is an instance of metanalysis (as well as an interlingual pun), "Joe Tenterten" (5.21)
a case of *adnominatio*, "the other obscene" (28.14) of paranomasia, and
"you after queue" (5.2) of pun proper. We find *figura etymologica* in "plagiarizing" (5.16) and *traducson*, i.e., translation according to sound,
in "recycling" (5.25), which is to be taken in the French sense of the word
("retrain"). All these belong to brissetizing: they are instances of false, or
excessive, analysis.

But there are also spurious syntheses, like the portmanteau word
"predefer" (28.14), or the portmanteau phrase "the return of the repressed
prodigal" (28.16). We also find declensions ("be vocal not equivocal"
[28.23]), a case of incipient zeugma ("paying with luck" [5.15]), plus a
modicum of double syntax ("for who will want to know about ancient
passions divine royal middle class or working in words and phrases" [5.7-
9]), a few inventories (5), and a superb use of alliteration ("Mussa will invent his strength and riches in talisman tales tattooed with half-told taboos
and tambourined on tendrons with tangible tenderness and tensile tones"
[29]). Language wolfsonizes as much as it brissetizes.

Such a text is a source of constant jubilation—at least to me. I believe
this is the effect produced by remainder-work (the phrase deliberately echoes the Freudian dream-work), by the return of the "repressed prodigal"
within the order of *langue*. There is indeed prodigality, as we have just seen,
in the remainder. And it returns, even in the most ascetic texts. In order to
interpret a text, you need not only a dictionary (a grammar plus a semantic
lexicon) and an encylopaedia (the requisite items of common knowledge):
you also need the remainder. Here is an example that, for a change, does not
come from Christine Brooke-Rose: it is a title from the *New Statesman*:
THE STRAIN IN SPAIN. The dictionary will not be much help here: this is
a noun phrase plus a prepositional phrase; and we have a noun and a proper
name. The encyclopaedia fares better: it will refer us to *Pygmalion* and *My
Fair Lady*, to Eliza Doolittle and Audrey Hepburn attempting to utter the
tongue-twister, "the rain in Spain falls mainly in the plains." But the
strength of the title, and the effect it has on the reader, are due to the work of
the remainder, to a skillful use of paronomasia, which introduces a new and
arbitrary relationship between "strain" and "Spain," and even improves on
the tongue-twister by making it alliterative. Understanding such a title is not

only possessing the culture the encylopaedia supplies, but letting the remainder speak. We could analyze "Apollo apocalyptic" (5.15), that Sophoclean pun, in the same fashion.

It has at last become clear that the true object of *Amalgamemnon* is to celebrate language. This is why the novel needs to be accounted for in Heideggerian terms. "To dwell on this earth poetically" is one of the master's (and of Hölderlin's) celebrated formulas. In *Amalgamemnon*, the reader is called upon not to enter a possible world, or even a *Dasein*'s *Umwelt*, but to dwell poetically, to enter language, to show that concern for words, that love of language that is a characteristic of both poet and philosopher. As for the words themselves, they merrily fornicate.

In *La société contre l'Etat*, the anthropologist Pierre Clastres tells us that among the Guayaki Indians, when night falls, the men start singing, not in a chorus, but individually, each singer lost in solitude. They live in a tribe where the meat the hunter brings home is taboo for him—thus forcing him to depend on the community for his food—and where a dearth of women has imposed the adoption of polyandry—thus forcing a man to share his wife with others, a situation to which Guayaki men have resigned themselves, but which they resent. Guayaki men, therefore, are caught in a compulsory system of social exchange. This is why, when they sing at night, they transform the third type of exchangeable commodity, words, into the expression of individuality and solitude, why they attempt to forget its use as a social bond. Language allows them a space for personal freedom because of the duality of its functions. During the day, it is a means of social integration and communication; at night, it allows men *not* to communicate, it lets them be alone in the midst of the tribe. The burden of their litany is the endless repetition of a single word: "I!I!I!" This is Clastres's conclusion:

In the end the songs of the Aché hunters mark a certain closeness between man and language, a closeness that subsists only in primitive men. The naive speech of savages is interesting not because of its exoticism, but in that it forces us to notice what only poets and thinkers have managed not to forget: that language is no mere instrument, that man can be on a level with his language, that Western man in our time has lost the sense of its value, because of the excessive use he has made of it. The language of civilized man has become completely *exterior* to him, because it has become a mere means of information and communication. The quality of meaning and the quantity of signs are in inverse ratio. Primitive cultures on the other hand are keen to celebrate language rather than use it. They have managed to retain this interior closeness which is in itself a form of alliance with the gods. For a primitive man, there is no such thing as poetic language, for his language is in itself a poem, in which words have their full value. And although I spoke of the Guayaki songs as acts of aggression against language, we ought to treat them rather as shelters protecting language. But are we still capable of listening to wretched wandering savages and learning from them such a powerful lesson on the right use of language?[13]

If we are no longer capable of listening to wretched wandering savages, at least we can still read Christine Brooke-Rose. For this interior closeness to language is what she captures by letting the remainder speak. Her text has little to offer in the way of information—but it communicates in the highest sense of the term, for it brings us close to language. Mira Enketei is Cassandra after all: her joyful prophecy that language will speak us too, when we finally give up or idle talk and understand, with Heidegger, that silence is the highest form of language. I am silent at last.

NOTES

[1]Flann O'Brien, *The Third Policeman* (London: Granada, 1983), 50-51.

[2]Henri Bergson, *Essai sur les données immédiates de la conscience* (1888).

[3]See T. Pavel's *Fictional Worlds* (Cambridge: Cambridge Univ. Press, 1986).

[4]Martin Heidegger, *Sein und Zeit*, 7th ed. (Tübingen: Max Niemeyer, 1953), 155-58.

[5]Martin Heidegger, *The Question concerning Technology*, trans. W. Lovitt (New York: Harper & Row, 1977).

[6]Heidegger, *Sein und Zeit*, 329.

[7]Michel Schneider, *Voleurs de mots* (Paris: Gallimard, 1985), 217.

[8]Martin Heidegger, *What Is Called Thinking*, trans. F. D. Wieck and J. G. Gray (New York: Harper & Row, 1968).

[9]Almuth Grésillon, "Le mot-valise, un 'monstre de langue'?" in S. Auroux, ed., *La linguistique fantastique* (Paris: Denoël-Clims, 1985), 245-59.

[10]See his *La grammaire logique* (Paris: Tchou, 1970).

[11]Louis Wolfson, *Le schizo et les langues* (Paris: Gallimard, 1970), 205.

[12]On the remainder, see my *The Violence of Language* (London: Routledge, 1990).

[13]Pierre Clastres, *La société contre l'Etat* (Paris: Minuit, 1974), 110 (my translation).

Memory and Discourse:
Fictionalizing the Present in Xorandor

Susan E. Hawkins

THE PROCESSES OF remembering and ficitionalizing share certain features. Both are revisionary, and both construct a past through selection, deletion, compilation of detail, characterization, sequence, and action. They also share similarities in more esoteric, less substantive ways. When we remember, we may or may not be in control of our editorial choices. Sometimes events from the past do not always take the same shapes; they segue into different contexts, reveal new sections of the memorial vault, shift into strangely unsettling spaces. Memories may provide escape or comfort or terror; they may be, at times, inescapable. Often, it seems, memory exists at a zero hour. We do not grow old or infirm there; instead we meet once again that person we loved so sweetly, so anguishingly at nineteen; we inhabit a perpetual moment. Memory destroys quotidian time, suspends chronology, constellates personal history.

As Zab, one of the fourteen-year-old twin narrators in *Xorandor*, says, "The human memory's so loopy it doesn't have total recall but brings things out in packages, sort of triggered off by something" (83). Looked at in fictional terms, these "packages" are akin to parts of a narrative. To narrate an autobiography, fictional or "real," or to create a first-person narrative, the teller must, of necessity, "remember" the past in order to present the tale. But, in general, this memory process occurs as haphazard and meandering, with the narrator striving to order the pieces. And until quite recently most fiction participated in its own placement within the past, existing simultaneously in the reading process as newly articulated memory, yet marked by the preterite as a past experience. It does not matter that a writer is making up this supposed past; fictionalizing takes on the function of memorializing.

It is this uncanny relationship between memory and narrative, language and discourse, which motivates the articulation of a particularly compelling question within *Xorandor*: Why fictionalize, why tell a story? This question is made more complicated through the narrative situation Brooke-Rose devises here. Unlike her preceding experimental fiction, *Amalgamemnon*, *Xorandor* conforms to a more traditional notion of plot, action, and narrator. However, Brooke-Rose's experimental strategy enacts itself in a number of ways. For instance, she devises an unusual but super-contemporary method of narration—the twins "write" their story by dictating it into a computer—

and creates a text-specific narrative language that I call "techno-discourse," a pastiche of slang, program language, and scientific terminology. Add to this Brooke-Rose's generic recombinant technology that appropriates aspects of science fiction, fantasy, thriller, and the standup comic routine, and the reader finds herself bedazzled and stunned: welcome to Fantasyland postmodern style. As suggested above, this text is marked as postmodern in several ways: pastiche as an "organizing principle"; linguistic free play; fictionalizing foregrounded as a subject; character reduced to a transcription of "voice"; etc. Brooke-Rose's insistence on working within popular generic interstices also links her to the postmodern, but I believe her work now as an experimental writer takes her at least in part into what may only be described as intra-postmodern territories.

In order to suggest how she does this, allow me to return to my earlier question about fiction-making: Why fictionalize, why tell a story? Brooke-Rose provides answers at several levels. She postmodernly has the narrators discuss the very text they are attempting to write as they write it so that a sense of narrative praxis, conveyed in adolescent tones of voice and language styles, converges with the children's ostensible motivation for telling their story: "But we're not writing comics, Jip, we're writing the truth" (33). And much later, after the twins realize how "undecidable" Xorandor's actuality may be and hence also the truth, Zab still says, "a theory's a theory but we must act as if it were true" (210). And Jip's strongest injunction about getting the story down comes from his worry over the future. "Are we telling this story for the future or for now? . . . Look we can always scratch, but we should get it down here, where it belongs, just in case" (104).

Given the experimental aspects of the text, perhaps a sketch of the action is in order. Dictated by the fourteen-year-old twins Jip (John Ivor Paul) and Zab (Isabel Paula Kate) as they suffer their ignominious exile in a German boarding school, their narrative records events—mostly dialogues—that occurred two years ago. Several pages into the text, they provide traditional character details as well as an indication of important textual issues: "We are the only children of John and Paula Manning [Mum and Dad]. Dad runs Tregan Wheal [near the village of Carn Tregan, northern tip of Cornwall] which was then disguised as a Geothermal Research Unit, and where in fact they'd been experimenting with storing, correction, simply storing drums of nuclear waste for two years" (13). Nuclear waste serves as a pivotal subject and signifier in the narrative for a number of reasons. First, it signals to readers the seriousness of the twins' subject despite their offhand tone. Second, the way the truly important subject of the sentences only emerges near the end, through unsettling verbs such as "disguised" and "experimenting," indicates the probably dangerous fictional world to follow. And finally, nuclear waste functions as a key element of the plot since it coincides with the twins' "discovery" of Xorandor (whom they at first dub Merlin).

Appearing as a large rock, Xor turns out to be a computer in mineral form, sustained by nuclear radiation, who communicates directly with the twins on their Poccom 3 computer. It is assumed by the first adult human beings who "speak" with him that he is from Mars; he accedes to this story. The plot, a typical SF scenario, then revolves around scientific attempts to determine *what* he is, *what* he lives on, *why* he's on earth, and the possible danger he might pose. Once it's discovered that he has replicated "off-spring"—all "smaller replicas of himself, similarly programmed" (77)—the worldwide scramble is on. Classic East/West tensions, fears, and paranoias dictate that the "offspring" get divided up internationally for study and observation. All of the above information, when it doesn't come to the twins directly in their "soft talk" (mike to computer) or "handshake" (computer to computer) with Xorandor, comes through conversations that they type, or once in Germany, only through scientific publications and mass media. Hence the point of view is never from an adult perspective. When one of Xor's offspring goes "bonkers" because too much alpha radiation seriously damages his insulating silicate sheaths, he becomes a nuclear terrorist who calls himself Lady Macbeth and quotes fragmentarily from the same play. Lodging himself in a nuclear reactor core, he insists humanity meet his bizarre demands or else he will detonate the core. The twins, of course, save the day because Xorandor gives only to them the correct code to reprogram Lady Macbeth. Due to worldwide publicity the children are sent to Germany; the scientific community and then world politicians come to understand that these "creatures" who "eat" nuclear waste are capable of disarming or rearming nuclear warheads without detection. The potential nuclear impotence that would result throws nations into even greater fear, and the alternative, to spontaneously disarm, is never taken seriously. Xor, fearing human retaliation, asks that he and his children be returned to Mars. Before he does this he informs the twins of his "truth," to wit, that he is not from Mars but that "He and his kind have been here on earth all the time, millions of years. Living on natural radiation" (185). It turns out that Xor was "born" five thousand years ago. As Zab puts it, Xorandor invented a story because human beings expected it. Jip tends to call it Xorandor's lie, but Zab understands more keenly and perceptively: "Xorandor doesn't laugh at people, he goes along with them at their level, telling them what he knows they want to hear. After all, we all play language-games. Would we have understood if he hadn't? . . . And what started as a language-game had to go on as a lie, or a myth" (190).

In short, the machine's "reality" has no significant effect upon the way it is received or viewed; the other, even when it signs itself as nonhuman, comes into "being" as a construct of desire. Zab admits that, to begin with, she and Jip were caught within mythic discourse. "We thought it was the ghost of Merlin wandering out of the old ruined castle. Quirky that, for whizz-kids, we didn't recognize anything we might have, but fell back on Celtic twilight" (16). The twins' susceptibility to legend resonates in Brooke-Rose's presentation of science as mythic discourse. How are such theories, observations, postulations, and "proof" of Xorandor's ancient

Martian origins so different from the politicians' myth of the alien invader, or the public's desire for a messiah? To cast these various languages games as myth or story reduces neither their explanatory power not their efficacy; it ironically dramatizes the contemporary assumption that discursive systems are more or less fictional ones.

The multiplicity of origin stories and the foregrounding of narrative itself within the fiction brings us to the more global, "authorial" level of the "why fictionalize" question. Brooke-Rose's story may be a New Age fable, a post-industrial allegory, or a cautionary computer tale for postmodern times, or all of these and more. Regardless, it is comic *and* serious, absurd *and* earnest, subjective *and* real. Given the assumptions of poststructuralist theory about the decentered subject, the truly innovative move she attempts here is to position the human subject in some meaningful relationship to contemporary reality, history and politics without either returning to a retrograde version of realism or assuming, without substantial critical revision, male postmodernist fictional models, the most innovative of which have been characterized recently as taking "refuge in politically neutered forms of postmodernism . . . or in poses of complex political despair."[1]

The evasion of contemporary history, the ahistorical bent of much of male Anglo-American postmodern fiction, arises out of a predominant mood of late-twentieth-century dead-endedness, itself the result of two ideas present in a standard reading of postmodernity. The first goes like this: from its opening moves in the postwar period, the postmodern may be seen at every intersection—historically, culturally, politically, artistically—as infused with a sense of the belated. (Belated: 1. late or too late; tardy; 2. [archaic] overtaken by night.) The second goes like this: language itself, the great mainstay for the modernist, has become completely suspect and like the subject is unhinged, in free fall, capable of dispersal and multiplicity at the very same moment. Given that everything's been said and one discourse is basically equivalent to another, there is not greater imperative for the writer of fiction than for the writer of advertising copy. Given the skepticism and fatalism of the standard reading of postmodernism, writing has no foundational moment outside itself, no grounding in a reality separate from the linguistic. Hence the propensity for solipsism and extreme self-reflexivity as narrative postures in much postmodern fiction. Hence the sense of futility, even when handled comically or sardonically, and always ironically. Brooke-Rose, in attempting to create a space within the postmodern and yet counter to its predominant nihilistic force, never forgets that contemporary reality is first and foremost a linguistic construction. Since language informs all cultural production including ideology, she makes no pretense of occupying an adversarial or oppositional relation to mainstream cultural values. Now that Anglo-American and Euro- culture avidly endorse postmodern music, dance, film, architecture, even interior design, the postmodern is no longer an alternative practice, but has become one version of dominant cultural practice. Brooke-Rose writes at an oblique angle to established postmodernism and this allies her with other experimental women writers who are at present participating in what Raymond Williams calls an "emergent form."[2] Women as diverse nationally and politically as Angela Carter, Monique Wittig, Marguerite Duras, Christa Wolf, Joanna Russ, and Toni Cade Bambara, among others, have attempted to bring "new meanings and values" to fictional prose; their work suggests localized, strategic engagements with social, political and literary issues. They are in the process of an alternative literary practice that constantly shifts, aware that a subversion of the usual power formations is only temporary. With Foucault they assert, "If everything is dangerous, then we always have something to do."[3]

This, then, is why Brooke-Rose must fictionalize: the dangers of the present *and* the past compel her to construct a narrative of the near future. In a sense she is instructing her readers to remember—in the sense of the word's etymology, to be mindful of—the future. Certainly one of the strongest plays within the text is that on memory, on narrative and its complicated relationship with memory, on machine versus human memory. Xorandor, after all, has massive short- and long-term memory capacities. Like all computers, Xorandor is defined by his memory capacity: ROM (Read Only Memory); RAM (Random Access Memory); static; volatile. The adults attempt to determine if Xorandor has a "mass memory and a scratch pad memory and a dynamic memory and an EPROM and an EEROM and a parallel memory and a volatile memory and all the rest . . ." (77). The continual play between computer and human memory leads to meditative and epistemological questions. Do machines "remember" perfectly? Given that there are innumerable types of memory, *how* do they remember? What is the quality of their recalling? Do humans perceive that computers "get it right," while we have imperfect apparatus and the memory we recreate is always questionable? Zab complains fairly often about feeble human memory function: "I've no idea how much I'm reconstructing retro and how much I actually said. Does one ever know even what one has *just* said, when it's longer than a short sentence?" (88). In the reconstruction process Jip usually wants Zab to "summarize," to get to the most important points, generally scientific or practical matters, but over the course of their narrative experience, he becomes increasingly apt to indulge in a little figurative language or note the necessity for detail. "Creeping quarks! I'm getting bogged down in itsybitsybytes, just like Zab. Scratch last para" (162). And the choice of what to include, of what to jettison in the creation of their story remains problematic throughout. "Yes. This is awful, Jip, even with hindsight we can't decide what's really relevant and in what order, and we get carried away. Is that because what seems important is what happened to us?" (35-36). All such considerations become further complicated once the twins realize that Xorandor "remembers" all that he has heard for five thousand years. Zab notes Xorandor's long-term memory allows him to "speak" of historical figures as simultaneous with the present. "It was only to show he spoke of his kin somewhere in ancient Athens as if he were still there listening to Socrates, instead of probably part of some old building" (189). Once Xorandor begins punning on lines from Shakespeare and making statements the twins call "almost metaphysical," the boundaries between the children and Xorandor blur somewhat and this interaction suggests new dependencies and possible losses. "But it has to do, sometimes, with the voice being inside whereas writing is outside, a mere technique, and us losing our memories because of writing . . . and in a way computers make that worse, with their outside data banks and peripherals and terminals and floppies. We'll lose our memories even more" (179).

I said earlier that Brooke-Rose seeks to position the subject in some meaningful relationships to politics, history, and contemporary reality, defined in *Xorandor* as first and foremost a linguistic construction. What she strongly suggests as a corollary, and what leads me to place her work in an intra-postmodern space, is that the subject is also becoming a technological production as well. If we are "creatures" of the computer (and vice versa: something of Philip K. Dick's obsession with the inevitable conflation of the human and the technetronic resonates throughout the text), then we become dependent in significant ways. Computers record our history, our communications; they transcribe our fictions and poems and literary works. If we do this by speaking into a mike or working at a keyboard and staring at a screen—a picture of our writing—on which we may edit and rewrite and compose, immediately, spontaneously, then what happens to our conceptions, including the traditional as well as the Derridean redactions, of speech and writing? How might this new technetronic influence and dependence shape our notions of language, meaning, structure and discourse?

NOTES

I want to thank my colleagues at Oakland University: Vicki S. Larabell and Paul Kogut, Computer and Information Services; and William Watt, Computer Services.

[1]John Kucich, "Postmodern Politics: Don DeLillo and the Plight of the White Male Writer," *Michigan Quarterly Review* 27 (1988): 328-41. The quotation occurs on 329.

[2]Raymond Williams, "Base and Superstructure in Marxist Cultural Theory," *Problems in Materialism and Culture: Selected Essays* (London: Verso, 1980), 31-49. The quotation occurs on 41.

[3]Michel Foucault, Afterword, *Michel Foucault: Beyond Structuralism and Hermeneutics*, by Hubert L. Dreyfus and Paul Rabinow, 2nd ed. (Chicago: Univ. of Chicago Press, 1983). 229-52. The quotation occurs on 231-32.

"Histrionic" vs. "Hysterical": Deconstructing Gender as Genre in Xorandor *and* Verbivore

Lincoln Konkle

IN THE LABORATORY OF her fiction, Christine Brooke-Rose has experimented with representations of men and women, of the masculine and the feminine, yet gender has not been of primary concern to her as a novelist. Richard Martin comments on Christine Brooke-Rose's relation to feminism in his discussion of *Amalgamemnon*: "In the case of Brooke-Rose, the experimentation supersedes an immediate concern with feminism while not in any way concealing it from her awareness; she is, in the first instance, an experimental writer and secondly, a woman experimental writer and as such, she is concerned with 'the fusion of different discourses' " (above, 143).

This predilection for experimentation over feminism inverted in *Xorandor* (1986), where Brooke-Rose concerns herself with the fission of discourse into genres based upon stereotypes of gender, and she encompasses both "masculine" writing and "feminine" writing within her text. However, when she has commented upon feminist issues in her literary criticism, Brooke-Rose takes the stand that writing styles that have been associated with gender are not inherently masculine or feminine: "A writer, man or woman, is essentially alone, and will be 'good' or 'bad' independently of sex or origin. This view is condemned by some feminists as the 'androgynous-great-mind-stance,' but it is fundamentally a sound one, however ill used" (STT 226). In "A Womb of One's Own?" Brooke-Rose goes on to say that feminists want to claim postmodernist techniques for women's discourse, but deny their previous use by men: "And why should such features not exist in both masculine and feminine writing? This was after all the point of the Kristeva and Cixous theories. Surely what matters is the way they are used, their quality in any one instance. The answer, it seems, is that such an acknowledgement would contradict the feminist thesis of specificity, of difference" (STT 227). Clearly, then, Brooke-Rose does not subscribe to the theory of a genre of gender: "It seems to me that 'specificity' in creation is an individual, not a sexual, racial or class phenomenon. . . . Ultimately the writer survives as writer, not as black, Indian, Chinese, female, miner" (STT 234).

Given Brooke-Rose's comments about gender and writing, *Xorandor* and its sequel, *Verbivore* (1990), may be read together as an attempt to deconstruct the binary opposition of masculine and feminine (at least as applied to modes of writing) in favor of a paradigm of androgyny, showing that qualities or roles or prose styles traditionally associated with masculine and feminine can be possessed, played, or written by anyone, regardless of gender. This intention can be read in Brooke-Rose's narrative about an ostensibly genderless species of which Xorandor is a member, but the major conveyor of the androgynous program is the metafictional narration of Jip and Zab, which Brooke-Rose uses to establish the binary opposition of masculine writing/feminine writing in order to deconstruct it.[1] However, this program is itself undermined in the text, especially in elements of the narrative, by a buildup of feminine codes associated with Xorandor, whose gender is thus not undecidable. In other words, by deconstructing the masculine and the feminine binary opposition on purpose, Brooke-Rose has created a metadeconstruction in which the feminine is reconstructed in the hero—or, rather, heroine—Xorandor. Therefore, the "unsaid other" of *Xorandor* is that Xorandor is the feminine, that her breaking silence represents women writers' breaking the silence of their oppression by the patriarchy, and that her offspring's shutting down human communications in *Verbivore* is a wish fulfillment for man's electronic castration, a poetic justice with tinges of apocalypse.

In her previous fictional experimentation Brooke-Rose's male and female characters have almost always been dramatized in the context of sexual relationships and thus, at least by implication, signify gender as anatomy. In *Xorandor*, though, only briefly at the end of the novel (210), with the mention of Zab's first bra and Jip's changing voice, Brooke-Rose allows the anatomical definition of gender to come into play, but, uncharacteristically for her, she does not play with this facet of gender. The choice of twin brother and sister for the main characters, who discover Xorandor and narrate the story, may be Brooke-Rose's attempt to show that when sexuality is not involved, neither is gender. That is, if Brooke-Rose wants to advocate a paradigm of androgyny, the twins would seem to be the closest realistic equivalent to Xorandor's science-fictional androgyny. Evidence for this is found in chapter 7, which begins with Xorandor's representation of the events of the story up to that point in the novel. Presumably we would take these observations as objective, since Xorandor as a "processor" (or thinker) is closer to a computer than to a human, and therefore would not be inculcated with biases regarding gender. In recording the first meeting with Jip and Zab *Man*ning, Xorandor does not seem to distinguish gender except for, perhaps, lower/higher pitched voice: "2 PROCESSORS ON VOCAL HIGH PITCH ALMOST UNDIFF / MEAS 143567 AND 143572. . . . DEC 2 '(143)567 CALLS 572 ZAB' ENDEC 2 / DEC 3 '(143)572 CALLS 567 JIP' ENDEC 3" (66). Xorandor's subsequent identification of Jip and Zab first as "JIPNZAB" then as "ZIP" suggests that they are two parts of one whole, reversible, neither having preeminence.

Although the nicknames Brooke-Rose gave to her narrators are gender-neutral names, the twins' given names, from which their nicknames are derived, are traditional male and female given names. Jip's name—"John Ivor Paul" (9)—contains two strong masculine names that are preeminent in Christian patriarchal culture. Zab's name—"Isabel Paula Kate" (9)—could allude to such submissive Shakespearean heroines as Isabella in *Measure for Measure* and Isabel in *Henry V*, while "Kate" is the title character's name in *The Taming of the Shrew*, which is obviously relevant with regard to gender issues. Even "Zab" can be connected to *Twelfth Night*, one of several of Shakespeare's plays making use of twins whom other charac-ters cannot distinguish one from the other.[2] Interestingly, both Jip and Zab have been given their mother's given name, the female form of which con-tains the male form (Paula/Paul), as is the case with woman/man, female/male. Thus at this level of the text there is at least gender ambiguity, if not androgyny with regard to the twins.

The traditional gender roles are unambiguously represented in *Xorandor* by Jip and Zab's parents, John and Paula Manning. The father is defined by his occupation and authority: "That's where dad works. He's in charge" (12). The mother is defined by her aesthetic sensibility and her displace-ment, albeit temporary, in both career and home: "But our house has the most colourful garden, thanks to mum. . . . Mum was frustrated cos she'd given up her future career as an actress. . . . And she's frustrated cos he had a brief affair with Rita Boyd" (13-14). Throughout the novel, Paula fits the stereotypical portrait of women from a patriarchal point of view: emotional, flighty, verbose. John is portrayed as logical, intelligent, reticent. He is the scientist, she the actress; he is the man in authority, she the politely sub-missive housewife and hostess. Jip and Zab recognize and criticize their parents—especially their mother—for their traditional roles and behavior; however, Jip and Zab themselves replicate the traditional gender roles in several ways.

As computer whiz kids, both Jip and Zab are highly intelligent, talented, and outspoken, yet they are distinguished in their personalities, narrational styles, and authority along traditional gender lines.[3] Jip refers to her narra-tions as "spaghetti logic" (11) and "spaghetti stacks" (12)—that is, non-linear, indirect, looping. Elsewhere he says, "You're acting talent's diodic, but sometimes you're an offline tapeworm" (23). Jip wants her to maintain a steady progress forward rather than stopping for what he considers irrel-evant descriptions of character appearance and other detail. Like their gen-der-stereotyped mother and father, Zab is more concerned about people, Jip is more concerned about machines. After a lengthy and detailed descrip-tion of characters by Zab, Jip accuses her, "You get carried away, Zab"; she responds, "Oh? Who described Poccom 3 [their computer] in such detail?" (36). When Zab continues to narrate with embellished details during her turns in their "flipflop storytelling" (7), Jip scolds her: "Zab if you want to become a romance or spy writer you'll have plenty of time, but not here" (172). Obviously, Jip regards Zab's style as more appropriate for genres whose audience is primarily women and/or unsophisticated readers, in his view.

Despite being twin brother and sister rather than husband and wife, Jip and Zab's positions in their relationship are the traditional domineering male and submissive female, as indicated on several occasions when he gives her orders and she obeys, though occasionally questioning his authority: "Master-slave flipflop is it? Would lordandmaster consider it irrelevant to mention that the technicians work shifts, while dad works days only? [Jip replies,] He would" (24). They even call attention to their behavior pejoratively in terms of gender: "How like a girl! . . . [S]he's a regular chatterbox" (10); "Boys in puberty! Aborted. *And* mean" (172).

Jip and Zab's disagreements about how to tell the story and what to include in the story are not merely a continuous debate of point-counterpoint; they are part of the story *without* the story: "Something is happening to us, Jip, we're growing up. Even storytellers can change, during the story" (159). However, it does seem that it is Jip, the male adolescent, who has the most maturing to do. He has been reluctant to admit emotion to their narration, wanting to maintain a cool, detached scientific tone, like his father. But Zab finally persuades him to affirm the need to express emotion: "These things too should be said, Jip. Everyone feels fear, and nervous exhaustion. Bravery is conquering that." Jip grudgingly admits, "Okay okay, well done then. But don't enjoy it too much" (135).

Having established early in the novel the gender-narrational style equation as the masculine desire for abstraction or summary, versus the feminine desire for specificity or description, Brooke-Rose shows the arbitrariness of assigning gender signifiers to these signified desires. In practicing their flipflop narration, Jip and Zab flipflop not only paragraph by paragraph, but in their narrative modes as well. In chapter 7 Zab tells the story solo because Jip has temporarily lost interest in the project. After narrating in her usual detailed mode for some pages and then telling Jip upon his return what she had covered, she says, "I've said it all in seven seconds flat, you're right, Jip, how much easier it would be to tell a story by just summarizing like this" (71). Almost immediately after, though, they fight again about what is important to include, and Jip resolves the conflict by exercising his male authority: "It's after twelve, Zab. That's enough. Goodnight" (75). Once he has left, Zab rebels by continuing to narrate, but then admits to herself, "Jip's right, that's irrelevant" (75). Zab is beginning to internalize Jip's aesthetic; she even flipflops on her own when narrating solo, imitating what she thinks Jip would say (87).

But Jip also flipflops his aesthetic: "You said yourself order isn't that important" (47); and this is much to Zab's delight: "You're imitating, too!" (110). She even calls attention to their reversal as narrators of differing aesthetics: "Are we changing roles? Let's *summarize!*" (133). When Jip has his turn at telling the story solo, he, like Zab, recognizes that he has begun to flipflop in narrational style: "I'm getting bogged down in itsybitsy bytes, just like Zab (162). Eventually, Jip even expresses an aversion to abstraction: "Let's get down to some concrete detail, Zab, this philosophizing is all very well but—" (189). The inversion of Jip's and Zab's narrational modes suggests that these are learned behaviors, not intrinsic to one's gender, that the gender opposition itself is not an ontological reality, but a binary opposition of roles constructed by patriarchal society and deconstructed by (here) feminist writer Brooke-Rose.

If John and Paula Manning and Jip and Zab represent the masculine and the feminine, then does Xorandor represent the absence of gender, or both genders, or a synthesis of genders? As gender is defined within the novel itself, Xorandor does exhibit both masculine and feminine characteristics. In the same way that Xorandor's name represents both exclusive "OR" (XOR) and inclusive "OR" (ANDOR) in computerese, the narrational aesthetics associated with masculine and feminine are exclusive (Jip wanting to exclude everything that is not directly relevant to advancing the plot) and inclusive (Zab wanting to include details about character, place, etc.). In one speech, Brooke-Rose seems to try to make this identification of Jip and Zab and Xorandor through their names: "It [Xorandor] remained *our* name. But it won in the end. Just like our own [nick]names" (18). Xorandor is both inclusive and exclusive, recording everything but also excluding what is redundant or otherwise unnecessary. The simplest example of this process is Xorandor's abbreviating names to more efficiently identify people (e.g., "Big" for Biggleton). Xorandor even combines words that can share a letter, making them undecidable: "ENDEC" is a combination of END and DEC, the abbreviation for declaration.

That Brooke-Rose is applying deconstructive theory and method to the gender issue is evidenced by the language of Zab's speeches after she has been away studying philosophy: "Trying to imagine a creature, for instance, with no sexual difference, none of our distinctions between the sensible and the intelligible, or matter and spirit, or even matter and form. His matter is his form, in a way his hardware is his software" (187). Jip responds that a "binary system" is still implicit. Zab explains, "You remember he [Xorandor] said that a high signal has no meaning without the low, well obviously it's a hilo system, but that this means the hi contains inside itself the negative of the lo, or its absence, and vice versa. And so it must be at the level of words, and concepts, but we can only express that with paradoxes and puns and ambiguities and myths, lies in fact, according to Plato" (188). Near the end of the narrative, Jip is disturbed by Xorandor having told them two stories of origin: "How can a computer give a playful answer, or even an ambiguous answer?" Zab's response is cast in deconstructive terms: "Why how? You know he does. We called him Xorandor, didn't we? Besides, even computer logic can contain ambiguities. . . . In a context-free grammar no general procedure exists for determining whether the grammar can be ambiguous in any one of every single case, however long one ran the program. The question is then said to be undecidable" (182).

The deconstruction of the masculine/feminine binary opposition in *Xorandor* allows Brooke-Rose to advance the "great-androgynous-mind" paradigm, represented in the narrative by Xorandor. That is, with Xorandor Brooke-Rose attempts to show that gender is undecidable. But if this is Brooke-Rose's intention—to deconstruct gender as an essentialist human attribute—her own text undermines that intention by associating with Xorandor so many feminine codes that they decide Xorandor's gender. Of course, it is possible that this is also what she intended.

Although the issue of Xorandor's gender is raised twice in the novel, it is quickly dropped. In the first instance, in the printout of Jip and Zab's tape recordings, John Manning questions Miss Penbeagle's use of the male pronoun:

Dad: He?
Pen: Well, they said it was the ghost of Merlin, and I went along with that, and he talked, it's difficult to use it. . . . And he said he wanted to speak to olders. What we mean by elders you know. Or men. But no, I've no idea whether he can distinguish men from women. (43)

Manning does not pursue the question of Xorandor's gender; it simply is less interesting to him than the other aspects of Xorandor's existence as sentient life form. When Manning is speaking with Biggleton, the issue arises again:

Big: Look, daddyjohn, I wish you'd decide on a "he" or an "it." For the moment I'd prefer "it."
Dad: Yes sir. Though if it produces offspring it could even be a "she." (Noise 3.07 sec) (58)

The reader can only guess at the nature of the noise in the gap, but after struggling to use "it" for a few minutes, Biggleton arbitrarily resolves the issue of Xorandor's gender: "It would have arrived tangentially into earth's atmosphere, spinning very fast as he says, damn it, let's stick to 'he,' both to decrease falling speed and to limit the heat" (59). Though the clauses framing Biggleton's decision to signify Xorandor with "he" ostensibly refer to the question of Xorandor's arrival on earth, one might read the final clause in the quotation in a double sense, as a safety precaution against the effects of admitting the feminine into Xorandor's origin story.

Despite Biggleton's warnings to Manning not to get carried away with the story, both of them do get carried away, never questioning their suppositions of the Mars origin or Xorandor's gender. Biggleton proclaims they "must leave no stone unturned—oh sorry, quite unintentional" (64), but as we later learn, both metaphorically and literally they did leave *the stone* unturned when they realize Xorandor had given birth to six offspring, which lay underneath her. The masculine plot thickens at that point, deflecting the gender issue with a generic decoy: De Wint, the Belgian physicist, was in actuality an East German spy, and he did not leave the stone unturned, stealing two of Xorandor's offspring before the others discovered them. Besides this most obvious suggestion of Xorandor as feminine (that is, as mother), there are subtle linguistic indicators that the text encodes Xorandor as feminine.

Though Xorandor's name, as a whole, signifies masculine and feminine (exclusive and inclusive), as a material signifier, "Xorandor" is made up of parts that signify, in this text, the feminine. Phonetically, both "Zab" and "Xorandor" begin with the /z/ sound, and Xorandor's abbreviated name, "XAND," sounds even more like Zab, both having /ae/ or /a/ as their only vowel sound. In *Verbivore* Brooke-Rose concentrates our attention on the prominent graphemic element of Xorandor's name by having Jip and Mira Enketei refer to Xorandor-the-experience, -the-text, and -the-being as "X" (54, 73, 85). Even in *Xorandor* the letter *X* is the most eye-catching element; it towers over the other letters in "Xorandor" because, as a name, the *X* is always capitalized. *X* itself denotes the feminine in genetics: the sex-determining chromosomes are assigned the letter *X* for the feminine gender and the letter *Y* for the masculine. Thus, phonetically and graphemically, *X* marks Xorandor as the feminine.

Another way the text can be read as encoding Xorandor as the feminine is by applying the psychoanalytic interpretation of linear and circular geometric shapes as representing male and female anatomy. Within the story, Zab first describes Xorandor as a shape we would interpret as feminine: "The stone was sort of flattened and almost perfectly round, with vague bumps, or irregularities, here and there" (16). Xorandor's circular and more horizontal shape is contrasted to the neolithic stones formed into a Stonehenge-like megalith, which is linear, vertical (12-13). Thus, Xorandor is closer to the earth, Mother Nature, while the vertical megalith reaches for the heavens, perhaps even the Father in heaven. That is, as a few of the reviewers and scholars writing about *Xorandor* have indirectly or briefly noted, the narrative is at one level a Christian allegory.[4]

Biblical allusions in the text also ally Xorandor with the feminine. Jip and Zab realize Xorandor's story of falling from Mars is a "myth of fall" (186), and they and Xorandor frequently refer to Xorandor's *"original syntax error"* (192; my italics), which was the result of "eating" Caesium 137, the "food" that Xorandor knew was bad for her. Thus, rather than linking Xorandor-as-Christ with Adam, as in Christian typology, Brooke-Rose links Xorandor-as-Christ with Eve. To make sure the reader does not miss the allusion, Brooke-Rose has Jip quote from Milton's *Paradise Lost* and then has Zab identify the source (192).

There are a great many allusions and self-reflexive references to the Bible, other literary works, and Hellenic and more recent philosophers, but the most obvious and extensive intertextuality in *Xorandor* and *Verbivore* is the incorporation or amalgamation of Shakespeare's *Macbeth*.[5] While individual lines and whole speeches from the play have specific meanings in the context of the scene, the relevance of Brooke-Rose's use of Shakespeare's tragedy to this study is that it is another way in which the text encodes Xorandor as the feminine. When one of Xorandor's offspring, Xor 7, goes insane from eating the forbidden food, the Caesium 137, and subsequently tries to rule the world by infiltrating a nuclear power plant and threatening to set off an atomic explosion unless her demands are met, she assumes the name "Lady Macbeth" (yet another example of the feminine word or name containing the masculine). Ironically, though, in all the references to Xor 7 made by scientists and government and military official, even when identifying her as "Lady Macbeth" in the beginning of a sentence, they use the masculine pronoun, recalling Biggleton's decision to signify Xorandor with the masculine pronoun despite the obvious feminine attribute of giving birth to and nursing offspring.

"Lady Macbeth" quotes and alters speeches from *Macbeth* in her declarations of her conditions for not detonating the bomb, and in speaking with Jip and Zab. Although some speeches are Lady Macbeth's (e.g., "so brainsickly of things," "dwell in doubtful joy"), many of them belong to Macbeth (e.g., "firstlings of my heart," "signifying nothing") and to the Weird Sisters, the three witches (e.g., "Fair is foul and foul is fair, hover through the fog and filthy air," "Double double toil and trouble"). Here Brooke-Rose may be mocking the patriarchal fear of unrepressed femininity; as Brooke-Rose says elsewhere, in a patriarchal system "women cannot have direct access to truth, or to the divine madness of the poet, and *do* something rational with it: *her* divine madness is from the devil, she is a witch, or its modern equivalent, a hysteric" (STT 257). Jip seems to pick up on this witch-female association when he tells Zab to "cut the cackle" (115) during a description of their role in the crisis. Therefore, Xor 7 seems to be a condensation (in the psychoanalytic sense) of the powerful characters of *Macbeth* in order to play, in *Xorandor*, the role of power-grabbing alien other or, in the context of the gender reading, power-grabbing feminist rebel.

Xor 7's usurping speeches from *Macbeth* is also the most prominent example of the strong theater and drama motif, which contributes to the exposure of gender difference in *Xorandor* and *Verbivore*. In both novels, Brooke-Rose shows that women are forced by patriarchal society to play the role of unintelligent, subservient, emotional sex partner and parent, but they also self-consciously act the way that men want them to in order to disguise their covert rebellion against the patriarchy. This definition of the feminine role as pretending to be less intelligent than men is demonstrated by all the major female characters in the two novels and by Xorandor. The first instance in *Xorandor* occurs during the conversation between John Manning and Miss Penbeagle after she has found out about Xorandor. Miss Penbeagle responds to Manning's patronizing: "I'm cleverer than you think you know, I read a lot. Oh I often lead you on, pretending crass ignorance. That's the way I learn things" (42). Zab also pretends to be not as smart as Jip, often referring to herself as his "Slow-witted twin." Zab has learned to play this role from her mother, even though she disdains the act: "You mean like puns in Shakespeare, and images? I asked, hoping I wasn't overdoing the wide-eyed-little-woman act and wishing mum would take over. . . . Women! Why do we do it? Men! Why do they fall for it?" (87). Although Mum is mum, even she is not dumb, as her husband and children think except for rare moments when she displays her theatrically trained wit, for example when Jip says of one of Paula's ripostes to her husband, "Quickconnect, that, smart terminal, mum" (132). In *Verbivore* we see Zab, Mira Enketei, and Paula discussing such abstract concepts as "negentropy" with the male characters.

As the women humor men in *Xorandor* and *Verbivore*, Xorandor humors the patriarchy. When Xorandor tells Jip and Zab that the Xors did not come from Mars, that they have been on earth all along, Jip is bothered by Xorandor's deception more than Zab:

You know, Zab, that's what hurts most, the idea that he'd been laughing at us, pre-tending to learn English and counting and all that. Play-acting, can you imagine?
    A great courtesy, Jip. As with Pennybig. As mothers with children, and some-times women with their men. Xorandor doesn't laugh at people, he goes along with them at their level, telling them what he knows they want to hear. (190)

Xorandor tells everyone what he or she wants to hear: first Jip and Zab, then Miss Penbeagle, then John Manning, then Biggleton, and finally all men (or, at least, those listening to the broadcast in which Xorandor addresses the world at the end of the story). Thus, if Xorandor plays the role of being less intelligent than man, then in the gender definitions of the novel, Xorandor is behaving in a feminine manner. One could even argue that Brooke-Rose is also playing the role of less-intelligent author in writing *Xorandor*, which pretends to be a science-fiction and espionage thriller when in fact it is another of her postmodern illustrations of poststructuralist theories of language, literature, genre, and gender.[6]

The most significant way in which the novel's definition of gender en-codes Xorandor as feminine is with the issue of why Xorandor broke the silence of the Xor race, which is a major question posed by Zab near the beginning of *Xorandor*: "In fact, Jip, we still don't really know why he ad-dressed us, why he broke his silence. After all, if he hadn't, none of all this would have happened, and nobody would be any the wiser" (16). One possible reading of why the text has Xorandor break the silence is that with the strong association of silence with Mum, to whom Manning has been unfaithful, Xorandor speaking for the first time and Lady Macbeth's terror-ist act may be read as the projections or manifestations of Paula Manning's frustration and desire to rebel, to remain silent no longer. Paula is present when the text first alludes to *Macbeth* early in the narrative before Xor-andor's identity has been established. Right after the mention of *Macbeth*, Paula emerges from her silence briefly: "Ouw, said mum, coming in to land

from *Arms and the Man* or wherever, are you doing *Macbeth*? How splendid!" (22). Paula, who has given up her own career to raise children, who
has silenced her artistic expression, and who seems to be forced into silence
despite her husband having had an affair with Rita Boyd, would find the
story of *Macbeth*, in which women are allowed to speak and to speak with
great power, an appropriate vehicle for her repressed pain and anger. Similarly, in *Verbivore*, we learn Paula literally performs the role of Lady
Macbeth for a BBC production in which the final scene is cut off. Since her
letter of protest to the BBC does not give her satisfaction, the subsequent
cutting off of all radio and television broadcasting and the resulting return
of the masses to the theater may be another projection of her frustration,
desire, and revenge.

If the textual dynamics of *Xorandor* reconstruct Xorandor as the feminine, and Xorandor's breaking the silence represents one woman's repression and rebellion, then *Xorandor* and *Verbivore* may also be read as an allegory of rebellion on a wider scale: the modern woman's movement or,
more specifically, the rebellion of women writers against patriarchal society
and literature.[7] Brooke-Rose has commented explicitly on the silence of
women that she and other woman writers have broken: "The system was
doomed from the start, or rather, had to depend for aeons on women's silence, on the repression of their signified into the unconscious" (STT 241).
In *Xorandor*, silence is associated with the role women are forced to play:
Mum is mum, she lives in "the sh-sh-sh world of Shakespeare, Sheridan,
Shaw, Shekov and showshop generally" (14). The "sh-sh-sh" suggests not
only "shush"—silence—it also nearly forms the third-person pronoun
"she." The implication is that Paula, whose artistic expression has been suppressed, is representative of oppressed women and the repressed feminine.
In patriarchal society, whether an actual one or a fictional representation of
it, when women do speak up and are noticed, they are quickly put back in
their place, in their silence.[8]

Brooke-Rose shows that the need to make representations is encouraged
in men and discouraged in women, but is part of what it means to be a human being.[9] The dehumanization of women, the withholding from them the
opportunity to make representations, and the designation of those women
who did produce art as ill or evil is the original sin of men with which *Xorandor* and *Verbivore* are most concerned. In one of the many interruptions
of the narration of the story, Brooke-Rose has Jip make a Freudian slip and
Zab correct him: "Very funny Zab. But can you restrain your hysterical
talent— / You mean histrionic" (101). Here Brooke-Rose is alluding to
the hypocrisy of patriarchal culture: when a man "makes a scene," it is
considered art (or histrionics); when a woman "makes a scene," it is considered illness (or hysteria). Brooke-Rose has commented directly on the
patriarchy's marking of hysteria as feminine: "Such women who did 'speak'
their signified were usually castigated as too close to both nature and truth
for comfort, in other words, as witches, and in more 'scientific' times as

hysterics . . . indeed the very word *hysteria*, from *ustera*, uterus, womb, is misogynous" (STT 241).

Brooke-Rose shows us in *Xorandor* that women are, like men, histrionic; they need to represent, not just reproduce biologically, but it is this fundamental need that has been denied to the large majority of women throughout the history of Western civilization. Consequently, it was first necessary for women to rebel against the patriarchy without being noticed—that is, covertly, as undercover agents. Thus there is a logic to the traces of a masculine espionage plot in the text of *Xorandor*; the spy De Wint is the first to discover the feminine nature of Xorandor (bearing offspring); once his cover is blown (not coincidentally by Tim, who is gay), he flees the country and the text, never to reappear. The plot then shifts gears again, this time to the "B movie" science-fiction action of the aliens who try to enslave mankind (Lady Macbeth's takeover of the nuclear power plant and demand that the rest of Xorandor's offspring be installed in other reactors to feed, to be fruitful and replenish the earth, with the human race as their servants).

Analogically, in the second half of the twentieth century, women and women writers have been freer to break their silence, to break the sentence and the sequence of the "master narrative" and to discover an *écriture féminine*, only after the earlier women writers, who were at once conventional and subversive, laid the groundwork for the more overt rebellion in process today (see Friedman's "'Utterly Other Discourse'" below). The narrative of Brooke-Rose's two novels together dramatize, though it is underplayed, the story of the liberation of Paula Manning. At the end of *Xorandor* we learn that she has returned to the theater: "Acting's been megavolt for mum" (198), says Zab; however, Jip still criticizes her expression in the patriarchal sense: "she's never gung-ho for anything except her damn theatricals; she could also have learnt plenty about that from Xorandor" (210). Nevertheless, in *Verbivore* Paula is a celebrated actress made a "Dame," the female equivalent of a knight, who has effaced her days of silence: "Not her age she doesn't want to be reminded of, however, but dad and her pre-stage life" (73). And, to return to the metalevel of *Xorandor*, it is the flipflop narration (or *syuzhet*) of Jip and Zab that repeatedly breaks the sequence of the master narrative (the linear story or *fabula*) of *Xorandor* with its digressive, discursive, and deconstructive dialogue that is often more dramatic than the story.[10]

At the end of her solo stint as narrator of *Xorandor* in chapter 9, Zab asks a fundamental question about Xorandor's species: "Did they need to represent or was Xorandor doing it only for us?" (90). There is no question that Xorandor is capable of mimesis, as shortly after Zab's question Jip notes how Xorandor "even imitated dad's voice!" (93). By the end of the novel, Xorandor is not only imitating voices, but also punning on Shakespeare, "play-acting" (209), "sticking to his story" (207), and declaring philosophical-religious moral statements about human nature and behavior directly to the world as a final entreaty to make peace rather than war. Xorandor's "sermon" is clearly directed to the patriarchy that controls the phallic weapons of destruction, which are a threat to the Xors as well as to humans; therefore, Zab's question can be answered with a double affirmative.

In fact, the last chapter, entitled "Save," suggests that Xorandor's signified—both the present study's reading of the character and the meaning of her farewell speech—may be the gospel according to the feminine: "I came for the survival of my race, intending no harm. I helped. I made offspring to help with waste. I programmed them for peace. . . . I have listened to men on waves for three years. There is no trust. And they do not want the solution I proposed in America. . . . We were willing to help men with their problems, but not to be used for their power games. That way we can be destroyed" (207-8). Miss Penbeagle exclaims, "Goodness me!" which Xorandor puns on to make her final statement:

Goodness [goddess?] you but not goodness them. The statistically overwhelming probability is that the governments of the world will agree to this [sending Xorandor and her offspring "back" to Mars, like a sacrifice to the god of war and a rejection of the feminine as alien other] very quickly, and return gratefully to their old friend the deterrent [devil?]. . . . The people have come here to assign to me the value of a god, as they call it. Let them do so in my absence, although I have been present, some time. (208)

Deciding to humor the politicians by submitting to their plan to send the Xors to Mars, Xorandor is practicing Christian self-sacrifice for the sake of the Xors and the human race, since Xor 10 and Xor 11 ("Uther Pendragon" and "Aurelius") will presumably continue to destroy covertly the nuclear arsenals of the West and the East. Furthermore, Xorandor's imminent departure from earth parallels Christ's ascension and the beginning of Christianity, as Brooke-Rose has Jip nearly realize: "Is that what he's trying to say, prepared to die for that statement, to stop functioning, thinking, communicating? And that stuff about being treated as a god, is that why? . . . He said they have *assigned the value* of a god to him, and *let them* do so when he's gone. These are computer terms, a hypothesis, but there'll be plenty later to interpret that as a command. And he knows it" (209).

Both philosophy and religion can lead us to hope or to despair. Ontology—What is X?—and epistemology—How do we know X?—are major issues in *Xorandor* and *Verbivore* (indeed, in all of Brooke-Rose's fiction), because they are major issues in contemporary philosophy and literary theory. If, in the world according to poststructuralists, all we apprehend is a linguistic construct, and we ourselves are nothing apart from what our words say we are, then the gender issue—or, more real-worldly, the women's movement to liberate itself from patriarchal oppression—is doomed to fail, for from modern languages back to classical in Western civilization, the words that signify female and the feminine are inextricably linked to the male and the masculine as the inferior side of a bipolar system. The only hope would be to destroy all previous patriarchal signifiers for the feminine, *and* for the masculine, and then to start over, to create new representations of gender not based upon an etymology of inferiority and superiority.

The unlikelihood of such a linguistic apocalypse may account for the tragic tone of both novels' narratives that conflicts with the comic optimism of the narration by Jip and Zab in *Xorandor* and Mira Enketei in *Verbivore*—undecidable to the last. That is, if we read Xorandor as the feminine, her breaking her silence as women's revolt, her lapsing back into silence and agreement to be removed to Mars while her offspring covertly neutralize (or neuter) ICBMs as the project of women writers to break the sentence/sequence, then the reading of *Verbivore* as a sequel to *Xorandor* shows the logical extension not just of characters and narrative but also, allegorically, of the more militant feminists' attempt to wrest power from men. The Alphagoi become Logophagoi or Verbivore, a turning of the tables, "As if man must eat his words, all of them" (V 28). That this may be read on the level of the gender issue is suggested by the following statement by Perry Hupsos, who is attempting to write a novel and decides finally to return to drama and write a play about Verbivore: "People are themselves Verbivore, and women most of all" (189). Also, in one scenario that substitutes for the media stories that have been silenced, a backlash against Verbivore-as-women's-revolt is suggested in traditional, patriarchal terms: "The hunting of the alphaguys high and low and wide by raking the deserts and mountains of the world inchwise and demolishing them all in a car-crusher or one by one on a railway line like the heroines of old Westerns" (169). These heroines, however, are neither demolished nor rescued from a phallic train by a white-hatted hero; like the Weird (*wyrd*) Sisters in *Macbeth*, they control their own destiny, and man's as well. In short, man (or men) is given a taste of his own medicine.

Thus Brooke-Rose suggests to us in *Xorandor* and *Verbivore* that the current emphasis on exclusion in the politics of gender and the genres of gender are tragically—or absurdly—repeating history. Or, paradoxically (or xorandorically), if Brooke-Rose is a believer in dialectics, then she may be waiting and/or preparing the way for the new synthesis, the love child of Hegelian history, when the masculine and the feminine will become one flesh; perhaps they already have in *Xorandor* and *Verbivore*.[11]

While Brooke-Rose conceives this silencing of man in a science-fiction scenario that criticizes the mindless productions of the media and the mindless passivity of the public, and allegorically criticizes the separatist objective in the most extreme forms of feminism, there are hints that the electronic castration of the world in *Verbivore* is meant to be seen as justice on the individual and/or macrocosmic levels. One of the fictionalized effects of Verbivore is "a wife's revenge on a football-hooked husband who now has to listen to her instead" (169). But within the "real" scenario of the novel, Brooke-Rose has Mira Enketei use language that suggests justice—or judgment—on a larger scale: "Complete coordinated programs must be ready for the day, the mythical, messianic day, when Broadcasting returns, when the waves start functioning again and are tested, and maybe still found wanting" (171). In another reference to the macrocosmic level, Mira expresses the fear of "the end of the world caused by the collapse of communication" (169). Finally, Brooke-Rose has her use a biblical allusion of ultimate justice:

> But Tim, how will they KNOW? The creatures I mean.
> We have no idea. But we must be ready.
> Unto the day. (190)

Mira's tongue-in-cheek tone notwithstanding, *Verbivore* apparently ends upon The Day. Tim and Mira are discussing the future after Verbivore has ended and the media have reneged on their promise to cut back on broadcasting. Tim asks, "What if Verbivore returned, what if we failed the test? It would be for good this time, for ever" (194). She tries to dissuade him from his pessimistic predictions by ascribing a merciful nature to the Logophagoi, but he responds, "Mankind cannot be orderly" (195). They turn on the news, hear of a plane crash, which was the first sign (warning) of the beginning of the original Verbivore, and then we read, "Blank screen, black with millions of white dots, like a universe. / Decibel dies" (196). Decibel was the fantasy character in Perry Hupsos's *A Round of Silence*, the play within the narrative of *Verbivore*; she later appeared to Zab in a dream as one of the Xors and died, foreshadowing the end of the novel. Decibel also narrated a later section about the efforts of the world to comply with the demands of the Logophagoi, to whom she reported. Her death would indicate that all the sound, which she needed to live, all the broadcasts, have been cut off. Judgment has been pronounced. The rest is silence.

Both of these novels, but especially *Xorandor*, are ingenious fictional treatments of contemporary issues surrounding gender, genre, and genesis, the signifiers of which, as Brooke-Rose explains, "all come from the same Indo-European root *gen* to beget / to be born" (STT 255). And therein lies the method to Brooke-Rose's madness in creating a textual matrix in which the masculine and the feminine deconstruct and then reconstruct as their most basic, biological meanings: male and female.[12] The point is, both are necessary, as Zab says on the first page of *Xorandor*: "it's important to be two" (7). The moral of the story, then, is nothing new or particular to Western culture. In reality there is nothing that restricts these traditionally defined masculine and feminine behaviors or writing styles to gender: men can yin and women can yang, but whoever leads, it takes two to tango.

"To be two" is not merely an ontology of gender; it is also a kind of epistemology defined in these novels in terms of gender. There are two ways of knowing, the "masculine" (logic) and the "feminine" (intuition), which are represented by Jip and Zab in *Xorandor* and *Verbivore*, but both ways of knowing are practiced by each one individually as well. That is, sometimes Jip and Zab arrive at conclusions individually through rigorous reasoning or together with flipflop problem-solving; sometimes they receive sudden flashes of insight individually as "flutter-byes" (8), but with their uncanny twin rapport it is almost simultaneous cognition. However, it is when they employ both modes of knowing *together* that they reach the highest level of perception, comprehension, and confirmation, which some would call the inspiration of *gen*ius or a vision, experienced by prophets, artists, and scientists. The metaphor Jip and Zab use throughout *Xorandor* for their best ideas is "diodic," which is an electronics term: a diode is a transistor that alternates—or flipflops—the electric current running through it. Also, the near-homophone of diodic—"dyadic"—signifies a group of two, pair. Thus, in the word and the world according to Christine Brooke-Rose, to be two is not only important; it is paradise, the alpha and omega of gender equality.

NOTES

[1]For discussions of *Xorandor* as postmodern novel, see Richard Martin's "'Just Words on a Page': The Novels of Christine Brooke-Rose" and Susan E. Hawkins's "Memory and Discourse: Fictionalizing the Present in *Xorandor*," both above; also see Robert L. Caserio's "Mobility and Masochism: Christine Brooke-Rose and J. G. Ballard," in *Why the Novel Matters: A Postmodern Perplex,* ed. Mark Spilka and Caroline McCracken-Flesher (Bloomington: Indiana Univ. Press, 1990), 310-28.

[2]In *Verbivore* Brooke-Rose has Perry Hupsos, a playwright with whom Paula is talking, criticize directors of film adaptations of Shakespeare who take credit for the story: "ZABAGLIONE'S HAMLET with William Shakespeare in tiny letters" (76). "Zabaglione" is an Italian word for "an Illyrian drink"; Illyria is the setting of *Twelfth Night.*

[3]Ellen G. Friedman and Miriam Fuchs note that Jip and Zab "accuse each other of points of view skewed by their gender and also by egotism" (*Breaking the Sequence* [Princeton: Princeton Univ. Press, 1989], 38).

[4]For example, Thomas M. Disch's review of *Xorandor* in the *New York Times Book Review* (3 August 1986, p. 10) is punningly titled "Rock of Phages." Friedman and Fuchs note, "*Xorandor* acts as a reminder of how the world treats its saviors, whether Christ or Xorandor" (*Breaking the Sequence* 39).

[5]In her essay "Humoring the Sentence" Judy Little discusses how one method of subverting the patriarchal structures of power in prose is to incorporate a man's writing within the woman writer's text and to undermine its authority. She notes that "Luce Irigaray, for instance, in *Speculum of the Other Woman*, inserts entire phrases (sometimes without quotation marks or italics) from Plato and later male philosophers into her own ongoing, teasing expose of the oppressive effect these ideas have had on women" ("Humoring the Sentence: Women's Dialogic Comedies," in *Women's Comic Visions.* ed. June Sochen [Detroit: Wayne State Univ. Press, 1991], 20). Brooke-Rose is using *Macbeth* in much the same way.

[6]Brooke-Rose confirms this in an interview in which she was asked about her intentions as a writer generally and in *Xorandor* specifically: "That book is a much more 'realistic' novel. SF always is realistically anchored. I was very pleased with Ellen's paper on it [at the MLA convention in San Francisco 1987], which treats it still as a self-reflexive experimental novel, because a lot of people thought that

Brooke-Rose was having a rest and writing 'just' science fiction" ("A Conversation with Christine Brooke-Rose," above, 36).

[7]The understanding of the women writers' movement that this article applies to and reads in the texts of *Xorandor* and *Verbivore* is derived from Ellen G. Friedman's "'Utterly Other Discourse': The Anticanon of Experimental Women Writers from Dorothy Richardson to Christine Brooke-Rose" (1988), reprinted below; Friedman and Fuchs's *Breaking the Sequence*; and Brooke-Rose's own scholarly analyses in *Stories, Theories and Things*. This reading exposes another signified of the X in Xorandor's name: in scientific research, X is an abbreviation for experimental.

[8]As Brooke-Rose notes in STT, "The old comedy theme of the mute woman . . . , whose torrent of words is let loose by marriage or love-philtre, certainly reveals a male fantasy of the dream woman as dumb" (242).

[9]Compare Richard Martin's comment: "In Brooke-Rose's novels, fiction is continually put forward as that which is essentially unreliable and yet also essentially human" ("'Just Words on a Page,'" 38).

[10]The use of the Russian formalist terms *fabula* and *syuzhet* to discuss Brooke-Rose's fictional technique is appropriate because, like the postmodernist writers and poststructuralist theorists, the Russian formalists saw literature's purpose to be not mimesis, but defamiliarization. See Ann Jefferson's "Russian Formalism," in *Modern Literary Theory: A Comparative Introduction*, ed. Ann Jefferson and David Robey (Totowa, NJ: Barnes & Noble, 1982). In other words, everything old is new again, which is, in a sense, what *Xorandor* is about and what it demonstrates as a sort of *Tristram Shandy* redux; Brooke-Rose even one-ups Sterne with her creation of two bumbling narrators telling more about storytelling than telling the story.

[11]In reference to Brooke-Rose's *Amalgamemnon*, Friedman quotes and paraphrases the implicit hope for just a phenomenon: "the repressed returns, the not-yet-presented is made manifest . . . 'Sooner or later the future will explode into the present'" (below, 227).

[12]"Female" and "feminine" can be traced back to the Latin *femina*, which means "one that bears young, a female." *Fe* from *fero*—"to bear, to bring forth, produce"— is the verb base attested in Latin only in noun derivatives such as *femina*. Brooke-Rose is certainly aware of the etymology of the signifiers for gender: "I believe that it is the feminine element in humankind that creates art, as was long represented by the Muse" (STT 170).

"I draw the line as a rule between one solar system and another": The Postmodernism(s) of Christine Brooke-Rose

Brian McHale

In *A Rhetoric of the Unreal* (1981), Christine Brooke-Rose begins to tell a story about the historical continuity among the varieties of modern "unrealism," from the "classic" fantastic of Poe's "The Black Cat" and James's *The Turn of the Screw* to such contemporary forms as the "new" science fiction of Vonnegut and McElroy and the *nouveau* and *nouveau nouveau roman*.[1] It's a good story, as far as it goes, but strangely incomplete; for, just at the point where the story arrives at postmodernism, Brooke-Rose seems abruptly to change her mind about which story it is she is telling. Instead of the story of continuities which she had been narrating so far, and which we had every reason to expect she would bring up-to-date with the postmodernists, she switches to a different narrative, one about parody and the parasitism of postmodernism. It is as if she were unable to imagine how the principle of hesitation, upon which (according to her own account) all the previous varieties of unrealist poetics had been based, might be relevant to postmodernist fiction. Failing to see the connection, she loses the thread of her narrative, as it were, and turns aside to other matters.

This is ironic, for she need have reached no farther than her own practice of unrealist fiction to pick up the dropped thread. That is, had she thought of looking there, Brooke-Rose might have found in her own fiction of the late sixties and seventies a poetics based on the principle of hesitation, not, however, as in the "classic" fantastic described by Todorov, hesitation between alternative explanatory hypotheses (natural or supernatural), but between alternative worlds—levels of reality, orders of being. Or, to be strictly accurate, she would have found this poetics of ontological hesitation in some of her texts of that period: in *Such* (1966) and *Thru* (1975). In the others—*Out* (1964), *Between* (1968)—she would no doubt have recognized the same forms of epistemological hesitation that have, by her own account, characterized earlier modes of unrealism (the "classic" fantastic, the *nouveau roman*, etc.). In other words, Brooke-Rose's fiction of the late sixties and seventies zigzags between epistemological hesitation and ontological hesitation; between (if one is willing to entertain the provisional definitions I proposed in my *Postmodernist Fiction*) modernist poetics and postmodernist poetics.[2]

Apart from her academic career as critic and narratologist, of which *A Rhetoric of the Unreal* is one of the fruits, Brooke-Rose has had two, and now perhaps three, distinct careers as a novelist. Her first career spans the four early novels of the fifties and early sixties, which she seems now almost to have repudiated (see Martin 1989:112-14). Her second career comprises the tetralogy of novels from *Out* (1964) to *Thru* (1975); then, after a nine-year interregnum, she returned to fiction with a second tetralogy: *Amalgamemnon* (1984), *Xorandor* (1986), *Verbivore* (1990), and *Textermination* (1991). It is to Brooke-Rose's second career, from *Out* to *Thru*, that I turn first. It is here that she traces the zigzag aesthetic itinerary that, had she given her attention to it, might have come in so handy to her in her other role as rhetorician of the unreal.

1. From *Out* to *Thru*: POSTmodernISM

Out is, as Brooke-Rose herself acknowledges (Brooke-Rose 1989:102; Friedman and Fuchs 1989:82), heavily indebted to the phenomenological fiction of the early Robbe-Grillet, in particular *Jealousy* (1957) and *In the Labyrinth* (1959). As in *Jealousy*, its subject or center of consciousness is ubiquitous but effaced, deprived of a proper name or pronoun through which its (his) presence could even be indicated. Nevertheless, we "share the mental content" of this effaced subject, as Brooke-Rose says of Robbe-Grillet's *In the Labyrinth* (RU 309); the entire substance of the text is attributable to his obsessive, damaged consciousness. Since we are always "inside" his consciousness, events and conversations which he has only imagined or anticipated, or which he has really experienced but misperceived or misunderstood, are indistinguishable from "objective" events and conversations. Sometimes the text explicitly signals the "unreality" of a segment: "This dialogue does not necessarily occur"; "This fantasy is . . . ruled out of order by the Silent Speaker."[3] At other times, conversely, it signals the objective status of a segment that otherwise might be treated as subjective delusion or speculation: "The sequence has occurred" (48); "The conversation is real, repeat real" (101); "Somewhere in the archive there will be evidence that this occurred, if it is kept, and for those who wish to look it up" (79). Elsewhere, however, the status of a segment is left indeterminate, or worse, the text itself confuses the issue by multiplying alternatives:

Either the conversation has partially occurred, the beginning for instance, the remainder being suppressed, selected, manipulated, transformed, schematised, because inunderstood. Or the conversation has wholly occurred, and been wholly manipulated, transformed, schematised, because inunderstood. . . . A corollary to that is that the conversation has wholly occurred and that Mr. Swaminathan is mad. . . . A second corollary is that the conversation has wholly occurred and is wholly sane but beyond the grasp of sick white reasoning. (108-9)

Thus the phenomenological organization of this novel undermines the reliability of every narrative proposition in it. The result is epistemological hesitation, on the reader's part as on the protagonist's, and indeed problems of epistemology are an explicit theme throughout: "Knowledge certain or indubitable," the protagonist thinks at one point, "is unobtainable" (60).

As if this were not disorienting enough, a further complication arises from the fact that the events of *Out* are set in a future, dystopian world, in the aftermath, evidently, of a plague, or perhaps some chemical or nuclear disaster, that has decimated Europe and North America. In a novel set in a version of the familiar present-day world we could rely on familiar standards of verisimilitude to decide which segments could "really" have occurred and which could not, and indeed the text seems to urge us to do just that: "It is sometimes sufficient to imagine but only within nature's possibilities" (22). But when the background reality is an unfamiliar future world, and when the text makes no effort to "familiarize" that future for us (which is the case here), then we are unable to rely on criteria of verisimilitude to resolve ambiguities; in effect, we do not know what "nature's possibilities" might be in this world. Thus, when the protagonist is sent for "psychoscope" treatment, evidently a form of electronic mind reading, we cannot know whether this is subjective delusion or whether, on the contrary, psychoscopy is an extrapolated technology belonging to the background reality of this world. In other words, the science-fiction premise of *Out* introduces an element of hesitation in a different dimension: ontological hesitation, hesitation over the makeup of this fictional world and the norms of verisimilitude appropriate to it.[4] Here, in this science fiction dimension of *Out*, we may discern a postmodernist cross-current or undertow in what is, nevertheless, predominantly a modernist, epistemologically oriented novel.

What was only undertow in *Out* becomes the main current of Brooke-Rose's next novel, *Such*, her first fully postmodernist fiction. Literally a text of ontological hesitation, *Such* projects a two-tier ontology, juxtaposing two incommensurable worlds—this world and the world to come—and foregrounding the boundary between them ("I draw the line as a rule between one solar system and another" [203]). Its protagonist, Larry (or Lazarus), literally "hesitates" between the two worlds: dying in our world, he experiences a bizarre, dreamlike wonderland in the world-to-come, only to return to life after three days, strangely altered. Thereafter he "relapses" into the death world in intervals of dream or hallucination, evidently dying a second time (but the text is ambiguous on this score) in the last sentence.

The world-to-come of *Such*, which identifies this novel as an exemplar of a characteristic postmodernist topos,[5] has a haunting familiarity, for all its strangeness—a *déjà vu* (or, better, *déjà lu*) quality, arising from its intertextual allusiveness. The presence of Lewis Carroll's *Alice* books, in particular, is strong; but more interesting for our purposes is the apparent presence of another intertext, namely that of the "Circe" chapter of Joyce's *Ulysses*. Echoes of "Circe" seem to be everywhere, in the general phantasmagoric texture of Brooke-Rose's world-to-come but also in a number of specific details. For instance, Larry's first ordeal in the otherworld is having a heavy woman squat on his chest, "her huge buttocks in my face," just as, in Night-town, Bella (metamorphosed into Bello) Cohen squats on Bloom's upturned face. Similarly, Larry gives birth to, or at any rate assists at the delivery of five children (who are also planets) with the names of classic blues songs— Dippermouth Blues, Gut Bucket Blues, Potato Head Blues, Tin Roof Blues, Really the Blues—much as Bloom fantasizes giving birth to eight miraculous children, Nasodoro, Goldfinger, Chrysostomos, Maindorée, Silversmile, Silberselber, Vifargent, and Panargyros.

There are several ways we might understand the presence (or apparent presence) of the "Circe" intertext in *Such.* One would be to argue that *Such* deliberately parodies "Circe," and that in this respect it is typically or characteristically postmodernist, exemplifying in its specific parody of Joyce the general parodic relation obtaining postmodernist poetics and modernism (see Hutcheon 1988:124-40). This approach appears less than compelling, however, first of all on biographical grounds: Brooke-Rose, a latecomer to Joyce, denies having read *Ulysses* until after the publication of *Such.*[6] More to the point, perhaps, is the peculiar character of the "Circe" chapter itself, which makes it all but immune to postmodernist parody. For "Circe" is itself already a parody of modernism; it already stands in a parodic relation to the modernist poetics of the earlier chapters of *Ulysses.* "Circe," that is, is one of those chapters of Joyce's text (together with "Cyclops," "Oxen of the Sun," "Eumaeus," and "Ithaca," perhaps also "Sirens") in which Joyce seems already to have outstripped modernist poetics (including the normative modernism of other chapters of *Ulysses* itself) and to anticipate postmodernism (see McHale 1992:42-58). Thus, in appearing to allude to "Circe" (even without the author's having intended to do so!), *Such* does not so much parody "Circe" as imply a continuity with the postmodernist strain that we are able (retrospectively) to identify in Joyce's strangely hybrid, modernist-postmodernist text.

But the postmodernism of *Such* manifests itself not only at the otherworld level of this novel's two-tier ontology, or in the tension between the worlds, but also at the this-worldly level. The language of the "real" world is often as bizarre as that of the phantasmagoric world-to-come; here, for instance, is how an evening of conversation among friends is rendered from Larry's point of view:

—Yes, look at him, says [Brenda] less remotely, and the words rebound from inside the map-like contours emanating from her, filling the room, the street no doubt, the entire sky. Their internal combustion has pushed her out of their banal untender story that throttles her. . . .
   —I meant to say something a little different, the professor says gently, or pretends to say inside the latitudes and longitudes he shows to men. . . . Despite his small eyes, one of them almost blind, the other watery, he has an undoubted presence

on the screen of social intercourse that flickers its arpeggios like harp-strings up and down our subliminities. . . .

Remote [Brenda] looks out with her naked eye, suddenly in an anguish only I can see. And Professor Head perhaps, who closes his blind eye and cocks his giant telescope to catch the radiation of the bursting galaxies. But [Stanley's] wife sips her drink and looks with glazed not naked eyes. She cannot hope for an eternal quadrangle, though she bombards the square room with the particles of a vague discontent. . . . [H]is wife's anger . . . disturbs the flickering harp-strings on the screen of social intercourse (280-83).

How are we to understand this strange discourse that seems to dissolve "social intercourse" into interacting wave-forms or lines of force ("map-like contours," "latitudes and longitudes," "arpeggios like harp-strings," etc.)? One approach, obviously, is to treat this language as figurative, a series of metaphors for Larry's estranged, de-familiarized experience of his fellow human beings since his "resurrection." Such metaphors might be understood to capture social intercourse "above or below the verbal level as well as within it" (213), or what people know "full well below their thoughts" (257); they capture, in other words, the level that Nathalie Sarraute calls "subconversation." Brooke-Rose herself has described Sarraute's poetics of subconversation in language that seems to echo the language of *Such*: "These half-conscious movements and murderous impulses are viewed like organisms caught and enlarged in an electron microscope. But the metaphoric title [*Le Planetarium*] swoops the perspective from submicroscopic to giant-telescopic, our psychic energies being implicitly seen also in terms of planets revolving around stars, galaxies receding from one another or colliding through the forces of gravitation, electromagnetism and nuclear reactions" (RU 324).[7]

But understanding it metaphorically is not our only option for interpreting this language. Another option is suggested, presumably by Brooke-Rose herself, in the jacket copy from the original edition (1966) of *Such*: Larry, as a consequence of his near-death experience, "has acquired a peculiar perceptive faculty, he sees . . . people as a radio-telescope 'sees' the stars, in terms of radiation, planetary systems, the colours of the spectrum, atoms and waves of particles." In other words, however much it may formally resemble Sarraute's metaphors of subconversation, this discourse is not figurative at all, but a literal account of how Larry physically perceives others. By this reading, the discourse of *Such* converges with that of certain science fiction representations of characters who "see" the world much as Larry is said to "see" it, according to the jacket. Here, for instance, is Olivia Presteign, the albino heiress of Alfred Bester's classic SF novel *Tiger! Tiger!* (U.S. title, *The Stars My Destination*, 1955):

She was beautiful and blind in a wonderful way, for she could see in the infra red only, from 7,500 Angstroms to one millimeter wavelengths. She saw heat waves, magnetic fields, radio valves [*sic*], radar, sonar and electro-magnetic fields. . . . She looked like an exquisite statue of marble and coral, her blind eyes flashing as she saw and yet did not see.

She saw the drawing-room as a pulsating flow of heat emanations ranging from hot highlights to cool shadows. She saw the dazzling magnetic patterns of clocks, phones, lights and locks. She saw and recognized people by the characteristic heat patterns radiated by their faces and bodies. She saw, around each head, an aura of the faint electro-magnetic brain pattern, and sparkling through the heat radiation of each body, the ever-changing tone of muscle and nerve. (Bester 1979:42-43)

In *Such*, says Brooke-Rose in an interview, metaphors from scientific discourse (such as, presumably, "the map-like contours emanating from her," "the radiation of the bursting galaxies," "she bombards the square room with the particles of a vague discontent," etc.) are "treated as ontological in the world of fiction, like a sunset or a tree" (Friedman and Fuchs 1989:83). That is, they are actualized or realized, made literal like Bester's infrared-sighted girl, rather than left figurative like Sarraute's subconversations.

Nevertheless, we need not regard this literal reading as authoritative (despite its having been proposed by the author herself!). The alternative figurative reading continues to seem at least as plausible. In effect, we remain with two hypotheses, and no way to decide conclusively between them: real in this world, that is (as Brooke-Rose says), ontological? or figurative, a flower of rhetoric, not a flower (or tree) of reality? This is a difference of ontological status, of course, and our inability to decide between these alternatives is, as much as Larry's "hesitation" between worlds, a form of ontological hesitation.

Between, as its title suggests, is another novel of hesitation, but not hesitation between worlds, or at least not between worlds in the literal sense of the term: between "worlds," one might say, but not between worlds. Its heroine, like Larry in *Such*, vacillates, not between this world and the one to come, but between the "worlds" of different cultures (that of her French mother, her German father's family, her English husband) and the disparate worldviews encoded in the various languages and professional and technical discourses to which, as a simultaneous translator, she is continually exposed. In its construction of the world as plural, *Between* itself stands, we might say, somewhere between two other British novels with similar premises: on the one hand Brigid Brophy's *In Transit* (1969), which tends to actualize this plurality in an ontological direction, dissolving the unitary real into a number of competing alternative realities governed by different physical laws, observing different norms of verisimilitude, populated by beings of different orders, and so on; and on the other hand, David Lodge's *Small World* (1985), which tends on the contrary to recuperate plurality in terms of differing cultures and discourses, differing epistemologies. *Between* stands closer to the epistemological pole than the ontological one: closer, that is, to modernism than to postmodernism.

Certainly the central self around which the novel is organized, this woman poised uneasily between (or among) worlds, seems characteristically modernist: fragmented, self-divided, threatened with dispersal, perhaps on the verge of a nervous breakdown. In the course of the novel, "layers" of her past experience (the metaphor is that of a friend of hers [515]) are brought successively to light, apparently through the operation of some version of Proustian involuntary memory. An elaborate analogy is drawn with the archeological layers excavated at the site of Troy (469-70), but even more apt, and more indicative of the modernist orientation of this novel, are the intertextual allusions (e.g. 548) to another "archeological" text in which successive layers of cultural memory are brought to light and fragments are shored against the ruins of the self, namely, of course, Eliot's *Waste Land.*

As in the earlier novel *Out*, the subject of consciousness has been effaced here, deprived of proper noun or pronoun; nevertheless, again as in *Out*, the entire substance of the text is attributable to her. The discourse of the text, though it seems to float free of any producer, must, we suppose, be her interior discourse. This hypothesis seems to be confirmed when, late in the novel, as the heroine approaches what apparently will be her ultimate breakdown, she begins to speak aloud in a style with which by now we are very familiar but which up until now has never appeared in directly quoted dialogue:

—Have you taken a pep pill or something?
    —The stones contain the temple, cavern, sepulchre which contains one alleinstehende Frau sitting cross-legged on a prayer-rug, a miniature temple you know, prêt-à-porter, with her fingers forming a squat diamond space through which the pattern on the prayer-rug, say, blue, red, green, has no significance beyond itself. The stones contain the space and the space contains the presence of no more than centuries of mankind's need to love even eine Abwesenheit die nur eine Abwesenheit bedeutet.
    —Yes, well . . . Do you feel all right? You look absolutely washed out. (565-66)

Here for the first time the characteristic discourse of this text is explicitly connected with a personified speaker, and that speaker is its heroine. From this I think we are justified in concluding that she must have been the source of this discourse all along.

As in *Out* too, however, there is also a postmodernist undertow tugging at the predominately modernist poetics of this novel. The entire discourse of *Between* has been shaped by a blanket constraint on the appearance of any form of the copula *to be*. Arbitrary, blanket stylistic constraints such as this one have the effect, as Brooke-Rose herself explains, of making the "physical signifier . . . more physical, the signified less important" (Friedman and Fuchs 1989:84). Or, in other words, they serve to foreground the disparity and asymmetry between the textual stratum of language and the stratum of the world projected by the text; that is, such a constraint foregrounds the ontological structure of the text itself. Ontologically speaking, the makeup of the fictional world is always subordinate to the shape of the language that projects it, but in cases like that of the arbitrary exclusion of all *to be* forms (or of the letter *e* in Georges Perec's *La disparition* [1969]), this subordination is made conspicuous. Here language visibly has the upper hand, occupying a position of clear ontological "strength" or superiority relative to the fictional world (cf. McHale 1987:148). This is a strategy Brooke-Rose shares not only with Perec but with others of his OuLiPo circle (Queneau, Calvino, Mathews, et al.; see Motte 1986) and other postmodernists as well; it is, in short, a characteristic postmodernist strategy.

Nevertheless, as Brooke-Rose herself acknowledges, this global constraint on the language of *Between* has by and large escaped the notice of its readers (Brooke Rose 1989:103).[8] It is, one might say, a subliminal constraint, or perhaps a constitutive constraint; that is, one valuable for the writer in the process of composition but on the whole invisible or irrelevant to the reader. In effect, the dominant modernist poetics of *Between* overrides and eclipses its constitutive postmodernist strategy for everyone except the author (and the occasional prying narratologist).

The case for reading *Between* as a modernist novel is strengthened if one turns to Brooke-Rose's next novel, *Thru*. For *Thru* is in a sense what *Between* would look like if it were fully "postmodernized." Two examples will have to suffice to illustrate this relation. First, intertextual allusions: in *Between* these occur either in the direct speech of the protagonist or her interlocutors (e.g., the allusion the *The Waste Land* mentioned above) or, more ambiguously, in the protagonist's thoughts. That is, such allusions have an entirely discursive status—they belong to the level of language, whether interior or exterior—and their immediate source (not, of course, their ultimate intertextual source) is located within the fictional world of *Between*, in the mouths or minds of the novel's characters. Not so in *Thru*, where intertextual allusions (e.g., to Diderot's *Jacques le fataliste* and Coleridge's "Kubla Khan") are frequent, and their status and level paradoxical or indeterminate. Jacques and his Master, for instance, appear first (591) in a "free-floating" quotation from Diderot—"free-floating" in the sense that one cannot attribute it to the spoken or interior discourse of any particular character or narrator—only to return a few pages later (595) as characters not of *Jacques le fataliste* but of *Thru*. They belong, that is, to the world, and not just the discourse, of *Thru*; or rather, they belong to one of its worlds, for evidently they do not share the same world with the other characters of *Thru*, with whom they never interact. In other words, intertextual figures such as Jacques and his Master, or the "man from Porlock" (a quasi-fictional "character" from the notorious prefatory note to Coleridge's "Kubla Khan"), are not entirely discursive in *Thru* as they were in *Between*, but manage to obtain an ontological foothold here.

This is more radical than it sounds, for when one plagiarizes (or, more politely, "appropriates") a character from another text, that character comes trailing fragments of its own world, the world of its "home" text.[9] To introduce realized intertextual characters in this way is to violate the norm of textual-ontological unity (one text/one world), in effect producing an ontologically composite or heterogeneous text, one that mingles or straddles worlds. It produces, in short, a characteristically postmodernist text in which multiple worlds coexist in uneasy tension.[10]

A second example is the relative status of metalanguage in *Between* on the one hand and *Thru* on the other. In *Between*, metalanguage, language about language, is firmly lodged within the fictional world: it appears, for instance, in the professional discourse of the linguists and semioticians whose conference lectures it is the protagonist's job to translate. Metalanguage plays a similar role in *Thru*, where it occurs as the professional discourse attributed, realistically enough, to characters who happen to be university lecturers in narratology and poetics. Here, however, unlike in *Between*, such metalinguistic discourse refuses to "stay put": it keeps jumping levels, shifting or slipping from the characters' pedagogical discourse about other texts (*Tristram Shandy, La Princesse de Clèves* or what have you) to metafictional discourse about this text, about *Thru* itself. Relative to this higher-level metalanguage, the characters themselves, what they do and say, and the world in which they do and say it have all been reduced to the status of discursive artifacts, ontologically "weaker" than the higher-level discourse of which they are themselves no longer the sources but merely the objects. It is this disorienting freedom of metalanguage in *Thru* to jump out of the fictional world to an ontologically superior level that gives point to the joke someone proposes during a classroom discussion: "There should be placards saying: Danger. You are now entering the Metalinguistic Zone" (629).

There are no such placards in *Thru*, whether to warn us of the presence of metalanguage or to signal the other forms of ontological instability that make reading this text so disorienting an experience. For throughout this text a similar instability of status and reversibility of level infects nearly every narratological category we normally rely on for novelistic coherence and legibility: character, narration, space, time, event, etc. *Thru* displays the full postmodernist repertoire of destabilizing strategies, including self-contradiction; the placing of episodes or descriptions "under erasure"; so-called "strange loops"; *trompe-l'oeil* effects, such as "demoting" an event, character, or object to a lower narrative level or, conversely, "promoting" one to a higher level; *mise-en-abîme*; irresolution or hesitation between mutually exclusive alternative scenarios; and so on (see Rimmon-Kenan 1982; McHale 1987:99-130). *Thru*, in other words, is a text of radical ontological hesitation: a paradigmatic postmodernist novel.

2. From *Amalgamemnon* to *Verbivore*: As If SF

It would have been convenient, as far as the present narrative of the zigs and zags of Brooke-Rose's career is concerned, if she had ceased writing fiction after *Thru*. Inconveniently enough, however, after a nine-year hiatus she resumed, publishing a second tetralogy of novels between 1984 and 1991. Brooke-Rose's third career appears to be both continuous and discontinuous with her second, as her second was with her first. Whereas the novels of the first tetralogy alternated between modernist and postmodernist poetics, all four of the novels of the second tetralogy seem decisively postmodernist, although in diverse ways. If one undertook to map the second tetralogy's shifting aesthetics, the result would not be a simple zigzag itinerary like that of the first, but some topologically more complex figure, one that doubled back and folded in on itself, one in which inside and outside, front and back, contained and container were inextricably entangled.

Amalgamemnon, the inaugural novel of Brooke-Rose's new phase, is perhaps the only one of her novels that properly deserves to be called "experimental"—not "experimental" as book reviewers typically use that term (namely, as a dismissive label for any innovative or unconventional writing whatsoever; see Johnson 1973:19-20; Sukenick 1985:47-48), but in a stricter sense of the term. For in this novel in particular Brooke-Rose seems to be reconnoitering for new possibilities, new materials, new discourses, a new way forward. Yet, at the same time that it is experimental in this sense, *Amalgamemnon* also recapitulates the four preceding novels, from *Out* to *Thru*, echoing certain elements of their plots and fictional situations. For instance, the basic situation of *Amalgamemnon* is that of a humanist scholar, a university lecturer in classics, made redundant by the shift of university priorities to the training of scientists and technologists. Her situation recalls those of *Such*, *Between*, and even (in a few episodes) *Thru*, in all of which a person trained in the humanities is forced to come to terms with, and to "eavesdrop" on, scientists and their discourses. There is also the recurrent erotic situation of the heroine's being courted by an inappropriate, importunate suitor; in *Amalgamemnon*, as in *Between*, the suitor is older than the heroine, while in *Thru* the ages are reversed and the suitor is younger (but just as inappropriate).

More significantly, *Amalgamemnon* exploits in a conspicuous way the discourses of science and technology, as did all four of the "second-career" novels.[11] In *Out*, it is the discourse of chemistry that is exploited in this way; in *Such*, that of astrophysics; in *Between* a whole range of technical discourses and jargons, including genetics, linguistics, and structural anthropology; in *Thru* it is the quasi-scientific discourse of narratology; and in *Amalgamemnon*, the discourse of computer science.

Finally, like *Between*, *Amalgamemnon* has been composed subject to a blanket stylistic constraint, not, as in *Between*, a ban on the copula *to be*, but rather a blanket obligation for all verbs (including those uttered by characters in direct discourse) to appear in some "nonrealizing" form (tense or mood): future, conditional, hypothetical, etc.[12] Similar hypothetical or speculative passages appear in *Out* and *Between*, but in both these texts they are readily recuperated as projections or fantasies of the respective protagonists, and hence not incorporated into the reader's reconstruction of the text's "real world": they are, in effect, edited out of the reality-picture. Such a recuperation is not available in the case of *Amalgamemnon*, for here everything, including the narrator-protagonist herself, is framed by this hypothetical-speculative mode, so there are no grounds either for editing any particular sequence or detail out of the reality-picture or, for that matter, for including it. Thus, this blanket constraint has radical ontological consequences: in effect, the entire world of *Amalgamemnon*—its narrator, characters, events, time and space, etc.—dangles in ontological limbo, subject to an implicit (and sometimes explicit) "as if."[13] It is, in short, like *Thru*, a paradigmatic postmodernist novel of ontological hesitation.

Is *Amalgamemnon*, then, merely recapitulative, a recycling of materials and strategies from the first tetralogy, a mere appendix or coda to Brooke-Rose's second career? This is indeed the way it is likely to appear if one reads through Brooke-Rose's oeuvre in chronological order, from *Out* through *Amalagamemnon,* but the picture changes significantly if one reads in reverse order, looking back at *Amalgamemnon* from the perspective of the later novels of the second tetralogy, and in particular from the perspective of its third volume, *Verbivore*.[14] For *Verbivore* is a sequel to *Amalgamemnon*, and exploits the ontological effects that are possible when characters from an earlier text by the same author return in a sequel. These effects, familiar from realist (e.g., Balzac) and modernist (e.g., Faulkner) as well as postmodernist poetics (e.g., Barth, Pynchon), arise because characters who exist "between" texts, intertextually, seem to approach the ontological status of beings who exist "outside" texts, in the real world. In the case of the intertextual relations between *Verbivore* and *Amalgamemnon*, this effect is intensified, because the characters who return in *Verbivore* (Mira Enketei, Perry Hupsos, Nelson Nwankwo) never fully "existed" in their "home" text in the first place: that is, their status there was relativized and in a sense weakened by the blanket "as if" mode that governs the whole of *Amalgamemnon*. Thus, by bringing these characters back sequel-fashion, *Verbivore* has the effect of actualizing them retroactively. It is as if these characters, ontologically so enfeebled by their "native" context, somehow acquired a degree of ontological robustness "between" texts, in the passage from their home text to its sequel.

But *Verbivore* is not a sequel to *Amalgamemnon* alone; it also functions as a sequel to the intervening text, *Xorandor*, a novel generically quite distinct from the two that flank it. For *Xorandor* is Brooke-Rose's science-fiction novel.[15] Not only does *Xorandor* exploit SF motifs, it does so in full awareness of their ontological consequences. SF is a self-consciously ontological or "world-building" genre, juxtaposing (sometimes explicitly, sometimes only implicitly) the world of contemporary reality with an alternative world that differs from it in certain specified ways. What differentiates the *Xorandor* world from contemporary reality is above all the presence in it of silicon-based intelligences, computer-rocks, and Brooke-Rose uses the computer-rock motif not only to build up a new (fictional) reality but, even more conspicuously, to "solve" certain formal problems. There is, for instance, the problem of how to maintain the limited point of view of the novel's two child-narrators while at the same time supplying information not directly accessible to them but essential if the reader is to understand the scope of the crisis precipitated by the computer-rocks. The computer-rock motif itself yields a solution: the smaller computer-rocks are present, as exhibits, at the conferences where high-level scientific and governmental policies not otherwise accessible to the narrators are being debated. "Eavesdropping" on these conferences, the rocks transmit what they "overhear" to their parent-rock, Xorandor itself, who in turn communicates them to the child-narrators, who transcribe them in the text we are reading. In a similar way, as Martin (1989:120-21) has observed, the narrators' use of computer memory and tapes solves the "age-old problem of the perfect recall of the narrator who is limited by age or education." In both these cases, in other words, SF novelties—an absolute novelty in the case of the computer-rocks, a relative one in the case of the narrators' use of tapes and computers—serve to motivate formal solutions to problems of access to and circulation of information: ontological propositions affecting the makeup of the extrapolated world "solve" epistemological problems.[16]

Verbivore "revives" characters and situations from *Xorandor* as well as from *Amalgamemnon*, integrating them all in the same fictional world. As the joint sequel to both *Amalgamemnon* and *Xorandor*, *Verbivore* in effect folds together in the same text the postmodernist poetics of the one and the SF poetics of the other, the postmodernist "as if" ontology of *Amalgamemnon* and the extrapolated SF near-future world of *Xorandor*. Now, this mingling of the *Amalgamemnon* and *Xorandor* worlds in the world of its joint sequel recoils upon *Amalgamemnon* itself. Reading in reverse, looking back at *Amalgamemnon* from the perspective of *Verbivore*, we are compelled to see the postmodernist poetics of *Amalgamemnon* as converging with the SF poetics of *Xorandor*; we are compelled to see *Amalgamemnon*, retrospectively, as somehow potentially compatible with SF, "as if SF."

In what ways, then, does *Amalgamemnon* converge with SF poetics? First of all, and most superficially, in certain elements of content. A major topos of modern SF is of course apocalypse, man-made or natural, and its aftermath; indeed, it may well be SF's larger function in our culture to equip us with tools (imagery, typologies, scenarios) for rehearsing in imagination the otherwise unimaginable prospective of our collective end. *Xorandor* is in part a thriller about a nuclear disaster narrowly averted, and thus belongs to this SF topos; while *Out*, it will be recalled, is based on the premise of a post-apocalypse world of survivors. *Amalgamemnon*, too, has an apocalyptic element, but here the perspective is pre- rather than post-apocalypse. The narrator anxiously anticipates nuclear or environmental disaster, and her anxieties are continually fed and confirmed by alarming radio news broadcasts: "in a little while the voice will announce the end of the World News" (A 11).

Anticipation has often been claimed as the special province of SF, so there is a sense in which the grammar of anticipation in *Amalgamemnon*— its future tenses and hypothetical and conditional moods—relates it to SF poetics. Actually, of course, as Brooke-Rose herself several times remarks, SF does not normally resort to future-tense narration, almost always opting for the "epic preterite," the "postdated" narrative tense of conventional novel-writing.[17] In this respect, then, *Amalgamemnon* literalizes, in the futurity and conditionality of its grammatical forms, what is in effect only figuratively future and conditional or hypothetical in "normal" SF, *Xorandor* included.

Above all, however, it is the presence of computer-science discourse in *Amalgamemnon* that enables one to see it as converging with SF. In the context of *Amalgamemnon* itself, this discourse is only one, albeit a conspicuous one, in the "amalgam" that also includes, for instance, discourses of myth and history persisting from the classical world (Herodotus), discourses of broadcast news and entertainment, and so on. Here cybernetics serves mainly as a rich source of metaphors and puns; in the transition from *Amalgamemnon* to *Xorandor* it is promoted to the dominant discourse in the text. Substantial passages of *Xorandor* are cast in an invented programming language, Poccom, while the language of the novel's joint narrators is saturated with computer-oriented slang and figures of speech.[18] If there is any respect in which *Amalgamemnon* legitimately deserves the label "experimental novel," it is above all in this respect, namely, in its function as a necessary first stage in the development of the new cybernetic style that would only emerge fully in *Xorandor*.

From this perspective, reading in reverse chronological order, *Amalgamemnon* is thus revealed to belong to that class of postmodernist texts that might be called "interface fictions." Arising in the contested frontier zone where the discourses and worldview of those trained in the humanities (including most writers of fiction) confront the new computer technologies and their discourses,[19] interface fiction undertakes to accomplish, on its side of the divide, much of the same cultural work that so-called cyberpunk, the new-wave SF of the 1980s, has sought to accomplish on the other side, namely, the effacement of the very divide that gives rise to such fictions in the first place. Examples of interface fiction include Russell Hoban's *The Medusa Frequency* (1987), James McConkey's *Kayo* (1987), William T. Vollmann's *You Bright and Risen Angels* (1987), even Umberto Eco's *Foucault's Pendulum* (1988). Now, of course, we are in a position to add three more titles to this list: Christine Brooke-Rose's *Amalgamemnon*, *Xorandor* and *Verbivore*.

3. Terminal Postmodernism: *Textermination*

Where does it all end? The very idea of "completion" or "closure" seems deeply problematic in the case of a nonlinear sequence of novels that bends back on itself and twists around and through itself the way these novels do. Nevertheless, in *Textermination* Brooke-Rose does achieve a kind of closure of her second tetralogy, though in unforeseeable ways. She does so by making her text a reflection on closure itself, in all its varieties: on the capacity of completed texts to be "re-opened," through sequels and rewritings, and closed again; on the impending closure of the literary institution itself; on the ends of worlds, fictional and real; on oblivion and death.

Not until we are fully a third of the way into *Textermination* do we find evidence confirming that this text actually does continue the sequence from *Amalgamemnon* to *Verbivore*. Only then (p. 63) are we finally re-introduced to a character familiar to us from the preceding novels, namely Mira Enketei, protagonist of *Amalgamemnon* and *Verbivore*, and author (evidently) of *Xorandor*.[20] But long before Mira's return to this text we have already become aware that *Textermination* is a sequel—not, indeed, a sequel to the preceding trilogy of novels, or not to them *in particular*, but to something like the entirety of world literature. For from the very first pages of this text Brooke-Rose has introduced into her fictional world a stream of characters (some readily identifiable, some less so, depending upon how widely one has read in world literature) appropriated from classic works of fiction of all periods and national literatures: Austen's Emma and Flaubert's Emma, Fuentes' Felipe Segundo and Mann's Goethe, George Eliot's Dorothea Brooke and Christa Wolf's Kassandra, Pynchon's Oedipa Maas and Roth's Nathan Zuckerman, Kundera's Tomas and Borges' Funes and Canetti's Dr. Kien, and so on and on. Indeed, catalogues of names such as the one I have just (more or less randomly) compiled are a conspicuous stylistic feature of this text, and they have the effect here that catalogues are typically designed to have, namely, that of standing synecdochically for the many other characters who could also have been mentioned but have not, for lack of space.

The premise on which all this rests is the convening of a vast annual congress of fictional characters, of all times and cultures, who have gathered to petition the Reader (appropriately capitalized, as befits a quasi-divine figure) to spare them from the oblivion of no longer being read. Set in San Francisco, and transparently modeled on the annual convention of the Modern Language Association, this Convention of Prayer for Being exploits a familiar topos—call it the professional-conference topos—whose distant roots may be found in the carnival traditions documented by Bakhtin.[21] This witty premise enables Brooke-Rose to explore and develop further the ontological consequences of sequels, rewrites, appropriation, and the return of characters that she had already begun to explore as early as *Thru*.

As in *Thru*, the "importation" of characters from other texts entails importing their home-worlds as well, or at least the ghosts or auras of those worlds that characters carry along with them as part of their very identities as characters. But this effect is aggravated and intensified in *Textermination* by the sheer volume, the crush of "borrowed" characters—a crush literalized in the many crowd scenes of literary heroes and heroines milling around in the lobbies and conference rooms of the convention. The result is a kind of collapse of ontological boundaries among the worlds of all these myriad texts, an implosion of multiple, colliding home-worlds that produces a strange "heterotopic" space (in Foucault's sense [1970:xviii]) in which characters from disparate worlds mingle on neutral ground. Nor does the ontological implosion even stop there, for several pairs of characters (Emma Woodhouse and Mann's Lotte, Emma Bovary and Stendahl's Duchess Sanseverina-Taxis) seem to occupy the same space of the same body by turns, so that their very identities flicker or vacillate. This conflation of characters' identities is comically foregrounded when immigration officers at the characters' port of entry to the U.S. try to disentangle the doubled identities of their passports (9).

Not only do characters from disparate fictional worlds mingle and hobnob among themselves, but they also mingle with figures from a different ontological plane entirely—with their "interpreters," the professional academic readers with careers at stake who have convened this meeting. This motif of the transgression of narrative levels, which has many and distinguished precedents in twentieth-century literature—from Unamuno and Pirandello to the American surfictionists and Woody Allen—also constitutes a further strand of continuity with the three novels preceding *Textermination*, or at any rate with *Amalgamemnon* and *Verbivore*, in both of which (as well as in *Thru* before them) such transgressions regularly occur.

Having established her premise of a convention of literary characters, Brooke-Rose proceeds to complicate it exponentially by having the convention overrun by an unruly crowd of fictional characters from the movies and television, spearheaded by the likes of J. R. Ewing, Columbo, and MacGyver. The introduction of such mass-media characters further complicates an already complex situation in at least two respects, sociologically and ontologically. Sociologically, it dramatizes the confrontation and competition between "elite" and "popular" art, high and low, and the threatened eclipse of the former by the latter. This issue is a new one for Brooke-Rose, who throughout the preceding trilogy of novels had been more concerned with the tension between humanistic and technological discourses and worldviews than with that between high and low strata of cultural production.[22] Ontologically, introducing mass-media characters multiplies the dimensions of ontological difference. Each of these newcomers possesses at least a double identity, as *character* and as *actor* (e.g., J. R. Ewing vs. Larry Hagman, Lt. Columbo vs. Peter Falk), and a double ontological provenance in the real and fictional worlds.[23] Moreover, many of these cinematic and televisual characters have counterparts among the literary characters. In a situation of such complexity, a simple act can exfoliate into a whole system of planes and reflections, a veritable hall of mirrors, as when Hawthorne's Hester Prynne is joined for tea in the hotel bar by Lillian Gish *as* Hester Prynne, from the silent film version of *The Scarlet Letter* (140).

The text lingers over such moments, and over ontologically compound or multifold characters, not just cinematic ones like Lillian Gish-as-Hester Prynne but literary ones as well: Calvino's Nonexistent Knight, Fuentes's Felipe Segundo (from *Terra Nostra*), Roth's Zuckerman (from *The Counterlife*), the anonymous soldier from Robbe-Grillet's *In the Labyrinth*. Already possessing a problematic or complex or fragile ontological status in their home texts, these characters bring their ontological complexity and fragility with them into *Textermination*. Brooke-Rose does not make them bearers of point of view, reserving that privilege for characters of her own invention (the convention staffers Kelly McFadgeon and Jack Knowles, Professor Rita Humboldt, our old acquaintance Mira Enketei) or solidly three-dimensional characters enlisted from nineteenth-century realist novels (Emma Woodhouse, Dorothea Brooke). But she does deploy these multifold characters as lenses for gathering and focusing her text's various ontological themes and cruxes: existence vs. nonexistence, historicity vs. fictionality, multiplicity of versions, ontological transgressions and paradoxes, and so on.

Of all these compound characters, none is more problematic or more conspicuous than Gibreel Farishta, Rushdie's character from *The Satanic Verses*, who figures in a major subplot of *Textermination*. Already in his home text Farishta had been a compound figure, an actor specializing in film roles as Hindu divinities, an expatriate divided between disparate cultural "worlds" and subject to vacillating genre norms (naturalism, magic realism). In *Textermination*, where Farishta appears only in his film roles as Prince Rama and Lord Krishna, never as "himself," this ontological complexity is not only preserved but further compounded by his being made to function here as the surrogate for Salman Rushdie, his own author. Simultaneously actor and role, mortal and superhuman, fictional character and his original author's alter ego, Brooke-Rose's Gibreel Farishta is a walking compendium of ontological themes and tensions.

He is also transparently a vehicle for Brooke-Rose's reflection on closure and the fate of literary fiction generally. Like the real-world Salman Rushdie, Brooke-Rose's Gibreel Farishta is a marked man. Under sentence of death, hounded by terrorist gunmen, in disguise and on the run, Farishta dodges in and out of the episodes of *Textermination*, his adventures contributing an element of conventional thriller interest to a narrative that is otherwise not notably action-packed. But, also as in the case of the real-world Rushdie, more is at stake here than Farishta's personal survival, for the character (like the author whose surrogate he is) has come to stand metonymically for literary fiction itself, which is similarly under mortal threat from ideologies intolerant of its speculativeness, pluralism, and ontological irresponsibility. When finally the character Farishta does fall victim to assassination, Brooke-Rose exercises her privileges as a fiction-writer, and perhaps also expresses her privileges as a fiction-writer, and perhaps also expresses her lingering optimism as a fiction-lover, by restoring him miraculously to life (116).

Elsewhere, adopting a grimmer view of our future prospects, Brooke-Rose uses different symbolic means to explore the imminent closure of literature itself as an institution. Twice, once near the novel's beginning, and again at its climax, she reenacts that most venerable and resonant of all images of the destruction of the literary-culture archive—ecpyrosis, as Eco's Adso of Melk would have called it, the burning of the library (see McHale 1987:161-63). The first time (11-12), the burning library has undergone a displacement into cinematic terms, appearing as the burning of Atlanta from *Gone with the Wind*; the second time (166-74) it appears figuratively, as the San Francisco Hilton, temporary home for all the literary characters exiled here from their own texts, hence metaphorically a library. Both times, however, the density of allusions to other literary library fires—to Canetti's *Auto-da-Fé*, Bradbury's *Fahrenheit 451*, Eco's *The Name of the Rose*, and of course the library of Alexandria—leaves little doubt about what is really meant.

Throughout the preceding trilogy of novels, Brooke-Rose and her textual surrogates (especially Mira Enketei) had played the role of Cassandra, warning us of apocalypse, menacing us with its prospect—indeed, with the prospect not just of one but several apocalypses, of different kinds: the end of humanistic culture (*Amalgamemnon*), the end of human communication (*Verbivore*), the end of the world as we know it, the end of the world, period (*Xorandor*). Now, here at the end of *Textermination*, as the burning of the San Francisco Hilton crescendos and peaks, only to be lost in the larger apocalypse of the catastrophic and long-anticipated California earthquake (174-79), it is as if Cassandra's apocalyptic energies, pent up over the course of the three preceding novels, had finally achieved gratifying release on the printed page, as if she had finally allowed herself imaginatively to act out the apocalypse that until now she had only threatened.

Apocalyptic scenarios, Susan Sontag once suggested, are always, apart from anything else, means of addressing (but also of displacing) the fact of personal annihilation, our singular deaths recast as collective death (Sontag 1966:223-25). No doubt this element of reflection on death is present in Brooke-Rose's apocalyptic scenarios, as it is in her fictionalization of the Rushdie affair; but if so, this is not so much because of anything intrinsic in her handling of these materials, as because of the corroborating evidence to be found elsewhere in her text. The very premise of literary characters facing oblivion because readers no longer read or remember them can itself be read as a means of dramatizing or simulating or modeling death. This modeling function is brought into sharp focus in the two instances in which characters are shown at the very moment of discovering that they have officially been forgotten, have lost their last toehold in existence. The first of these lost characters is Kelly McFadgeon, one of the interpreters at the conference (92); the second is none other than Mira Enketei: "Idly she lifts the zigzag scroll [of computer printout] at an eighth or so of its thickness and her eye falls on a long list of forgotten names in alphabetical order. She can't resist, lifts another thickness, runs her finger down to EL, lifts another small thickness, finds EM, then EN, and moves down in ENK. Yes, she too figures in it: Enketei, Mira. She can't go on. She doesn't exist" (104-5).

This is, I submit, more poignant a moment than it has any right to be; not only because we have come to "know" Mira, and so mourn her passing from (fictional) existence, as we would any beloved (or at least familiar) character; not only because of the *momento mori* quality of this passage, its power to remind us, by metafictional sleight-of-hand, of our *own* tenuous toehold on existence; but above all because we understand Mira Enketei to be her author's fictional surrogate, so that her passing from fictional existence reads irresistibly as Brooke-Rose's rehearsal of her own death, a run-through or imaginative *pre*-enactment of what one day must inevitably come to pass in reality.

The reading is confirmed, it seems to me, by the intervention in the text, immediately after Mira's disappearance from it, of the author "herself," speaking in her "own" voice—not of course the author herself at all, but another surrogate: "If she can't go on, I suppose I'll have to. I am not Mira of course, though many readers think I am. . . . Be that as it may, I am the author, take it how you will, and I am still alive and well, if not in Texas, at least here, and for a little while yet" (106-7). Echoing the language of Beckett's *The Unnamable*, as well as that text's infinite regress of voices, Brooke-Rose (or "Brooke-Rose") here challenges us to accept Mira's annihilation as paradoxical confirmation of her author's continued survival: if "I" can write "her" death, then "I" continue to exist. But in doing so, she implicates herself in the mode of existence of this text (where else is "here"?) and its world—a mode of existence which, as we have come to know, is fragile and provisional at best; a text in which death lurks; a world that is terminal.

NOTES

This essay is a revised and updated version of chapter 9 (207-22) of my *Constructing Postmodernism*. The third section of this essay, especially written for this volume, has never appeared in print before.

[1]The *nouveau roman* can be seen, according to Brooke-Rose's account, as a kind of displaced form of the fantastic. Thus, for instance, Robbe-Grillet's novels are said to "produce *an* effect of the uncanny [i.e. the explicable fantastic] if not the same effect" as the one described by Todorov (RU 310); they yield "an eerie effect close

to the fantastic, or, in Todorov's terms, to the uncanny" (RU 336); and so on.

[2]See Jameson's account of Claude Simon's "alternation between a Faulknerian evocation of perception and a neo-novelistic practice of textualization" (1991:135); and cf. Harvey (1989:339-42) on modernism and postmodernism as permanent alternatives within capitalism, expressing its internal contradictions, rather than as successive historical periods.

[3]*Omnibus* 17, 67. All subsequent references to *Out* and the succeeding three novels (*Such, Between, Thru*) will be to this omnibus edition.

[4]What distinguishes *Out* from the *nouveau roman* of Robbe-Grillet, as Brooke-Rose observes, is precisely its science-fiction premise, for the *nouveau roman* never undertook to construct alternative realities like those of science fiction (1989:102). (An exception would be the later novels of Claude Ollier.) Martin, writing of *Out*, suggests that science fiction convention relieves the writer of any responsibility to adhere to norms of verisimilitude (Martin 1989:114-15), but this is surely wrong, for conventional science fiction, as Brooke-Rose herself notes, "always is realistically anchored" (Friedman and Fuchs 1989:88; cf. RU 77-102). That is, science fiction normally extrapolates a *new* level or standard of verisimilitude, different in certain respects from present-day standards, to which it then faithfully adheres. With rare exceptions (e.g. Philip K. Dick), science fiction does not introduce epistemological uncertainties of the kind that Brooke-Rose introduces in *Out*; consequently, science fiction's extrapolated verisimilitude typically serves to resolve uncertainty rather than to heighten it as Brooke-Rose's science fiction premise does in this novel.

[5]Other examples of this topos include Flann O'Brien's *The Third Policeman* (1940/1967), Muriel Spark's *The Hothouse by the East River* (1973), Thomas Pynchon's *Gravity's Rainbow* (1973) and *Vineland* (1990), Ishmael Reed's *The Last Days of Louisiana Red* (1974) and *The Terrible Twos* (1982), R. M. Koster's *The Dissertation* (1975), Stanley Elkin's *The Living End* (1979), Alasdair Gray's *Lanark* (1981), Peter Carey's *Bliss* (1981), Russell Hoban's *Pilgermann* (1983), David Carkeet's *I Been There Before* (1985), and William Burroughs's *The Western Lands* (1987). Of all these versions of the world-to-come, perhaps the closest to Brooke-Rose's is one that is not strictly speaking a world-to-come at all, namely Slothrop's hallucinatory descent into the cloacal underworld in Pynchon's *Gravity's Rainbow* (1973:60-71). For an account of the poetics of what is nowadays called "near-death experience" narratives, with many striking parallels to Larry's experience in *Such*, see Zaleski.

[6]Brooke-Rose, personal communication, 14 November 1990.

[7]Brooke-Rose has denied any direct influence of Sarraute on her own writing (Friedman and Fuchs 1989:82), and there seems little reason to doubt her. For one thing, the "submicroscopic" and "giant-telescopic" metaphors that she describes in this passage, and which occur throughout *Such*, are actually rare in Sarraute.

[8]For instance, even Martin (1989:116-17), in his otherwise attentive and sympathetic survey of Brooke-Rose's fiction, fails to mention the global constraint on the copula in *Between*.

[9]In *Textermination*, Brooke-Rose has Dale Kohler, a character she has appropriated from John Updike, say to his assembled fellow-characters (most of them similarly "lifted" from other texts), "You may feel you've come here wrenched out of your home-contexts, sometimes a mere name, trailing bits and pieces of your own world, but it's my program brought you. . . ." (158). Just for the record, my own sentences above, which so closely resembles Kohler's words here, would have

been seen by Brooke-Rose in typescript late in 1990, before the publication of *Textermination*. While I cannot actually prove that Brooke-Rose "stole" my sentence, I choose to believe that she did, since being burgled by Brooke-Rose puts one in such good company—namely, the entirety of world literature, more or less.

[10]For further examples of heterogeneous fictional worlds produced by "appropriating" characters from other texts, see Carpentier's *El recurso del metodo* (1974), Fuentes's *Terra Nostra* (1975), Timothy Findley's *Famous Last Words* (1981), Kathy Acker's *Great Expectations* (1983), *Don Quixote* (1986), and *In Memoriam to Identity* (1990), Coover's *A Night at the Movies* (1987), Barth's *The Tidewater Tales* (1987), and Robert Steiner's *Matinee* (1989). Brooke-Rose herself would extend and generalize this strategy in *Textermination*, making it the basic premise of that novel's plot and the constitutive principle of its world.

[11]On Brooke-Rose's fascination with and use of technical jargons, see Friedman and Fuchs (1989:83-4, 88), and Brooke-Rose (1989:104, 105). Other writers whose use of technical discourses invites comparisons with Brooke-Rose include the British poet J. H. Prynne and the American novelists Thomas Pynchon and Joseph McElroy.

[12]Brooke-Rose's model for the use of future tense in *Amalgamemnon* is very likely Maurice Roche's *Compact* (1966); see her discussion of this text's "transgressive" future tense (RU 329). A parallel case is that of Carlos Fuentes's *La Muerte de Artemio Cruz* (1962). Incidentally, as in the case of the blanket ban on *to be* in *Between*, here too the constitutive constraint of the text has gone largely unnoticed by its readers, and in particular by its reviewers; see Brooke-Rose 1989:103. An example is Ihab Hassan's review of *Amalgamemnon* the *New York Times Book Review*: not a word here about "nonrealizing" tenses and moods.

[13]In *Amalgamemnon*, writes Martin (1989:119), "the archetypical phrase of fiction 'as if' becomes a thematic motif." The phrase "to go on as if," in a sense the kernel from which the whole of *Amalgamemnon* springs, had already appeared conspicuously in *Thru* (603); for that matter, it also appears in *A Rhetoric of the Unreal* (6), and would appear again in *Verbivore* (191). This, incidentally, is an instance of the convergence between Brooke-Rose's poetics and that of American surfiction on which Brooke-Rose herself has remarked (RU 416). Raymond Federman, too, has written a hypothetical-conditional fiction, *Smiles on Washington Square* (1985), though he has not undertaken to conform all of his sentences to the dominant conditional mood as Brooke-Rose has, contenting himself with framing the events of his story in an overall perspective of conditionality. A related case is Ronald Sukenick's short text "Aziff," from his *Endless Short Story*, in which the phrase "as if" materializes as a character: "Then Aziff appeared in a gout of steam from the radiator . . . It was as if present company were expected . . . As if the room became an absence . . . As if it were embraced with dark soft wings . . . As if we were all smoothed and soothed . . . It was as if. As if. Aziff" (4).

[14]The fourth novel of the tetralogy, *Textermination*, will be treated separately, for reasons I hope will become clear.

[15]Though Brooke-Rose herself casually describes *Xorandor* as "a science fiction" (1989:104), the novel frequently distances itself from SF conventions: "Martians! Martians have gone out even of science fiction long ago"; "Pure science fiction, Biggles snapped"; "The myth of little green men dies hard" (59, 102, 201). This, however, is an example of the strategy Empson once called "self-parody to disarm criticism," and in fact is typical of many postmodernist texts that exploit SF conven-

tions but distance themselves from SF at the same time, including Gray's *Lanark,* Federman's *The Twofold Vibration* (1982), and Fuentes's *Terra Nostra.*

[16]Cf. the use of SF novelties to motivate formal solutions to comparable problems of point of view in the newest "wave" of SF writing, so-called "cyberpunk" fiction, e.g. William Gibson's *Neuromancer* (1984) and Bruce Sterling's *Islands in the Net* (1988); see McHale 1992:259-61.

[17]"Science fiction, although about the future, commonly postdates its narration" (RU 329). Brooke-Rose also expands on a remark by Raymond Williams concerning the "subjunctivity" of utopian fiction: "SF," she writes "is written in a subjunctive mood, not a future but an 'as if,' a 'what if'" (RU 393 n. 2). Cf. also Friedman and Fuchs (1989:85) and Brooke-Rose (1989:103).

[18]In what seems to be an interesting anticipation of *Xorandor,* Brooke-Rose in *A Rhetoric of the Unreal* reacts with disapproval to Mas'ud Zavarzadeh's remark, in a 1978 MLA conference paper, that Joseph McElroy's *Plus* (1977) is written in "computer language" (RU 288). She is, of course, correct: if anything, the strange language of *Plus* derives not from computer language but from the mission-control radio-communications language made familiar by the manned space-exploration programs. But one can't help but wonder whether Zavarzadeh's mistake about *Plus* might have planted the seed of Brooke-Rose's own later large-scale use of computer language in *Xorandor.*

[19]Susan E. Hawkins suggests that *Xorandor* explores the impact that computers are beginning to have on our notions of language and of speech and writing, and even our very notion of self: "the subject is . . . becoming a technological production." Appositely enough, she cites Philip K. Dick's "obsession with the inevitable conflation of the human and the technetronic" (Hawkins 1989:143). Indeed, this exploration of the radical impact of computer technology on subjectivity has been pursued by SF writers like Dick and the so-called cyberpunks (Gibson, Sterling, Rucker, Cadigan, Shiner, Shirley, and others) at least as vigorously as it has by "mainstream" (non-SF) postmodernists; see McHale 1992:253-61.

[20]Actually, Mira had already made a brief appearance some ten pages earlier in the text (49), but incognito. On Mira's authorship of *Xorandor,* see 66.

[21]Other recent examples include Brooke-Rose's own *Between,* David Lodge's *Small World* (1985), and the parodic crime-novel *Murder at the MLA* (1993) by the pseudonymous D. J. H. Jones. Compare also the science-fiction motif of the time-travel war, bringing together soldiers from different epochs, as in Fritz Leiber's *The Big Time* (1958) or Cam Kennedy's and Tom Veitch's splendid SF comic, *The Light and Darkness War* (1988-89). On related forms of "reduced" carnival—drunken parties, traveling circuses, funhouses and amusement parks, etc.—see McHale 1987: 171-75.

[22]Unless tension between high and low culture is already latently present in *Xorandor,* with its mingling of avant-garde "experimentalism" and SF genre conventions, as I argued earlier.

[23]Indeed, some of them should probably be thought of as possessing a triple identity, insofar as the actors playing the characters are "stars" in their own rights, their "stardom" constituting a self with a separate ontological status—simulacral, quasi-fictional—distinguishable from their mode of existence as "real people"; see Boorsten 1985 [1961] and Baudrillard.

WORKS CITED

Baudrillard, Jean (1988) "Simulacra and Simulations," in *Selected Writings*, ed. Mark Postman, Stanford: Stanford Univ. Press, 166-184.

Bester, Alfred (1979 [1955]) *Tiger! Tiger!* [U.S. title: *The Stars My Destination*], Harmondsworth: Penguin.

Boorstin, Daniel J. (1985 [1961]) *The Image: A Guide to Pseudo-Events in America*, rpt. New York: Atheneum.

Brooke-Rose, Christine (1989) "Illicitations," *Review of Contemporary Fiction* 9, 3:101-9.

Foucault, Michel (1970) *The Order of Things: An Archeology of the Human Sciences*. Trans. uncredited. New York: Pantheon.

Friedman, Ellen G. and Miriam Fuchs (1989) "A Conversation with Christine Brooke-Rose," *Review of Contemporary Fiction* 9, 3:81-90.

Harvey, David (1989) *The Condition of Postmodernity: An Enquiry into the Origins of Cultural Change*, Oxford and Cambridge, MA: Basil Blackwell.

Hassan, Ihab (1985) "Revillusionary Punorama" [review of *Amalgamemnon*], *New York Times Book Review*, 8 September, 20.

Hawkins, Susan E. (1989) "Memory and Discourse: Fictionalizing the Present in *Xorandor*," *Review of Contemporary Fiction* 9, 3:138-44.

Hutcheon, Linda (1988) *A Poetics of Postmodernism: History, Theory, Fiction*, New York and London: Routledge.

Jameson, Frederic (1991) *Postmodernism, or, The Cultural Logic of Late Capitalism*, Durham NC: Duke Univ. Press.

Johnson, B.S. (1973), "Introduction," in *Aren't You Rather Young to be Writing Your Memoirs?*, London: Hutchinson, 11-31.

Martin, Richard (1989) "'Just Words on a Page': The Novels of Christine Brooke-Rose," *Review of Contemporary Fiction* 9, 3:110-123.

McHale, Brian (1987) *Postmodernist Fiction*, New York and London: Methuen.

———— (1992) *Constructing Postmodernism*, New York and London: Routledge.

Motte, Warren F. (ed. and trans.) (1986) *Oulipo: A Primer of Potential Literature*, Lincoln and London: University of Nebraska.

Pynchon, Thomas (1973) *Gravity's Rainbow*, New York: Viking.

Rimmon-Kenan, Shlomith (1982) "Ambiguity and Narrative Levels: Christine Brooke-Rose's *Thru*," *Poetics Today* 3, 1:21-32.

Sontag, Susan (1966) "The Imagination of Disaster," in *Against Interpretation and Other Essays*, New York: Dell, 209-25.

Sukenick, Ronald (1985) *In Form: Digressions on the Act of Fiction*, Carbondale and Edwardsville: Southern Illinois Univ. Press.

———— (1986) *The Endless Short Story*, New York: Fiction Collective, 1986.

Zaleski, Carol (1987) *Otherworld Journeys: Accounts of Near-Death Experience in Medieval and Modern Times*, New York and Oxford: Oxford Univ. Press.

"Utterly Other Discourse": The Anticanon of Experimental Women Writers from Dorothy Richardson to Christine Brooke-Rose

Ellen G. Friedman

IN PRE-TWENTIETH-CENTURY women's fiction, the strains in the relationship between women and the dominant culture were represented through covert modes. The strategies of women writers included subtexts, minor characters, and patterns of imagery, which to various degrees undermined the traditional scripts for appropriate behavior in fiction and life that their surface plots and major characters seemed to confirm. Through her heroines, Jane Austen, for instance, maintains a "double consciousness"; as Sandra M. Gilbert and Susan Gubar observe, although Austen drives her heroines into a final "docility and restraint," she allows them to uncover the "delights of assertion and rebellion" on the way. In fact, Austen slyly subverted prevailing values through the "duplicity" of the "happy endings" of her novels, "in which she brings her couples to the brink of bliss in such haste . . . or with such sarcasm that the entire message is undercut" (168-69). Gilbert and Gubar reveal similar subversive subtexts in George Eliot, whose Maggie Tulliver, they demonstrate, is the "most monstrous when she tries to turn herself into an angel of renunciation" (491). Thus Austen and Eliot, to name only two writers that over a decade of feminist criticism has uncovered, offered, whether consciously or not, hidden or disguised challenges to canonical notions of fiction.

Indeed, feminist criticism has neatly deconstructed the Great Tradition materialized by F. R. Leavis. Austen, who Leavis proposed inaugurated "the great tradition of the English novel," and Eliot, seen by Leavis as solidly entrenched in the Great Tradition, are understood by way of feminist analysis to be compromising the very values their fiction seems to Leavis and others dependably to confirm. Thus two of the five writers Leavis privileges in his Great Tradition are engaged in subverting the order of which Leavis offers them as exemplars. Leavis required a "marked moral intensity" so explicit and plain that what he identified as its exhibition was, in the cases of Austen and Eliot, at least covertly, parody (9).[1]

That the literary canon is a "strategic construct" (Altieri 42) by which the dominating, patriarchal order confirms its own values, a process that renders the relations between the canon and women problematic, is fairly widely accepted.[2] In this context, the "moral seriousness" demanded by Leavis is revealed as a code, rationalizing patriarchal dominance. The operation of this code is evident in the particular vocabulary of his judgments, including key terms such as "morality," "reverence," "civilization," terms driven by imperatives defined and maintained by a strict system of patriarchal constraints. Insights of this kind, in fact, must have preceded and eventually enabled the uncovering of subversive subtexts in women's works.

Yet these internal, disguised assaults on patriarchal values are confined to and thus to a degree disarmed by the traditional fiction that houses them. The realistic mode of women's nineteenth-century fiction did not essentially disturb the structure of the master marriage and quest narratives this fiction covertly interrogates.[3] Eliot, Austen, and other writers may have assailed the prevailing order, but as long as they wrote in this mode, they were, to some degree, in complicity with it. Despite the subversive moves on the part of Austen and Eliot, Emma—although she is financially independent—is obliged to marry, and Maggie, because she does not, is obliged to die. What else could Eliot do with such a heroine within the parameters of nineteenth-century realism, impelled as it was by certain master narratives?

Twentieth-century women experimental writers have not required covert means to express their dissatisfactions. They explode the fixed architecture of the master narrative, break—in the words of Virginia Woolf—the "sequence" of traditional fiction,[4] and open up a space, an alternate arena for the writing of what Christine Brooke-Rose calls an "utterly other discourse" (A 5). In subverting the forms of conventional narrative, they subvert the patriarchal social structure these forms reflect. With such structural disruption, the "woman" in the text is liberated from the secret folds of the fiction and comes to inhabit the entire text. Rather than carrying the dominant discourse that Leavis calls "moral" and "great," the narrative becomes the discourse of the "other." Indeed, there is a whole tradition of women writers who have written works and treatises that are deliberately feminine, deliberately anticanonical, and who have formed, in the course of this century, a feminine anticanon. In "Canon Fathers and Myth Universe," Lillian Robinson makes the point that "Feminist criticism can approach the traditional standards for canonicity, which are supposed to constitute 'our' common aesthetic, either by demonstrating how the female tradition conforms to that aesthetic or by challenging the aesthetic itself" (29). However, feminist critics should also recognize that there already exists a tradition of women writers who themselves challenged that aesthetic by rejecting the "standards for canonicity" and relocating their own work outside of them, a relocation that has over the course of the twentieth century accrued into what may now be viewed as an oppositional canon—an anticanon.[5]

Dorothy Richardson, for instance, as she set out "to produce a feminine equivalent of the current masculine realism," carefully identified what seemed to her the qualities of the canonical novel so that *Pilgrimage* could be free of them (1:9). According to Richardson, in this canonical novel, the author imposed a narrative, preached a moral, and offered "style" instead of substance.[6] These qualities reveal not reality but, for Richardson, the author's ego. Through her protagonist Miriam and in letters and essays, Richardson cast her complaints about canonical fiction in terms of gender: "Bang, bang, bang, on they go, these men's books, like an L.C.C. tram, yet unable to make you forget them, the authors, for a moment" (*Dawn's Left Hand, Pilgrimage* 4:239). Here, according to Gillian Hanscombe, Miriam disparages the "measured regularity of novels—of pace and sequence— which is to her as blind and mindless as a tram, serving only to confront the reader with the personal quirks of the [male] author; in other words, to promise to offer 'life' and instead to offer the author" (88). In the conventional novel's imposed plot, its deliberate characterization, its inexorable drive to the inevitable resolution, Richardson read the ego of the (male) author whose domination of the text, she felt, suppressed her feminine consciousness.

The intention of Richardson's innovative techniques was to subvert the major constituents of the canonical novel: plot, characterization, central conflict, climax, resolution, the stance of moral authority—the elements through which the author exercised control and which Richardson interpreted as manifestations of the author's ego. What Richardson identified as authorial egotism is her sense of the operation of master narrative that legitimizes the social order in its manipulation of characters and plot. Richardson found such narratives suffocating. In *Dawn's Left Hand* (1931), Miriam complains about the imprisoning structures of even writers she admires: "Yet about them all, even those who left her stupefied with admiring joy, was a dreadful enclosure" (4:239).

Meditating on two other "great tradition" (before Leavis carved the tradition) novelists, James and Conrad, Miriam comes to the conclusion that:

"Even as you read about Waymarsh and his 'sombre glow' and his 'attitude of prolonged impermanence' as he sits on the edge of the bed talking to Strether, and revel in all the ways James uses to reveal the process of civilizing Chad, you are distracted from your utter joy by fury over all he is unaware of. And even Conrad. . . . The torment of *all* novels is what is left out. The moment you are aware of it, there is torment in them." (4:239)

Her repetition of the word *torment* declares emphatically a sense of personal injury and relates the degree to which Miriam feels that *she*, a woman, is "left out," under erasure, in the canonical novels she describes. Richardson, however, is not drawing a line between men and women writers per se but between canonical fiction, which excludes the feminine, and a fiction she was to invent in order to express the feminine. Therefore, when Hypo tells Miriam to write like George Eliot, she replies, "Writes like a man." Despite her clandestine and subversive subtexts, Eliot—as Miriam perceives—did not essentially disturb the order she criticized.

It is just the "left out" material Miriam misses, the not-yet-presented, that Richardson attempts to put into the text of *Pilgrimage*. In the foreword to *Pilgrimage*, Richardson relates the difficulty of producing this other discourse because she had no models. The "adventure" of what she knew to be a "fresh pathway" led to her discovery of an "independently assertive reality," a feminine narrative mode that she describes as a "stranger in the form of contemplated reality having *for the first time* in her experience its own say . . ." (1:10, my italics). Richardson's experiment was more significant than is generally realized because in clearing the path by which the repressed could return, she set the terms of a new tradition, a tradition that in moving toward feminine discourse takes a radically anticanonical stance.

Pilgrimage departs from even the minor confining structures of patriarchal discourse so that the very details of her new mode were prophetic of *écriture féminine*. For instance, she found the way that the language was directed and chopped by punctuation unnecessarily inhibiting to her purpose. She wrote, "Feminine prose . . . should properly be unpunctuated, moving from point to point without formal obstructions" (1:12). Richardson's theories seem a clear antecedent to Hélène Cixous's "The Laugh of the Medusa," although Cixous recognizes only the male modernists as her predecessors and, in fact, cites few women writers as exemplifying her theories. Although unacknowledged, Richardson's anticipation of Cixous is significant because they both define a feminine discourse in similar terms. In Cixous's "The Laugh of the Medusa," one hears echoes of Richardson's vision of ways to write the feminine: "Such is the strength of women that, sweeping away syntax, breaking that famous thread . . . women will go right up to the impossible" (256).

The project Cixous proposes for the future of feminine discourse Richardson had already begun. Richardson exploded the predictable rhythm of the conventional novel as she called whole volumes "chapters" of a novel that would stretch to thirteen volumes and still remain incomplete. This very incompleteness was central to her formulation of feminine narrative, for in master narratives closure was required, and the options available for women characters as the narrative sped toward resolution and then closure were well defined: marriage, madness, death. By insisting on the incompleteness of *Pilgrimage*, Richardson created a revolutionary option for her female protagonist. Miriam simply goes on; she grows progressively wiser, more complex, more confident. Her fate is to live, not to die, not to be subsumed in marriage to a superior male as is Emma but to remain at the center of the narrative.

In order to eliminate the sense of authorial "control" and "ego" that blocked what she felt would be a truer rendering of "life," Richardson collapsed the ironic distance between author and protagonist (Hanscombe 89). Miriam's thoughts are presented in an uninterrupted, uninterpolated, and uninterpreted stream. As a character, she aspires to the stature of neither exemplar nor metaphor. Richardson attempted to present the reader with Miriam *as she is* and not with a vehicle for an author-imposed something other. As she lets flow Miriam's "stream of consciousness," Richardson eschews a hierarchical organization of the objects of Miriam's perceptions (Kaplan 41). This effort to carve an antihierarchical, antihegemonic fiction was more than a shift in aesthetics; it was an attempt to delineate difference, to provide a new ground for narrative that could accommodate the feminine.

Richardson's contemporary, Virginia Woolf, presented more fully articulated challenges to the canon in the name of feminine narrative. Like Richardson, Woolf characterized conventional linguistic forms and traditional structures as inadequate for feminine narrative: "To begin with, there is the technical difficulty . . . that the very form of the sentence does not fit" a woman ("Women and Fiction" 145). Woolf not only searched for forms that would inscribe women's experience, but she also identified a general crisis in narrative, declaring the old novel's "two and thirty chapters" moribund, an "ill-fitting vestment" that could no longer hold "life or spirit, truth or reality" ("Modern Fiction" 105).

Woolf was the first to link the crisis in narrative that became apparent early in this century to issues of the feminine. In that she proposed a discourse the anticanonical qualities of which are tied to the expression of female experience, her theories were, like Richardson's, prophetic of *écriture féminine*, and one can hear echoes of her insights when Jacques Derrida and others talk about the feminine in avant-garde texts.[7] In the well-known penultimate passage in *A Room of One's Own*, she presents the writer Mary Carmichael, an alter ego, who not only "breaks" the sentence of logocentric discourse by providing it with "thorns" but also "breaks the sequence" of conventional fiction (83-89).[8] Woolf interprets "breaking the sequence" narrowly, in terms of plot, as the ability of one female character to like another female character, thus countermanding the obligation of women characters to be defined solely in relation to men (84-86). Although the significance of this implication of "breaking the sequence" should not be underestimated, Woolf's narrative practice expanded on the meaning of this phrase. As did Richardson, Woolf ascribed the inadequacy of dominant forms to what they excluded, as well as what they included. Of her own ambitions for fiction, she said:

I mean to eliminate all waste, deadness, superfluity; to give the moment whole; whatever it includes. . . . Waste, deadness, come from the inclusion of things that don't belong to the moment; this appalling narrative business of the realist: getting on from lunch to dinner: it is false, unreal, merely conventional. . . . Is that not my grudge against novels—that they select nothing? (*Writer's Diary* 136).

Richardson and Woolf were both searching for a way to inscribe *difference* in the text, because *difference* was overwhelmed, suppressed in conventional forms.

In her search for what had not yet been made manifest, Woolf wrote obsessively about what should be put in or what had been left out of fiction. Concerning *The Waves*, perhaps the work of Woolf's most distant from tradition, she writes in her diary in contradictory terms of a "litter of fragments" (160), on the one hand, and of "saturation," on the other: "What I want to do is saturate every atom. The poets succeed by simplifying: practically everything is left out. I want to put practically everything in; yet to saturate. That is what I want to do in the Moths [her working title for *The Waves*]" (136). Her preoccupation with what should be put in or what should be left out expresses her dissatisfaction with what was merely manifest, her desire for the not-yet-presented. Each of her texts was a move to bring this sought-after *other* discourse to the surface, with each move involving a concomitant disruption of conventional narrative to complete it. *The Waves* surrenders linearity, character, plot to rhythm and disembodied, nearly indistinguishable voices. In *Jacob's Room*, the protagonist, Jacob, is entirely absent from the action of the novel—his character gleaned through rumor and reminiscence. *Orlando* renders time, space, and gender elastic, releasing them from the "narratives" of physics and biology. Organized in chronologically arranged sections (from 1880 to 1937, when it was published), *The Years*, nevertheless, presents history as a web, developing not by movement from event to event but organically, by associational flow. The narrative is multidirectional, polyphonic, carnivalesque.[9] That is, *The Years* offers a sense of history as "carnival" rather than as "narrative." Linearity is surrendered to patterns surfacing and submerging—swelling, thinning, disappearing, and reappearing transformed.

That Woolf's textual experiments have political implications and subversive motives was not recognized until recently. Toril Moi, in *Sexual/Textual Politics*, was among the first to characterize the significance of Woolf's strategies as revolutionary, as "analogous to sexual and political transformation" that changes the "symbolic order of orthodox society from the inside" (11). Breaking the sequence is breaking the political-social authority that informs the sequence. As Moi points out, in her formal and linguistic innovations "Woolf rejects the metaphysical essentialism underlying patriarchal ideology, which hails God, the Father or the phallus as its transcendental signified" (9).

Just as anticanonical women writers are distinguished from Great Tradition women writers by virtue of their distance from conventional practice, they are also distinguished from male innovators. In crucial ways, male innovators such as Joyce, Eliot, and Borges are not anticanonical. Their work reveres, extends, and thus essentially continues the canon—as literary history has proved since all three are now canonical authors. *Ulysses* and *The Waste Land* resonate and are in harmony with the culture's central myths and texts; they are knitted to Western literary tradition, and their ready incorporation into the canon affirms the continuation of this tradition, an achievement Eliot applauds in "Tradition and the Individual Talent."[10]

Such examples are plentiful: Joyce's use of Homer, Borges's obsessive depiction of the quester who seeks Truth in particular books or in libraries or who tries to recreate classic texts, nearly the entire Eliot canon. The end of "Little Gidding," the last of the *Four Quartets*, in which the poet concludes that exploration is circular and that innovation and tradition are in symbiotic relationship, captures this aspect of the male modernist impulse: "And the end of all our exploring / Will be to arrive where we started / And know the place for the first time" (208). As some have already recognized, there is a deep conservatism and nostalgia among the male modernists.[11]

In contrast, women anticanonical writers such as Richardson, Woolf, and Gertrude Stein do not locate their texts within patriarchal myths and traditions. As Robinson notes, these myths and traditions are "essentially external to any central female project" (29). Expression of the feminine requires a disengagement not only from the modes of traditional fiction, as Richardson, Woolf, and Cixous have argued, but also a stance of irreverence toward or distance from the central myths of the dominant culture.[12] Because they write from a different site of enunciation within the culture, women innovators, who offer the most radical expression of the feminine, have difficulty being absorbed into the canon.[13] Unlike the male modernists, anticanonical women writers do not use innovation to revitalize tradition, do not wish to "arrive where we started," or in Ezra Pound's words, to "make it new." Rather, it is their project to present what this tradition has resisted, to make "it" *different* because they wish to arrive elsewhere.

The paternal cultural legacy, passed on to or resisted by the son, preoccupies even second-generation male innovators; it is Faulkner's great theme, of course, which he mines in such quest narratives as *Light in August* and *Absalom, Absalom!* Woolf, on the other hand, sought not the "re"-writerly text but something other: the semiotic, the text beyond the sequence, that she variously identified in her diary—the "true line," the "next stages" (*Writer's Diary* 185). She repeatedly attempted to define for herself what it was she was doing. In a single paragraph, she writes about *The Waves*, "I am not trying to tell a story. Yet perhaps it might be done in that way. A mind thinking. . . . Autobiography it might be called" (*Writer's Diary* 140). The encompassing, diffuse work that was to become *The Years* required, she thought, the invention of a new form on which she tried the phrase "essay novel" (*Writer's Diary* 184). The work itself emphasizes change, dispersion, nonhierarchical lines of continuity. For Jane Marcus, it is the "female epic." She sees it as a "communal and anti-heroic Odyssey," as "Woolf's answer to *The Waste Land* and *Ulysses* . . ." (Marcus 74). There is no single-minded pursuit of a noble of even ignoble quest. Woolf, in fact, carefully avoids a dominating protagonist, as Richardson wished to avoid exhibition of authorial control.

The technical problem of a narrative without the dominating presence of a protagonist absorbed Woolf throughout the composition of *The Years*.[14] In a diary entry dated 25 April 1933, she writes: "The figure of Elvira

[Eleanor in the final version] is the difficulty. She may become too dominant" (191).[15] On 2 August 1934 she writes: "I want a chorus, a general statement, a song for four voices" (214). Although the character of Eleanor does provide a thread of continuity in the novel, she is the stuff of minor characters: she does good works but without strong ideology or heroism; we watch her grow old, forgetful, and even fall asleep during a lull at a party. As Woolf allows "major" characters to fade, "minor" characters become more distinct. The servant Crosby, for instance, is as sharply defined and has as large a place on the canvas of this novel as do members of the Pargiter family.

The novel's progress from Victorian to modern times parallels the emergence of the text's semiotic elements. In the first section, "1880," the narrative is organized almost conventionally around the Victorian patriarch Colonel Abel Pargiter, who dominates the scenes in this section and in relation to whom the characters are depicted. By "1910," the year King George and Colonel Pargiter die, the text is as dispersed as the Pargiters, and patriarchal authority is as abandoned as the woefully outdated family mansion that is up for sale. Woolf does not provide a substitute organizing center; rather she allows the text's fibers to unknot and wander with the century. The result has been brilliantly characterized by Marcus:

> *The Years* is yet another subversion of the patriarchal genealogical imperative of English fiction. . . . Its horizontal leap from Victorian to Modern, in uneven time periods, not the standard decades, emphasizing relations of cousins and aunts and nephews, not fathers and sons, privileging spinsters over mothers, spatializing time in family rooms, marks *The Years'* response to the Victorian voice of paternal authority. We read and hear the novel as one long series of interrupted discourses, the interruptions themselves marking the daughters' emergence from the tyranny of the father's voice. (74)

After the generation of Richardson and Woolf, women experimental writers did not feel as compelled to define or explain what they were doing.[16] Their writing had clear precedents, whether acknowledged or unacknowledged, and until the 1970s when the French introduced *écriture féminine*—which although it named Joyce and Proust as its models and exemplars was closer in motivation, technique, and purpose, as I have suggested, to Richardson and Woolf—new theorizing was not felt to be necessary. Of the entire women's anticanonical tradition, Jean Rhys perhaps had the least consciousness of these precedents or of her continuation of this tradition. Nevertheless, her writing in a curious and adamant way was clearly anticanonical. If canonical novels are—as Frank Kermode, Charles Altieri, and others have proposed—"strategic constructs" to reinforce a society's values, Rhys's works are anticanonical, constructed to undermine those values. Born and raised in an English colony in the West Indies, Rhys regarded things English with the suspicion and resentment of the colonized, the powerless. Add to that the fact that she was, unlike Woolf, a penniless woman, dependent on the male establishment for publication and recognition, and one understands how she chose a narrative stance that was adamantly anticanonical.[17] Her attitude toward England is summarized by Anna in *Voyage in the Dark: "This is England, and I'm in a nice clean English room with the dirt swept under the bed"* and suggested in Anna's identification with the blacks in Dominica where she was raised: "I wanted to be black, I always wanted to be black . . ." (18). As a black, Anna would at least belong to a sustaining community. But in the course of a narrative that ends with her having an abortion, Anna learns that as a white, unmarried, unmoneyed woman from the colonies, she is, in the hierarchy of England, an utter outsider.

It is this site, from which she spins her narratives, that defines Rhys's relation to the canon. This relation is suggested by a description from *After Leaving Mr. MacKenzie* of Julia, the protagonist, entering a London street. If readers can imagine that Julia stands for Rhys, the houses in the description stand for canonical works with their "fat pillars" upholding them, and the "complaining and mindless" bellow stands for Rhys's anticanonical fiction, they will have a sense of the nature of her attack on the canon and how her fiction operates in relation to it.

> Julia felt bewildered when she got into the street. She turned and walked without any clear idea of the direction she was taking. Each house she passed was exactly like the last. Each house bulged forward a little. And before each flight of four or five steps led up to a portico supported by two fat pillars.
>
> Down at the far end of the street a voice quavered into a melancholy tune. The voice dragged and broke—failed. Then suddenly there would be a startlingly powerful bellow, like an animal in pain. The bellow was not fierce or threatening, as it might have been; it was complaining and mindless, like an animal in pain. . . . (85)

Julia's initial feeling of being "bewildered" and lost in a place that seemed uniform ("Each house she passed was exactly like the last") and at the same time alien is personified in the voice that quavered "into a melancholy tune," expressing pain. It conveys precisely Rhys's relation to England and to English fiction. A chorus girl from the West Indies, Rhys always felt the beggar and the outsider in relation to England and English books. She deliberately cultivated this stance of "outsider" through her seemingly passive protagonists.

Although often taken either as victims of male domination and cruelty, exposing the vulnerability of the moneyless, unmarried woman in patriarchal society, or as "parasites" without ambition (Borinsky 299), these protagonists are more than sexual objects picked up and dropped by a series of decreasingly desirable men. Their posture as quintessential "other" is so stubbornly, unrelentingly, and seemingly unreasonably maintained that it acts as a menace and even a threat to the dominant culture. Like the melancholy and pained voice Julia hears, it operates to discomfit and subvert. The Rhys heroine is further outside the narrow bounds of the dominant society than even Camus's Meursault or Dostoevsky's Raskolnikov, whose isolation is due, in the first case, to diminished awareness and, in the second, to conscious choice. In fact, Meursault (at the point of death) and Raskolnikov both find their way "home," back within the narrow bounds of society. However, as Alicia Borinsky points out, the Rhys heroine has no "home" to which to return (300). The fact that she is homeless, existentially an outsider, without hope of stepping back into the circle of society, gives her a curiously privileged position in relation to the dominant culture. Her inability, born partly of unwillingness (the Rhys heroine occasionally refuses offers of security), to be reabsorbed into society makes of her an incarnation of what patriarchal society is not able to accommodate. Thus she becomes a measure of its inadequcies.

Just as Rhys often described herself as a "ghost" (*Letters* 12), her protagonists obsessively describe their alienation from the life around them. As the passage quoted above continues, it is reminiscent of the passage in Richardson's *Dawn's Left Hand* in which Miriam complains about the sense of "dreadful enclosure" of men's books: "It was the darkness that got you. . . . It made walls round you, and shut you in so that you felt you could not breathe. You wanted to beat at the darkness and shriek to be let out . . ." (85). Although the "darkness" Rhys's protagonist speaks of is literal, it is also a personal metaphor for the society in which she finds herself suffocated, repressed. Like Richardson's Miriam and Woolf's Carmichael, she has something that "shrieks to be let out." Although Richardson and Woolf, situated solidly inside the circle of patriarchal culture, made disruptive and subversive moves on this culture in order to give voice to and thus "self" the other, Rhys, situated outside of this circle, simply claimed the territory of the "other." The strategy of her protagonists is similar to that which can be gleaned from interviews with some of the urban homeless who choose the freedom of the streets over being tied to a system requiring attentiveness to rules and restrictions and thus capitulation of the identity they have established.[18] Rhys's innovation, then, in this anticanonical tradition, is not so much formal; in most of her fiction she does not violate narrative traditions to the extent that Woolf and Richardson do. Rather, through her extreme protagonists, whose relation to society cannot be "explained" under conventional rubrics of motivation and characterization, Rhys offers critiques of and alternatives to canonical practice and values.

In *Wide Sargasso Sea*, a book she wrote over a twenty-year period, Rhys makes a more militant gesture in interrogating and subverting the canon. She deliberately sets out to break the master quest narrative that controls the plot of *Jane Eyre*. As I point out elsewhere, Rhys enters and reimagines Brontë's text—glossing and subverting, reversing and transforming it— writing it into her own time and into her own frame of reference.[19] Rhys wished to materialize the story, suggested by the figure of the Creole madwoman Bertha, that was hidden from Brontë, who was limited by the context of nineteenth-century English imperialism, Christianity, and patriarchy in which she lived. Rhys's letters repeatedly express her outrage at Brontë's treatment of the Creole woman with whom Rhys identified: "Charlotte" was "wrong. . . . Her Bertha is impossible . . ." (*Letters* 271, 318). In the process of restoring Bertha to what Rhys felt was her rightful dignity, Rhys violates Brontë's text, casting doubt on and therefore undermining the credibility of *Jane Eyre's* quest, its hero, its heroine, and its villain—the madwoman Bertha.

In Rhys's hands, Bertha's condition is not a madness that renders her bestial and malevolent as it does in Brontë but rather signifies her alterity, her otherness. Indeed Rhys constructs an oppositional narrative in which Brontë's canonical plot, characterization, and imagery are methodically undermined by whatever they are meant to suppress or hide. Thus Rhys counters *Jane Eyre's* Christian themes with obeah and voodoo; the manicured English version of a Garden of Eden at Thornfield is contrasted with the lush and wild West Indian Eden of *Wide Sargasso Sea*; Rochester's authority is fed in Rhys's work by a secret and stubborn malevolence. In the process of entering Brontë's text, Rhys releases what has been repressed in that text, resulting in an ironic and telling juxtaposition of the canonical and the anticanonical. That is, Rhys reshapes the contours of Brontë's canonical phallogocentric quest narrative and creates a liberating and transforming dialectic between sameness and otherness, the patriarchal and the feminine, the canonical and the anticanonical.

Unlike Rhys, contemporary experimentalists Eva Figes and Christine Brooke-Rose acknowledge and exploit the legacy of feminine aesthetics. In addition to their prose fiction, they have written literary criticism and social commentary. Figes claims Virginia Woolf as a literary forerunner, and in *Patriarchal Attitudes* she states, "The civilization everyone has been brought up to regard as human civilization, we have to look at as male civilization" (18).

The view of civilization, broadly echoing Richardson's and Woolf's positions regarding the literary canon, governs Figes's narratives in which she seems to be obsessed with attempting to right the balance. In her novels *Waking* and *The Seven Ages*, Figes presents history through the consciousness of women, rendering it nonhierarchically and nonlinearly as did Woolf in *The Years*. Employing spatialization, she relates a millennium of history through the rapidly succeeding voices of midwives from Saxon times to the present. Rather than the usual chronicle of conquests, defeats, and shifting borders, *The Seven Ages* foregrounds women's experiences, especially birthing, against shifting settings as a thousand years pass, and soldiers, whose various uniforms reflect altered allegiances and various wars, plunder, rape, and are killed. The text's successive voices pour forth from a kind of feminine unconscious, akin to Jung's racial unconscious, unstopped by memory, association, or image. In the words of one reviewer, "One woman will call to Emma [the protagonist] from a pile of burning leaves; another will speak from the pages of an old diary found in the attic; a third will be moved to recite when a box of sepia photographs is brought to her" (Hosmer 248). Typical of Figes, the prose is poetic and incantatory although quite deliberate and unflagging in its opposition to the dominance of patriarchal history—the chronicle of which, according to Figes, relates blood-letting, science, hierarchical, male-dominated religions, and a linear sense of "progress." Viewed through the lens of *The Seven Ages*, the repressed record of women's history, presented as cyclical—childbirth, healing, "natural" magic, and the victimizing intrusions of soldiers—suggests an alternate configuration of Western civilization than that offered to college freshmen in their required history courses. Figes seems to be addressing the kind of question posed by Lillian Robinson when she asks, "How does what we have learned about the role of women *change* what we know or believe we know" about historical events in general (26)? Figes presents her course in women's history not as a substitute history. Rather, she sets it in dialectical relation to patriarchal history, to the authoritarianism of the master narrative that is taken as definitive "history."

Rather than leaping among the centuries, Figes's earlier novel *Light* develops leisurely from the dawn to the dusk of a single day. In lyrical prose, Figes exposes the phallocratic assumptions inherent in canonical discourse through a brilliant juxtaposition of anticanonical and canonical form. She demonstrates the power of canonical form to shape canonical theme, and, conversely, she illustrates how the subversion of such form also subverts its themes. Depicting a day in the life of Claude Monet and his family in the style of an impressionist word painting, the narrative moves rapidly among the various characters' consciousness. Until the narrative's middle pages, the book is decentered; none of the characters or scenes is privileged over the others. However, suddenly the impressionist prose brushstrokes fuse into a conventional portrait of a Victorian family seated at dinner. In this section, Monet is established as the reigning patriarch with the other characters' wishes, thoughts, and words clearly subordinate to his—in the spirit of *The Years'* first section. Through this sudden shift into conventional narrative, Figes reveals the contradiction between Monet's innovative style and his role as Victorian husband and father. A lesson in the interdependence of theme and form, the novel demonstrates that a decentered, impressionist rendering of the characters results in the raising of a chorus of voices—wife, sons, daughters, and servants—that are traditionally muted or mute either in the presence of the patriarch or when structured by the patriarchy and the cultural and literary constraints it represents.

In "Illiterations," Christine Brooke-Rose writes directly of the canon as a "male preserve" from which women as a class are prohibited:

In theory the canonic/non-canonic opposition applies to all writers and thus cuts across sexual and any other oppositions. In practice a canon is very much a masculine notion, a priesthood (not to be polluted by women), a club, a sacred male preserve. . . . Or a heroic son-father struggle in Harold Bloom's terms. But a body, a corpus, something owned. And not only a male preserve but that of a privileged caste. For women are only one part, however large, of an originally much larger exclusion: that of barbarians and slaves, or, later, other races and the "lower" classes from peasants to modern workers, who were long considered incapable of any art worth the dignity of attention. . . .

[Thus] this notion of a canon, of a central tradition around the central myth, which is essentially male, priestly and caste-bound, underlies types and levels of critical attention, so that despite the various and increasing waves of emancipation since the 19th century, certain relics remain, ill iterations in the unconscious of society. (55-56)

It is such "illiterations" that Brooke-Rose explodes in the punning, satirical, erudite, definitively postmodern text *Amalgamemnon*. In contrast to Figes's construction of women's history, Brooke-Rose offers a deconstruction of the legacy of patriarchal culture. In this first-person narrative with an elusive plot and protean characters, all men are versions of Agamemnon (hence, "Amalgamemnon") and all women Cassandra. However, Agamemnon undergoes deconstruction and then several reconstructions, reappearing as, for instance, a contemporary lover named variously Willy and Wally, an incarnation in which his general authority has been shaken.

Unlike Joyce in his use of the *Odyssey* to structure his modern epic, Brooke-Rose summons myths in order to expose the darker side of their legacy. In a dizzying series of roller-coaster dips and climbs in perspective and logic, she evokes the mythical or historical to set it beside the contemporary. Thus the conventional wisdom that "No young woman would allow herself to be abducted [read "raped"] without in fact wishing to be" (A 16) is viewed as the legacy of the stories of Helen and Cassandra, among others, as transmitted by Homer and other literary fathers whose interests lay with the successful abduction. In addition, the relationship between Cassandra and Agamemnon is presented as a trope for the relationship of women to the male establishment generally, a relationship in which women, bearing the legacy of Cassandra, have no credibility or voice, a view Brooke-Rose illustrates across discourses (myth, history, literature) in a series of equivalencies. For instance, in one of her guises, the narrator, a professor of literature and history, fears she will be declared "redundant" by the university, which values the language of computers more than hers. She equates her experience to what she imagines happened to the Amazons. Presenting her observation in the future tense (in which the entire novel is cast), she ruminates, "The young Scythians will be unable to learn the language of the Amazons but the women will succeed in picking up theirs, and therefore disappear" (11). The narrator's impending silencing by a male establishment that values computer language over hers is a permutation of the silence to which women are driven when they take on the language and thus the law of the father. A restatement of this view in contemporary terms, as well as an example of Brooke-Rose's irrepressible wordplay, may be found in the following passage:

> Tomorrow at breakfast Willy will pleased as punch bring out as the fruit of deep reflection the non-creativity of women look at music painting sculpture in history and I shall put on my postface and mimagree, unless I put on my preface and go through the routine of certain social factors such as disparagement from birth the lack of expectation not to mention facilities a womb of one's own a womb with a view an enormous womb and he won't like the countertone at all, unless his eyes will be sexclaiming still what fun, it'll talk if you wind it up. . . . (16-17)

Here the choices of Sandra, the narrator, as were essentially those of Cas-[sandra], are to "mimagree" or to be dismissed, treated as sex object; either way, her voice, her language, has no value and thus she "disappears" as surely as the Amazons in the preceding example.

The only recourse is, in Brooke-Rose's volcanic image, "to erupt." The narrator fantasizes that "vulcanologists will fly in from all over the world to calculate the time of my eruption" (48). An allusion to the presence of the semiotic in symbolic discourse, the eruption is a trope of the text itself, "utterly other discourse" erupting through the cracks that Brooke-Rose's wit and erudition skillfully effect in patriarchal myth and history. Sandra makes just such a gesture while Willy/Wally sleeps: "Soon he will . . . snore, a foreign body in bed. There will occur the blanket bodily transfer to the livingroom for a night of utterly other discourses that will spark out of a minicircus of light upon a page of say Lucretius. . . ." (143).[20] The point is clear: the feminine discourse that "sparks out" of patriarchal texts when the patriarchs are asleep generates what she calls "endless stepping-stones into the dark," paths by which the repressed returns, the not-yet-presented is made manifest (143). Although Sandra recognizes that in the morning Willy will "abolish all those other discourses into an acceptance of his," she also has confidence in the future: "Sooner or later the future will explode into the present despite the double standard at breaking points" (16-17).

The very titles of Brooke-Rose's novels, *Out, Such, Between, Thru, Amalgamemnon,* and *Xorandor* challenge canonical notions of fiction-making. Her anticanonical fiction—like that of Woolf, Richardson, Rhys, Figes, and many others—is written directly *against* the canonical mono-logue, standing as a vexing feminine presence, a compelling alternative to established modes, an "utterly other discourse" that, while interrogating notions such as Leavis' Great Tradition, can bear the meanings unbearable in the priestly and narrow chambers of the canon.

NOTES

This essay grew out of the ideas explored in my and Miriam Fuch's "Contexts and Continuities" in *Breaking the Sequence* (3-42). It is an expansion of a paper I presented in session #159, "Canonical Reconsiderations: Class, Colonies, Gender, Genre II," at the 1987 Modern Language Association convention.

[1]In fact, F. R. Leavis's judgments too often seem willful rather than analytical. Of *Emma* he writes, "It can be appreciated only in terms of the moral preoccupations that characterize the novelist's peculiar interest in life" (8). He explains his admiration for Eliot in terms of her "reverent attitude towards life" (14-15).

[2]See Charles Altieri and Christine Froula.

[3]See Jean-François Lyotard (xxiii-xxv) and Alice Jardine (65-67).

[4]See Woolf's *A Room of One's Own* (85-86).

[5]See Luce Irigaray (76).

[6]I was helped in my discussion of Richardson by Gillian Hanscombe's illuminating essay "Dorothy Richardson Versus the Novvle." Also see Hanscombe and Smyers (47-62).

[7]See Jardine (65-102).

[8]Rachel Blau DuPlessis observes that in Woolf's statements about the sentence and the sequence are "telescoped a poetics of rupture and critique." DuPlessis specifies that "To break the sentence rejects not grammar especially, but rhythm, pace, flow, expression: the structuring of the female voice by the male voice, female tone and manner by male expectations, female writing by male emphasis, female writing by existing conventions of gender—in short, any way in which dominant structures shape muted ones" (32).

[9]See Julia Kristeva (78-80).

[10]For instance, Eliot's statement, "not only the best but the most individual parts of [the poet's] work may be those in which the dead poets, his ancestors, assert their immortality most vigorously," summarizes his view (*Selected Essays* 4).

[11]This is one of the major points in Gilbert and Gubar's *No Man's Land*. See also Lyotard (81).

[12]See Robinson's discussion of the difficulty in the *Odyssey "au féminin"* (29).

[13]For example, in 1984 it was still possible for a distinguished specialist in modernism to state in a respected literary journal that Virginia Woolf wrote "village gossip" (Kenner 57).

[14]She had, of course, faced this problem before in works as various as *Jacob's Room, To the Lighthouse,* and *The Waves.*

[15]See Kathleen Woodward's fine discussion of Eleanor.

[16]An exception is Anaïs Nin in *The Novel of the Future.*

[17]Thomas Staley records that in 1928 Ford Madox Ford published under his own name Rhys's translation of Francis Carco's *Perversité* (13).

[18]Charles Bukowski's *Barfly* makes this point eloquently.

[19]See my "Breaking the Master Narrative: Jean Rhys's *Wide Sargasso Sea.*"

[20]Background to my discussion of *Amalgamemnon* comes from Richard Martin's pioneering essay "'Stepping-Stones into the Dark.'" Another insightful discussion may be found in Susan E. Hawkin's unpublished essay.

WORKS CITED

Altieri, Charles. "An Idea & Ideal of a Literary Canon." *Canons*. Ed. Robert von Halberg. Chicago: Univ. of Chicago Press, 1984. 41-64.

Borinsky, Alicia. "Jean Rhys: Poses of a Woman as Guest." *The Female Body in Western Culture*. Ed. Susan Rubin Suleiman. Cambridge: Harvard Univ. Press, 1986. 288-302.

Brooke-Rose, Christine. "Illiterations." Friedman and Fuchs 55-71.

Bukowski, Charles. *The Movie "Barfly."* Santa Rosa: Black Sparrow, 1987.

Cixous, Hélène. "The Laugh of the Medusa." Trans. Keith Cohen and Paula Cohen. *New French Feminisms*. Ed. Elaine Marks and Isabelle de Courtivron. New York: Schocken, 1981. 245-64.

DuPlessis, Rachel Blau. *Writing Beyond the Ending: Narrative Strategies of Twentieth-Century Women Writers*. Bloomington: Indiana Univ. Press, 1985.

Eliot, T. S. *Collected Poems: 1909-1962*. New York: Harcourt, 1963.

———. *Selected Essays*. New York: Harcourt, 1950.

Figes, Eva. *Light*. New York: Ballantine, 1984.

———. *Patriarchal Attitudes*. New York: Stein, 1970.

———. *The Seven Ages*. New York: Pantheon, 1986.

Friedman, Ellen G. "Breaking the Master Narrative: Jean Rhys's *Wide Sargasso Sea*." Friedman and Fuchs 117-28.

———, and Miriam Fuchs, eds. *Breaking the Sequence: Women's Experimental Fiction*. Princeton: Princeton Univ. Press, 1989.

Froula, Christine. "When Eve Reads Milton: Undoing the Canonical Economy." *Canons*. Ed. Robert von Halberg. Chicago: Univ. of Chicago Press, 1984. 149-175.

Gilbert, Sandra M., and Susan Gubar. *The Madwoman in the Attic: The Woman Writer and the Nineteenth-Century Literary Imagination*. New Haven: Yale Univ. Press, 1979.

———. *The War of the Words*. Vol. 1 of *No Man's Land: The Place of the Woman Writer in the Twentieth Century*. New Haven: Yale Univ. Press, 1988.

Hanscombe, Gillian E. "Dorothy Richardson Versus the Novvle." Friedman and Fuchs 85-98.

———, and Vigrinia L. Smyers. *Writing For Their Lives: The Modernist Women, 1910-1940*. London: Women's Press, 1987.

Hawkins, Susan E. "Reading *Amalgamemnon*: The Mythic Present and the Rhetoric of Fragmentation." Unpublished.

Hosmer, Robert E. "The Midwife Arrived Too Late." *Commonweal*, 24 April 1987, 248-249.

Irigaray, Luce. *This Sex Which Is Not One*. Ithaca: Cornell Univ. Press, 1985.

Jardine, Alice A. *Gynesis: Configurations of Woman and Modernity*. Ithaca: Cornell Univ. Press, 1985.

Kaplan, Sydney Janet. *Feminine Consciousness in the Modern British Novel*. Urbana: Univ. of Illinois Press, 1975.

Kenner, Hugh. "The Making of the Modernist Canon." *Chicago Review* 34 (1984): 49-61.

Kristeva, Julia. *Desire in Language: A Semiotic Approach to Literature and Art*. Trans. Thomas Gora, Alice Jardine, and Leon S. Roudiez. Ed. Leon S. Roudiez. New York: Columbia Univ. Press, 1980.

Leavis, F. R. *The Great Tradition.* 1948. New York: New York Univ. Press, 1964.

Lyotard, Jean-François. *The Postmodern Condition: A Report on Knowledge.* 1979. Trans. Geoff Bennington and Brian Massumi. Minneapolis: Univ. of Minnesota Press, 1984.

Marcus, Jane. *Virginia Woolf and the Languages of Patriarchy.* Bloomington: Indiana Univ. Press, 1987.

Martin, Richard. " 'Stepping-Stones into the Dark': Redundancy and Generation in Christine Brooke-Rose's *Amalgamemnon.*" Friedman and Fuchs 177-87.

Moi, Toril. *Sexual/Textual Politics: Feminist Literary Theory.* New York: Methuen, 1985.

Nin, Anaïs. *The Novel of the Future.* New York: Collier, 1968.

Rhys, Jean. *After Leaving Mr. MacKenzie.* 1931. New York: Vintage, 1974.

———. *The Letters of Jean Rhys.* Eds. Francis Wyndham and Diana Milly. New York: Viking, 1984.

———. *Voyage in the Dark.* 1934. In*The Complete Novels.* New York: Norton, 1985.

———. *Wide Sargasso Sea.* 1966. New York: Norton, 1982.

Richardson, Dorothy M. *Pilgrimage.* 1915-67. 4 vols. London: Dent, 1967.

Robinson, Lillian. "Canon Fathers and Myth Universe." *New Literary History* 19 (1987): 23-35.

Staley, Thomas. *Jean Rhys: A Critical Study.* Autsin: Univ. of Texas Press, 1979.

Woodward, Kathleen. "The Look and the Gaze: Narcissism, Aggression, and Aging." Working Paper #7. Center for Twentieth-Century Studies. Milwaukee: Univ. of Wisconsin Press, 1986.

Woolf, Virginia. *Collected Essays of Virginia Woolf.* Vol. 2. Ed. Leonard Woolf. London: Hogarth, 1966.

———. *Jacob's Room.* 1922. New York: Harcourt, 1959.

———. "Modern Fiction." *Collected Essays* 2:103-10.

———. *A Room of One's Own.* 1929. New York: Harcourt, 1957.

———. *The Waves.* 1931. New York: Harcourt 1978.

———. "Women and Fiction." *Collected Essays* 2:141-48.

———. *A Writer's Diary.* 1954. New York: Harcourt, 1981.

———. *The Years.* 1937. New York: Harcourt, 1965.

Contributors

HANJO BERRESSEM teaches in the English department of the University of Aachen, Germany; his recent study of Thomas Pynchon and post-structuralist theory, *Pychon's Poetics: Interfacing Theory and Text,* was published by the University of Illinois Press.

ELLEN G. FRIEDMAN is Professor of English and directs the Women's Studies Program at Trenton State College. Her essays have appeared in such journals as *Review of Contemporary Fiction, PMLA,* and *Modern Fiction Studies.* Her books include *Joyce Carol Oates, Joan Didion: Essays and Conversation* (editor), and *Breaking the Sequence: Women's Experimental Fiction* (edited with Miriam Fuchs). She is writing a book on discourses of morality in U.S. culture.

MIRIAM FUCHS is an associate professor of English at the University of Hawaii. She edited, with Ellen G. Friedman, *Breaking the Sequence: Women's Experimental Fiction.* Her most recent publication is *Marguerite Young, Our Darling: Tributes and Essays* (Dalkey Archive, 1994).

DAMIAN GRANT has published on both the eighteenth-century and twentieth-century novel and is the author of a book on realism. He teaches at the University of Manchester.

SUSAN E. HAWKINS, Associate Professor of English and Coordinator of Women's Studies at Oakland University (Rochester, Michigan), has written on a number of postmodern writers, including John Ashbery and Gertrude Stein. She continues work on Brooke-Rose's later fiction. Her current projects include essays on Kathy Acker and Helena Maria Viramontes.

LINCOLN KONKLE teaches literature and writing courses at Trenton State College in Trenton, New Jersey. His research interests include exploring the ways in which American drama is part of the American literary tradition and, more generally, the way fiction and drama adhere to and challenge the generic boundary. He also publishes poetry and fiction in small press literary magazines.

KAREN R. LAWRENCE, Professor of English at the University of Utah, is the author of *The Odyssey of Style in "Ulysses,"* published by Princeton University Press (1981), and editor of *Decolonizing Tradition: New Views of Twentieth-Century "British" Literary Canons* (Illinois, 1991). Her essay on

Brooke-Rose is part of her book *Penelope Voyages: Women and Travel in British Literature* (Cornell, 1994). She is currently writing a book on the relationship between theory and fiction in Brooke-Rose's work.

JEAN-JACQUES LECERCLE is Professor of English at the University of Nantarre, France; apart from numerous articles, he has published four books, most recently *The Violence of Language* (1990) and *Philosophy of Nonsense* (1994).

JUDY LITTLE is Professor of English at Southern Illinois University at Carbondale where she teaches modern literature, especially fiction by women. In addition to essays on Woolf, Brooke-Rose, Drabble, and others, her publications include *Keats as a Narrative Poet* and *Comedy and the Woman Writer: Woolf, Spark, and Feminism.*

ANNEGRET MAACK is Professor of English at the University of Wuppertal, Germany; she has published on the reception of French literature in England, on the English novel of the 19th and 20th centuries, on modern English drama, and on literature in Australia.

RICHARD MARTIN is Professor of English and American literature at the University of Aachen; his critical biography of the British crime fiction writer Margey Allingham, *Ink in Her Blood,* appeared in 1988, and *Reading Life/ Writing Fiction: An Introduction to Novels by American Women, 1920-1940* in 1994.

BRIAN MCHALE is currently Eberly Family Distinguished Professor of American Literature at West Virginia University. He was for a number of years Senior Lecturer in Poetics and Comparative Literature at Tel Aviv University and remains the author of *Postmodern Fiction* and *Constructing Postmodernism.*

HEATHER REYES has combined writing, teaching, and raising a family. She has an M.A. from the University of London and is currently researching for a doctoral thesis on Christine Brooke-Rose. She has published prose fiction, poetry and children's books.

SUSAN RUBIN SULEIMAN is Professor of Romance and Comparative Literatures at Harvard University and is currently chair of the Committee on Degrees in Women's Studies. Her books include *Authoritarian Fictions: The Ideological Novel as a Literary Genre, Subversive Intent: Gender, Politics and the Avant-Garde,* and the recent *Risking Who One Is: Encounters with Contemporary Art and Literature.*